The Safe Airline

THE SAFE AIRLINE

J.M. Ramsden

MACDONALD AND JANE'S · LONDON

Printed in Great Britain by
REDWOOD BURN LIMITED
Trowbridge & Esher

ISBN 0354 01029 8

Contents

Foreword

The first principles of any professional subject can easily get lost in jargon and technical detail. This can happen in air safety, to the bewilderment of the profession, and perhaps the confusion of air safety itself.

This book is my collection and explanation of all the important airline safety principles and numbers, put for the first time between two covers. The collection is mine, and so are any omissions and inadequacies. I would like to thank *Flight*, in whose pages I originally published some of the material, and also the many air-safety professionals who have inspired, informed and helped me.

Air transport is now one of the world's biggest industries, carrying hundreds of millions of passengers a year. It employs several million people in research, design and manufacturing; air traffic control; airports; the travel industry; banks and insurance; government departments and public authorities; and of course the airline operators themselves — of which there are now more than 1,000 flying more than 7,000 airliners of all ranges and sizes.

Few nations, however small, are without a flag airline. Indeed, for some new nations an airline is the first investment — before roads and even shoes for their people. Air transport is in fact the road and rail of many countries, lifting the whole economy on its wings.

Airlines have brought to ordinary people easy, cheap and safe travel to places which their parents and grandparents could only dream about. A European or American family can have a fortnight's holiday in the Mediterranean or the West Indies for less money than it would have cost in the 19th century, even taking into account inflation. Technology, rebuked though it often is for noise and pollution, has done this. The airliner has brought ordinary people closer together, revolutionising trade and diplomacy, ignoring frontiers, and setting international technical and safety standards unmatched by those of any other industry.

The convenience, speed and comfort of air transport could not have been sold without safety. Safety is air transport's priority, because the price of carelessness or neglect in the air is so much greater than it is on the surface.

The chances of being killed in an airliner crash are now less than they are of being killed in the family car. This astonishing achievement, in half a mere lifetime since flying was a daredevil pursuit, is the theme of this book.

I have tried to make the style and vocabulary accessible to the layman without, I hope, offending the professionals — in whose hangars and cockpits jargon and *Yuckspeak* are gremlins they would not much miss anyway.

J.M.R.

1   How safe?

Flying, being an unnatural form of human locomotion, arouses natural human fears. Even those who love flying, either as pilots or as passengers, do so partly because they have conquered fear. There is the aesthetic delight, which never palls, even with 20,000-hour pilots, of attaining the dream world of cloud and sky and sun. But there is always the sudden reminder, perhaps in turbulence or bad weather, that unforgiving gravity always tries to reclaim its own. The safe pilots and operators are the ones who never forget to respect this fact.

A few people have sworn never to travel by air. They would not think twice about going in a train, bus or car. Statistical pleas on behalf of air travel do not touch them. A quarter of a million people die violently on the world's roads each year, compared with less than 2,000 in airliners. In one country, the United Kingdom, 8,000 people a year die in accidents in their homes.

Each passenger nowadays has to fly in an airliner for more years than he has to ride in the family car before he becomes involved in a fatal crash. The Tutankhamen and Peking treasures go by air. In 1960 for the first time more people crossed the Atlantic by ship than by air; today nearly twenty cross by air for every one by sea. Nothing can persuade the true aerophobe to be an aerophile. He just says, as the caterpillar did when the butterfly flew over: "You'll never get me up in one of those things." Young people particularly, once they have made their first flight, seem to accept air travel as perfectly ordinary. For first-riders of all ages the sight of so many other people coming and going at the airport, and professional service, help to reassure and to achieve that defeat of natural human fear which airline marketing men call "the acceptance factor".

Acceptance, together with population growth, gross national product and fares, increases air traffic. Acceptance is proportional to the number of flights which arrive without incident. News media are not interested

1

in such flights. Those who spend their lives working for air safety are often angered by sensational Press treatment of air disasters. Yet their very anger may actually further air safety; the big black headlines and terrible photographs spur action, and they do not appear to affect traffic growth. Airlines which have suffered accidents have found that they get a few cancellations for 24 or 48 hours, but that bookings quickly return thereafter to normal.

The safest mode of machine transport, according to estimates by Sir Peter Masefield, is the railway. The least safe is the motor-cycle.

Assume groups of 100 people using each of five modes of transport for 5,000 miles a year, the average distance mechanically travelled in a year by a European. For how long could each group travel before one among them could expect to be killed? By rail, 1,540 years; by bus, 1,000 years; by scheduled air transport, 370 years; by private motor-car, 133 years; and by motor-cycle, 7 years.

Over the whole of the 1960s, the safety standard of passenger travel in Europe, in terms of million passenger-miles travelled per passenger killed, was: rail, 770; bus, 500; scheduled air transport, 185; non-scheduled air transport, 100; motor-cars, 67; private and general aviation, 6; motor-cycles, 3.6.

Stratton* has listed the risk per hour of all forms of transport as follows: bus, 0.03 deaths per million hours; rail, 0.05; private car (UK), 0.6; airline flying, 1.0; motor-cycling (UK), 9.0; canoeing, 10; private and sporting flying, 27; mountaineering, 27; motor-cycle racing, 35; rock-climbing, 40.

The risk of being killed in an air crash is one fatality per million hours of exposure. The risk of being killed in a car is 0.6 per million hours of exposure. The average person travels 10,000 miles a year in a car, that is to say 250 hours. This is equivalent in terms of risk to 150 hours of flying. But the average person flies much less than 150 hours a year. Therefore the chance of being killed in a car is, say, 10 or 15 times greater. Roughly speaking, the record suggests that a passenger has to make nearly half a million flights before he or she can expect to become involved in an air accident causing deaths.

GENERAL STATISTICS The annual world number of airliner crashes — "the newspaper-headline" index — has remained surprisingly constant throughout massive post-1945 increases in airline traffic. There are on average just under 60 fatal accidents a year, of which 35 are non-survivable. About half are on scheduled services and half are on non-scheduled — usually called charter-services.

---

*Journal of Navigation, London, October 1974.

The risk of dying from all causes averages just over 1.0 per million hours. The risk of dying from accidents of all sorts, including those in the home, and assuming a 16-hour day, is about 0.1 per million hours. The risk of being killed on a passenger airline service is now just about exactly 1 per million hours. In other words it is the same as the risk of dying from all causes. Assuming that scheduled and charter services are similarly safe, which now appears to be so, it follows that flying on air-transport services of all kinds produces the same risk of death as the general one from all causes.

This "death rate per million hours from all causes" is below 1.0 until the age of 35 or 40, when it starts to rise, reaching five by the age of 70 and more than ten by the age of 80. As Stratton has put it, flying as a passenger today is no more risky than being 55 years old.

On scheduled services the average number of passengers killed per year, though increasing slightly since 1950, has been 685. The risk measured in terms of fatal accidents per million aircraft hours has decreased from 5 to 2; and the risk in terms of passengers killed per million passenger hours has decreased from 6 to 1.

CHARTER SAFETY Are charter flights as safe as scheduled flights? Because of the relatively irregular nature of charters, crews may be less familiar with airports, instrument procedures and route facilities, and may often have to operate to the less well equipped airports.

A question often considered in the United Kingdom is the relative safety of corporations and independent airlines. This is more of a political than a safety question, because in aviation when the bell tolls it tolls for all.

There are many well established passenger-carrying independent airlines which can claim that they have not had a fatal accident. In the decade 1963-1972 British independent airlines suffered about 60 per cent of the accidents and fatalities while carrying about 25 per cent of the traffic. In the previous decade 1953-1962, British independent airlines suffered 75 per cent of the accidents and fatalities while carrying about 15 per cent of the traffic.

The conclusion was drawn by the British Government's *Air Safety Review*, and later by the Edwards Committee, that compared with British Airways the independent airlines as a whole, notwithstanding those which have a completely clean record, have a relatively lower safety performance. But the evidence is that the charter safety record is coming closer to that of scheduled airlines.

Data for the American airline industry make possible direct comparison between the safety of US scheduled airlines ("certificated route carriers") and non-scheduled ("supplementary air carriers").

3

The number of scheduled fatal accidents in 1970-72 was 2 per 1,000 million aircraft miles, down from 4 in 1967-69. The equivalent non-scheduled rates (but not, of course, actual numbers) were, respectively, 10 and 6. No data are available to obtain comparisons in terms of hours and flights. But on the mileage basis it is clear that, statistically, the records of both sectors are close. It would be statistically unacceptable to deduce that the non-scheduled accident rate is twice the scheduled rate. But it would be reasonable to conclude that the non-scheduled accident rate is not as good. The important point is that both scheduled and non-scheduled safety is improving, and that both are good.

AIRLINERS COMPARED Is one type of airliner safer than another? It is possible to compare the safety rates of the various types, taking as the measure the number of "reportable" accidents* per million hours, as shown in the table. Figures are rounded off:

	First million hr	Second million hr	Fifth million hr
Aerospatiale Caravelle	13	5	—
Boeing 707/720	18	13	8
Boeing 727	9	7	5
Boeing 737	2†	—	—
BAC One-Eleven	8	—	—
BAC VC10	5†	—	—
Convair 880/990	6	7	—
Hawker Siddeley Comet 4	15	—	—
McDonnell Douglas DC-8	14	5	5
McDonnell Douglas DC-9	5	4	—
Hawker Siddeley Trident	5†	—	—

Source: Based on a graph by H.C. Black, United Kingdom Civil Aviation Authority, Airworthiness Division, published in the Aeronautical Journal, Royal Aeronautical Society, August 1971.

The trend in the case of each aircraft is similar. Incidents and accidents are most frequent in the first ½ million hours, as crews learn to fly and operate their new aircraft, and as mechanical defects and other snags are removed. The percentage of reportable incidents attributed to

---

*This generally is defined as an accident involving extensive damage to the aircraft or injury or serious hazard to passengers. Training and test accidents are excluded. The number of accidents in a three-year period has been averaged and plotted against the middle year.
†At about ½ million hour.

crew error falls from around 70 per cent in the first two years of service to around 40 after six years and around 30 after 12 years, averaging around 50 per cent. There is very often an upward trend in the accident rate of a type after some years in service. This usually coincides with the sale of the aircraft to non-scheduled operators, who have to go through the learning process again.

AIRLINES COMPARED How does one airline compare with another? The differences can be very wide. The average airline has between 2 and 3 fatal accidents per million flights. The best, for example, the big United States domestic airlines, suffer less than 1. The worst airlines have a rate as high as 30. Some of these are airlines of less developed countries, usually formed for prestige reasons by governments with little appreciation of the cost of safety or of the technical standards required — both of the airline and of the national airports and their technical facilities and staff.

Paradoxically, safety level can increase when there is an increase in hazard level. The best example of this is the difficult approach to Hong Kong, where the combination of terrain and weather and procedures would be unacceptable to pilots at "normal" airports. Yet there has never been a serious accident at Hong Kong arising from the difficulty of the approach. Similarly, the approach to Runway 18 at Washington National, which follows the Potomac River, involves a winding, "unstabilised" approach. Again, there has never been a serious accident at this airport arising from this difficult procedure, presumably because it raises pilot alertness level.

The trouble with this airline's safety is that we have ten-year problems, five-year plans, three-year people, and now one-year dollars.

2 Safety Philosophy and Law

Air safety is assured best by the quality of the airline itself, its management and physical resources. These in turn are a function of money. But safety is still the subject of the most stringent rules and regulations known to any industry.

National laws governing air transport safety differ in the letter, interpretation and implementation. But practically all, including those of such a traditionally reticent country as the Soviet Union, are based in principle — and many according to the exact letter — on the recommended standards and practices of Icao, the International Civil Aviation Organisation. Icao is an agency of the United Nations, and is financed by its 100-plus member countries in proportion to their air traffic.

The word "recommended" has helped to make the world of air safety nearly one. The standards and procedures observed by pilots and air traffic control officers are the same almost everywhere international air services operate. Icao's standards are also purely technical, avoiding economic and political matters such as traffic rights and fares, with their delicate overtones of national sovereignty.

Most countries have signed the 1946 Chicago Convention. This set up Icao, which in turn drafted a series of operating handbooks. These take the form of Annexes to the Chicago Convention, covering air-traffic control, airworthiness, airport standards, radio communications, search and rescue services, accident investigation, and so on. They are listed at the end of this chapter. The civil aviation countries of the world may differ over the sovereignty-sensitive politics and economics of air transport, but there is virtually only one law governing technical standards. This is a unique achievement by the air-transport industry.

The Icao Annexes go into extensive detail, even defining, for instance, the shape and size of airliner registration lettering. Because they are voluntary they have become generally accepted. Not all are implemented. Some countries are just too backward or too poor to install the radio and navigation aids and airport facilities that Icao recommends. This is obviously unsafe, and it is the reason for the Icao experts whose job it is to advise and train local personnel. In many instances Icao actually supplies beacons or radars or radio equipment. The cost is borne by the subscriptions paid by States contracting to Icao. The financial burden falls most heavily on the biggest air-transport nations, which also supply many of the experts and the equipment.

Licences, like passports, are the property of each State, which by grant or revocation controls professional standards. Each individual aircraft, pilot, engineer and airline is licensed. An airliner without a Certificate of Airworthiness may not fly. A pilot or navigator or engineer who loses his licence, or fails to qualify for its renewal, loses his job. An airline which loses its Operator's Certificate is grounded.

Pilots and engineers employed by a government or its civil-aviation agency supervise and enforce standards. A Flight Inspector is likely to board an airliner anywhere at any time, checking flight plans, procedures, load documentation, flight-time limitations, the general professional performance of the crew and the way they conform with the requirements of the Operations and Flight Manuals. These are the statutory documents, part of the Certificate of Airworthiness, defining the operating procedures and limits of the aircraft and its crew. Engineer inspectors similarly check maintenance standards and the airworthiness of the aircraft, every component of which has its own approved maintenance schedule, overhaul life, and modification standard.

The working language of airline operations is English. The Russian pilot of an Aeroflot airliner will talk to the tower at Moscow airport in English. Russian is spoken at domestic airports, as is the mother tongue of other countries on domestic operations. Difficulties have arisen in Canada where French and English are equal languages officially under the law. But English has been standardised for international airline operations.

Fewer hazards arise when language is standardised, although confusion can arise — especially when a pilot is working in unfamiliar units as well as words. For example, a Brazilian pilot reported an incident arising from an instruction given to him while approaching a

European airport: "Set altimeter to 997." The pilot set his altimeter to 29.97. During the subsequent back-course ILS the pilot found, on visual contact, that he was 500ft lower than his altimeter indicated. He had set the altimeter to 29.97in of mercury instead of to 997mb.

Communications are important in all walks of life, but especially so in air safety. Communications become more difficult as technical complexity increases, and with it the amount of regulation and legal language in which regulations are couched, often incomprehensible to busy operators. A tragically large number of accidents could have been avoided if only there had been better communications as a result of previous incidents and accidents.

INCIDENT-REPORTING One of the most important air-safety rules is incident-reporting. Some countries make incident-reporting mandatory. An airline that does not report to the authorities an engine failure, a fire, a fault in the flying-control system or any other "reportable" incident as defined by the safety authority risks a fine or, at worst, loses its licence. Other countries prefer incident-reporting to be voluntary. There is controversy as to which is the better procedure: to leave what is obviously "reportable" to the professional conscience, or to enforce it at law. The best systems provide for voluntary as well as mandatory incident reporting.

The "mandatory" incident-reporting school argues that professional and commercial interests will tend to suppress incident information. A manufacturer is not necessarily going to tell the world about the shortcomings of his product, and other airlines may suffer avoidable accidents. This has happened.

The "voluntary" school argues that mandatory incident-reporting floods the authorities with paperwork so that the really useful incidents get buried beneath piles of trivia. It argues also that the fear of punishment is not the best inducement to confession.

The regulatory purpose of incident-reporting should be to get professionals sharing their experience with other professionals in the interests of air safety as a whole. The voluntary school does not want this debased by bureaucracy. The best incident information, it is argued, is forthcoming when the personnel involved know that their names will not be published or their frankness rewarded by disciplinary action.

There is much to be said for both systems. In America the Federal Aviation Administration has the power to fine airlines or personnel and to suspend their licences if they fail to report notifiable incidents or defects. There is little doubt that air-safety is well served by the mandatory reporting of defects and incidents, but only if voluntary reporting — especially of the subtle human-error type of incident — can be preserved. The Americans have complemented their mandatory incident-reporting system with a voluntary system, undertaking not to prosecute except in cases of gross indiscipline. As from 1976, all voluntary reports to the FAA went first to Nasa (National Aeronautics and Space Administration) for analysis and checking out, and the deletion of all identities.

Far more can be learnt from incidents than from a disaster and the forensic public inquiry which may follow, valuable though the uniquely penetrating examination of lawyers can be. The best form of accident-prevention is incident investigation. Incidents provide bigger samples from which to anticipate trends, and crews are alive to help. The International Air Transport Association, Iata, runs an Incident Exchange to which all airlines are invited to contribute, usually through their safety managers, on the understanding that anonymity will be respected. Reports of incidents are circulated round the operations departments of all Iata members. This is an effective way of learning from incidents which, for all that Fate cared, could have been a tragedy.

Other bodies in the experience-sharing business are the Flight Safety Foundation in America and the Flight Safety Committee in Britain.

Thousands of airliners with millions of components fly three or four thousand hours a year. The number of notifiable defects which go into the Technical Log of each aircraft is formidable, and 90 per cent of them are not really safety-sensitive. The job of the safety authority is to ensure that manufacturers and airlines identify and catch the serious ones, take the appropriate action, and alert all other affected operators — not only in the same country but all over the world. This is the objective, but because it depends on human beings it is not always attained.

There was the case of an Australian-operated airliner crashing with heavy loss of life following a cabin-air compressor fire. The inquiry found that if the operator had known about two similar compressor incidents with the same type of aircraft, one in Canada and another in the West Indies, a modification would have been incorporated. The inquiry blamed the manufacturer of the equipment for not having notified all operators of the defect and rebuked the airworthiness authority of the country in which the aircraft and component were manufactured for not having seen that this was done.

There was the case of the airliner which crashed in France when a cargo door blew off — a repetition of an accident which had befallen a similar type of aircraft operated by another airline in another country nearly two years before. Again, the manufacturer and its parent airworthiness authority were reproached. The incident-reporting system had failed.

The most powerful incident alert is the Airworthiness Directive, or

AD, to use the American Federal Aviation Administration term. For example:

"Effective immediately, a one-time inspection of the tailplane attachment angles for cracks, and the rework or replacement if cracks are found, and installation of stiffener brackets on all series airplanes in accordance with manufacturer's Service Bulletin SEB70-32."

By the time such an AD goes out, the manufacturer should already have taken action through his normal customer-support Service Bulletin. The role of the government air-safety agency is to ensure that public-transport operators are alerted to serious defects, and that action is not compromised by commercial interests.

Human defects are not easily made the subject of the law, and perhaps for the best results they never should be. Incident-reporting may be achieved by law or persuasion, or both. However achieved, no philosophy of air safety can be complete without it.

The international law governing crimes against aircraft, and liability for aircraft accidents, is the subject of Chapters 7 and 11 respectively.

RULES AND RESPONSIBILITY As the machine takes over more and more human functions it tends to diminish human responsibility. Also encroaching more and more upon the individual are State and law-makers. Airlines can say "well, we haven't been told to do this, so let's not bother." This tendency is apparent not only in aviation; when a trawler with 11 crew members sank, and was found to have only one five-man life craft, the owners were able to claim that they had "met Government regulations". But what did the owner thing he was doing? More to the point, what did the seamen think they were doing, and what had happened to their sense of individual responsibility?

The regulator's job is to create the environment in which the airline professionals recognise their own responsibility for safety.

Safety is important in times of growth and, paradoxically, in times of recession. There is an economic relationship between safety and the operational pressure of growth, and between safety and the parsimony and low morale of recession. Air safety requires constant investment by airline management in equipment, training, operational research, data-processing and analysis, and research. Regulations set only the minimum standards. The safest airlines set their own, higher, standards.

The law does not require an airline to buy, say, an airborne Flight Data Recorder (FDR). The financially strong airline will do so. Such a system monitors and measures every flight: take-off speed, flap settings, climb, cruise, descent, landing speeds, and so on. At the end of the desired period the tapes are removed for analysis. This may show where crews departed from correct procedures, allowing training methods to be changed, or even individual pilots' bad habits to be corrected.

The engineering department might want flight-recorder channels to monitor the engines, systems, flying-control surfaces, or highly stressed parts of the airframe structure. Data-processing and analysis will identify and anticipate faults. Reports go immediately to the engineering department, which will take more professional pride in fault-prevention than in fault-correction. And if the national regulatory body is really good, it will require all operators to report defect and incident information, and will have an organisation dedicated to ensuring that the right information about the serious defects and incidents gets to the right people so that they do not become accidents.

Spending on air safety is often hard to justify in the airline boardroom when next year's budget is reviewed against the usual pressure of rising costs. The voice of the operations director or chief engineer is more likely to prevail in the boardrooms of financially strong airlines. This is where air safety really begins, important though government regulations and inspectors may be.

OPERATING DOCUMENTS A number of technical reference books are essential to the safe operation of an airliner. Carried either on the flight deck or on the library shelves and desks of the flight-operations and engineering departments, they are typically as follows:

Certificate of Airworthiness No airliner may fly without a Certificate of Airworthiness, which is issued by the appropriate government authority. The certificate relates primarily to the type of aircraft, and its engines and equipment; but each aircraft individually must have a Certificate of Airworthiness. The certificate confirms that the airliner meets the airworthiness requirements of the authorities in respect of design, construction, workmanship, performance, operating limitations, modifications, and so on. A C of A can be revoked by the airworthiness authority if the aircraft is not maintained or modified according to the prescribed standards, or if any question of safety arises following an accident.

Certificate of Maintenance is part of the Certificate of Airworthiness. Certificates of Maintenance may be issued only by fully qualified licensed engineers approved by the airworthiness authority.

Technical Log At the end of every flight the captain enters in the airliner's Technical Log the take-off and landing times and particulars of any defects. Copies of the Certificate of Compliance, confirming that the defect has been corrected (see below), are later entered in the Technical Log — copies of which have to be kept by the engineering department for at least two years.

Certificate of Compliance This verifies that part of the aircraft or its equipment has been overhauled or replaced or modified in accordance with the requirements of the airworthiness authority. A Certificate of Compliance may be issued by a licensed aircraft engineer. Variations of the Certificate of Compliance are the Certificate of Release and the Certificate of Fitness for Flight.

Operations Manual This has to be supplied by the operator, and copies made available to all operating staff and kept up to date with amendments. The Operations Manual has to be approved by the airworthiness authority. It specifies the number of crew to be carried in each aircraft type, defines their duties, and — to quote the British requirements — "such technical particulars concerning the aircraft, its engine and equipment and concerning the performance of the aircraft as may be necessary to enable the flight crew... to perform their respective duties". Further, it contains all the check lists and standard procedures for emergencies, approach and landing, communications, weather reports; it prescribes minimum safe altitudes, and provides airport and route guides including all maps and charts (usually in a separate volume).

Flight Manual This document is provided by the manufacturer as part of the Certificate of Airworthiness. It sets out all the operating and structural limitations of the aircraft. Loading limitations include weights, centres of gravity, weight distributions, and floor strengths (Chapter 12). Airspeed limitations include all speeds which are limiting from the standpoint of structural integrity or handling qualities. Operating speeds are defined in Chapter 6.

Although the Operations Manual is prepared by each airline, and is peculiar to it, a standard typical Operations Manual is provided by most airworthiness authorities. Typical of these is the United Kingdom Civil Aviation Authority document CAP 360.

Performance and Weight Schedules These are part of the aircraft Flight Manual, and set out the standard performance and weights of the aircraft as measured and approved by the airworthiness authority. The International Civil Aviation Organisation in its Annex 8, *Airworthiness of Aircraft*, recommends that:

"sufficient data on the performance of the aeroplane shall be determined and scheduled in the aeroplane Flight Manual to provide operators with the necessary information for the purpose of determining the total weight of the aeroplane on the basis of the values, peculiar to the proposed flight, of the relevant operational parameters, in order that the flight may be made with the reasonable assurance that a safe minimum performance for that flight will be achieved."

The Weight Schedule, or Aircraft Weight and Balance Manual (see

Chapter 12), includes the maximum certificated weights for take-off, taxying, landing, and for "zero fuel". The most forward and rearward centre-of-gravity positions for the various configurations (take-off, cruising, landing) are specified.

Load Sheet For every flight the weight of the aircraft must be computed and entered on the Load Sheet. This sets out the weight of the Aircraft Prepared for Service (APS); and the respective total weights of baggage and cargo (crew and fuel weights are usually included in the APS weight). The manner in which the load is distributed and the centre-of-gravity positioned are all seen by the captain, who signs the Load Sheet before each flight.

Training Manual Airlines are required to prepare a Training Manual for everyone concerned in the training and testing of crews. The manual sets out training procedures, the minimum qualifications of instructors and check pilots, and of the trainees, and includes forms for recording training and tests. It also sets out simulator procedures, the extent to which training can be carried out on normal public transport flights, and defines the use of approved simulators and other training equipment.

The training records of each crewmember must legally be available to the authorities before he makes any public-transport flight carrying passengers. In practice the flight inspectors of the relevant authority ensure that Training Manuals are comprehensive, up-to-date, and amended in line with the best professional practice.

Log Books Every aircraft, and each of its engines and certain items of equipment, are required to have a Log Book. These are permanent records of defect and maintenance history, flying hours, and so on.

Air Operators Certificate This is an airline's licence to operate, and is awarded by the authorities when they are satisfied with the airline's competence, organisation, staffing and other arrangements.

Aeronautical Information Publication (AIP) This is provided by each State, in accordance with Icao Annex 15. It contains full information on the State's aeronautical facilities and regulations. The AIP is in fact the pilot's bible, providing him with all the detailed operating information he needs concerning:

Airports (AGA — Airports and Ground Aids)
Communications (COM)
Meteorology (MET)
Air Traffic Rules and Services (RAC)
Facilitation (FAL)
Search and Rescue (SAR)
Aeronautical Charts (MAP)
General (GEN)

13

Although too big and bulky to be carried on the flight deck, the AIP (*Air Pilot* as it is known in the United Kingdom) is the source of all route information in the Operations Manual. It is one of the most used documents in any airline's operations department.

Notams, or Notices to Airmen, supplement the AIP (above). They are not necessarily a part of the AIP or its amendment service. They provide usually temporary navigational information and warnings. Notams are typically published weekly. They are classed according to urgency as Class I (immediate telex) and Class II (post).

Civil Aviation Information Circulars These further supplement the AIP, and usually provide notice of proposed changes to operational procedures, or safety warnings following incidents or accidents (see Chapter 10). Like the AIP and the Notam, they are published by the Aeronautical Information Service of the State civil aviation authority. (An AIS office is usually open 24 hours a day to provide operational information on request).

Airline Transport Pilot's Licence This is the highest civil-pilot qualification. The holder must have an Instrument Rating, and Aircraft Ratings specifying those types which he has been cleared to fly as commander or as copilot. The minimum qualifications for an ALTP are typically at least 1,500 flying hours, of which 250 hours shall have been as pilot-in-command. He must have flown at least 100 hours at night, either in command or as copilot, and at least 75 hours instrument-flying of which not more than 25 hours may have been in a flight simulator. He must also have flown "a reasonable amount" in the type of aircraft on which he is to be qualified.

Applicants for an ALTP or its renewal must carry out a General Flying Test and a Type Rating Flight Test, demonstrating their competence in instrument flying, cross-country flying by day and night, and basic aircraft handling as well as all the manoeuvres and drills — including emergencies — appropriate to the aircraft type. Emergencies in instrument conditions may be carried out in the simulator. The holder of an ALTP has to undergo a flight-competence check every six months, and his Instrument Rating has to be renewed every 13 months. Medical requirements are discussed in Chapter 19. He may not carry passengers in heavy aircraft (usually defined as those weighing more than 20,000kg) over a certain age, the highest being typically 60.

Other pilot licences, with more limited privileges, are the Commercial Pilot's Licence (CPL) and the Senior CPL, holders of which are typically allowed to fly aircraft for hire and reward weighing respectively not more than 5,700kg and 20,000kg, and provided they have an Instrument Rating for public-transport flying.

Icao Annexes There are 16 Annexes to the Chicago Convention, setting out the recommended International Standards of the operation of aircraft. These "Annexes to the Convention", as they are known, are as follows:

Annex 1 Personnel Licensing
Annex 2 Rules of the Air
Annex 3 Meteorology
Annex 4 Aeronautical Charts
Annex 5 Units of Measurement
Annex 6 Operation of Aircraft
Annex 7 Aircraft Nationality and Registration Marks
Annex 8 Airworthiness of Aircraft
Annex 9 Facilitation
Annex 10 Aeronautical Telecommunications
Annex 11 Air Traffic Services
Annex 12 Search and Rescue
Annex 13 Aircraft Accident Investigation
Annex 14 Aerodromes
Annex 15 Aeronautical Information
Annex 16 Aircraft Noise

Belgrade tower to Aeroflot: "Can't you not speak English?"

---

3 Measuring Air Safety

How is airline safety measured? The criterion most commonly used is the number of passenger fatalities per 100 million scheduled passenger-miles. The scheduled airlines reckon that one passenger killed per 100 million passenger-miles is "acceptable". The trend is steadily down; but this is thanks partly to the greater passenger-mile productivity of increasingly big airliners. The passenger-mile criterion is of limited usefulness, except perhaps for public relations purposes.

Fatal airline accidents are so few that variations from one year to another, or between one airline or country and another, can be the result of wholly random effects. Statistical treatment of safety has therefore to be approached with special caution. There is a high element of chance whether an accident goes into the fatal record, or involves an aircraft which is a 350-seater or a 10-seater, or is 30, 60 or 100 per cent full. Even accident investigators feel that too much effort goes into following up one isolated accident which just happened to be fatal, perhaps by the narrowest of margins.

Whatever the measure, aircraft carrying 300 or more people are now so commonplace that there must be major improvements in safety if a steep rise in the number of fatalities is to be avoided.

The average passenger wants to know before he flies:

What are the chances of this aircraft crashing?

What are my chances of being killed if it crashes?

The measure of fatalities per so-many scheduled passenger-miles is unsatisfactory. A big airline with a very large volume of passenger-miles might suffer over a period of time one accident a year in which a few passenger fatalities are involved. The same airline might also, in the same period, get away with a number of scrapes. Yet this airline appears to have a safety record better than that of a small airline which flies for 20 or 30 years without scratching a passenger and which suffers, through no fault of its own, a tragedy which kills 100 passengers. Obviously unfair.

Airline A might suffer a series of, say, six culpable accidents, killing 50 passengers. The similar-sized Airline B might suffer over the same period — through no fault of its own — one accident killing 150 passengers. Airline B would appear in the statistics to be three times more dangerous than Airline A. Again, obviously absurd.

Airline C might fly the same volume of passenger-miles as Airline D and both might in the same period suffer one accident each, killing the same number of passengers. Yet it might well be that Airline C operates five times as many flights, and in a more adverse climate. Airline C is obviously the safer operator; but it appears equal in terms of fatalities per passenger-mile.

Another important flaw in this index is that it does not take into account non-scheduled flying. Nor does it take account of scheduled cargo operations. Together these two activities comprise perhaps 30 per cent of total world air transport, a proportion which is tending to increase. Nor does it differentiate between high-load-factor and low-load-factor operators, tending to discriminate against the former. It also ignores crew lives lost.

Passenger fatalities per 100 million scheduled passenger-miles provide a fair measure of general air transport safety. But even if one fatality per 100 million passenger-miles is "acceptable" today, it certainly is not going to be in 20 years' time, when the passenger-mileage volume will be so great that it would mean 10,000 people killed per year and big, black air-crash headlines every other day.

In order to compensate for the limitations of this most commonly accepted index, four other measures of air transport safety are adopted for this analysis. By these measures 15 leading air transport countries are assessed over what is felt to be an adequately long period — ten years. Obviously, air crashes are rare enough for comparisons over anything much less than five years to produce a distorted picture.

ACCIDENTS The accident tables list all crashes from January 1, 1963, to December 31, 1972, to transport-category aircraft of more than 12,500lb a.u.w. registered in the 15 countries concerned. The accidents all occurred to revenue flights, scheduled or non-scheduled, and killed passengers or crew. Cabin deaths caused by turbulence, and ground fatalities, are omitted.

TRAFFIC Total air transport *production*, measured in available capacity tonne-km (CTK), and total air transport *flights*, measured as departures, are assessed for both scheduled and non-scheduled operations for each country for the ten years.

The British Government publication *Business Monitor* provides figures for UK airlines while the *CAB Handbook of Airline Statistics* gives total CTKs and scheduled departures for US airlines. Non-scheduled US departures are estimated using average CTK/departure for scheduled traffic as a guide. The *Icao Digest of Statistics* gives scheduled and non-scheduled traffic for scheduled airlines and is used to up-date the US figures and to calculate the scheduled airlines' contribution to the ten-year totals of other nations. Non-scheduled traffic carried by non-scheduled airlines not covered by Icao is estimated airline by airline, using the annual *Flight* World Airline Surveys and Commercial Aircraft Surveys and typical average utilisations and block times. The available capacity and number of flights for each nation's non-Icao non-scheduled operators is assessed. These figures are adjusted for the growth in the charter market and the changes in equipment and the pattern of charter operations over the ten-year period and added to the basic data obtained from the Icao digest.

We now have two measures of total air transport *activity*, production and flights, against which to assess two measures of air transport *safety*: number of fatal accidents and number of fatalities to passengers and crew.

We can now work out for each country: (1) number of fatal accidents per unit of total transport production; (2) number of fatal accidents per flight; (3) number of fatalities per unit of total transport production; (4) number of fatalities per flight. These four criteria compensate for many of the deficiencies of the commonly accepted safety index of passenger fatalities per 100 million scheduled passenger-miles.

Probably the best single index of airline safety is the number of fatal accidents per departure. A passenger asks himself what his chances are of surviving a particular flight. He does not really consider the risk different if it lasts 10 hours or 1, if it goes fast or slow, or if he is with 400 or 40 passengers.

There were around four fatal accidents per million flights at the beginning of the 1960s (scheduled services). The British figure in 1935 was 67. The British and world rate is now just below 3. The "magic" rate of 1 is achieved by a few airlines. The target —if in our imperfect world it cannot be 0 — should be not more than 1 fatal crash per million flights, including charters.

THE SAFEST AIR TRANSPORT COUNTRIES The results are shown in the table below. They show that, of the 15 leading air transport countries examined, five are above average by every measure of air safety. They are, in order: Netherlands; Australia; Scandinavia; United States; West Germany.

The safest of all the world's leading air transport countries is the Netherlands. The Dutch record must be due to observance of all the best professional practices, and above all perhaps to the country's highly developed system of incident reporting.

AIR TRANSPORT SAFETY:
15 LEADING AIR TRANSPORT NATIONS COMPARED
1963-1972

All revenue flights, scheduled and non-scheduled,
involving fatalities to passengers or crew

Country	Accidents		Activity		Accident rates				Rank†
	No of fatal crashes	No of pass & crew killed	Capacity tonne-km (CTK) × 1,000 million	Flights × million	Fatal crashes/ million million CTK	Fatal crashes/ million flights	Fatali-ties/ 1,000 million CTK	Fatali-ties/ million flights	
Australia	2	50	16.356	2.551	122	0.785	3.06	19.6	2
Belgium	3	17	7.441	0.442	404	6.787	2.28	38.4	6
Brazil	12	298	7.751	1.574	1,550	7.620	38.42	189.3	13
Canada	11	364	28.529	2.732	386	4.030	12.75	133.2	8
France	13	532	26.037	1.834	500	7.090	20.42	290.0	12
Germany (W)	3	79	21.476	1.374	140	2.181	3.68	57.5	5
India	12	351	6.313	0.739	1,900	16.238	55.55	475.0	14
Italy	7	158	14.847	1.487	471	4.705	10.63	106.1	7
Japan	10	583	19.905	2.224	502	4.495	29.30	262.0	11
Netherlands	None	None	17.183	0.893	None	None	None	None	1
Scandinavia (1)	3	86	16.754	2.225	179	1.348	5.13	38.6	3
UK	16	949	46.900	4.411	341	3.620	20.25	215.1	9
USA	91	2,449	500.638	54.100	182	1.680	4.90	45.3	4
Country A (2)	7	279	1.889	0.184	3,705	38.000	148.00	1,516.0	15
Country B (3)	5	78	4.202	0.680	1,190	7.350	18.55	114.8	10
Totals/averages	195	6,273	736.2	77.450	265	2.52	8.51	80.9	

Sources: *Flight*, May 17, 1973; Icao Digest of Statistics No. 169; Business Monitor; CAB Handbook of Airline Statistics. For all countries except USA and UK non-scheduled operations by non-scheduled operators estimated airline-by-airline. †N.B. This ranking has no mathematical validity—see explanatory note. (1) Denmark, Norway and Sweden (2) A Middle East country (3) A South American country.

AS ABOVE, 1953-1962

Country	Accidents		Activity		Accident Rate				Rank
	No of fatal crashes	No of pass & crew killed	CTK × 1,000m	km × 100m	Fatal crashes/ 1,000m CTK	Fatal crashes/ 100m km	Fatali-ties/ 1,000m CTK	Fatali-ties/ 100m km	
Australia	6	68	4.932	9.238	1.22	0.65	13.8	7.4	1
Belgium	8	244	1.776	3.575	4.51	2.24	137.5	68.3	10
Brazil	32	657	5.071	11.850	6.31	2.70	129.5	55.4	11
Canada	18	261	6.203	9.712	2.90	1.85	42.0	26.9	7
France	33	908	8.335	18.735	3.96	1.76	109.0	48.4	9
Germany (W)	4	46	1.870	3.625	2.14	1.10	24.6	12.7	5
India	28	220	2.020	4.188	13.85	6.70	109.0	52.5	13
Italy	8	239	2.040	2.801	3.92	2.85	117.0	85.4	12
Japan	2	36	1.336	2.177	1.50	0.92	27.0	16.5	4
Netherlands	6	267	5.008	6.794	1.20	0.88	53.2	39.2	6
Scandinavia	4	62	3.871	5.647	1.03	0.71	16.0	11.0	2
UK	35	818	11.789	19.435	2.97	1.80	69.4	42.0	8
USA	94	2,406	109.145	149.926	0.86	0.63	22.0	16.1	3
Country A	5	66	0.288	0.656	17.35	7.62	229.0	100.5	14
Country B	15	394	1.098	2.586	13.65	5.80	359.0	152.0	15
Totals/averages	298	6,692	164.700	250.900	1.81	1.19	40.6	26.6	

Second comes Australia. This country's safety record is often attributed to good weather, but it could also be due to the general air-mindedness of the country and hence of its leaders. Air-safety regulation — toughly enforced — is led by professionals who have been in the job for many years. Australia's safety record may also owe something to its long-established system of mandatory defect and incident reporting with strict follow-up action, and to full publication of financial information. Australia has been described as a "police state" in its air safety regulation and enforcement.

Third comes Scandinavia (Sweden, Norway, Denmark). The Scandinavian record is particularly fine when it is considered that SAS is a triple-nationality airline — and that its home bases are amid some of the worst flying terrain and weather in the world.

Fourth comes the United States. The sheer volume of this country's airline activity — nearly 70 per cent of the total considered — illuminates the fact that US airlines account for less than half the world's airline accidents. The US record may also be partly attributable to full defect, incident and financial reporting, and to the fact that its main safety body, the Federal Aviation Administration, has always been led by professional aviators. The US philosophy is that in technical regulation only professionals can best judge the advice, work and motivation of professionals.

West Germany comes fifth, above average on every count. This is particularly commendable considering Lufthansa's rapid expansion, which is known to cause operating problems in the airline industry, as Japanese airlines especially appear to have learnt.

These were almost the findings of a similar *Flight* analysis covering the previous decade, 1953-1962 (issue of May 30, 1963). The results of that study are above. Two of the yardsticks were different, measuring accidents and fatalities per km rather than per departure or flight (because full departures data were not available then). But the overall 1953-1962 rankings show the safest countries still the safest ten years later.

The safest air transport countries over the whole 20-year period emerge in alpahabetical order as: Australia, Netherlands, Scandinavia, United States.

METHOD OF RANKING The final column in each table gives the nations a ranking based on their performance in each of the measures of accident rate. It is computed for each table by giving the four best individual accident rates the index 100, relating the other individual rates to this index, and then adding together each country's resultant scores. In the case of the table covering the period 1963-1972, the

Netherlands, with no accidents, is ranked first and the index 100 is related to the second-best individual score. It is emphasised that this computation has no mathematical validity, since one is not adding together homogeneous criteria; but it probably produces as fair an overall picture as can be devised.

Countries which are below average by each measure share a safety record which can be incontrovertibly described as below average.

THE SMALLER AIR TRANSPORT COUNTRIES Important air transport countries which rarely, if ever, appear in the annual *Flight* world airline accident tables, but which are not in the first 15 in terms of size, include, in alphabetical order: Austria, Finland, Iceland, Ireland, Israel, New Zealand, Portugal, South Africa, Switzerland.

In the 3½ years since the decade reviewed up to the time this book went to press, the countries listed recorded the following fatal accidents according to the same definitions (that is, accidents to all fixed-wing public-transport aircraft on scheduled or non-scheduled flights, passenger or freight, causing the death of one or more occupants):

	No of fatal crashes	No of passengers and crew killed
Australia	1	11
Belgium	1	105
Brazil	7	178
Canada	5	53
France	1	8
Germany (W)	1	59
India	1	48
Italy	1	38
Japan	—	—
Netherlands	1	191
Scandinavia	1	14
UK	1	104
USA	25	917
Country A	2	38
Country B	1	6

The countries whose airlines appear to be getting safer, in accord with the world trend, are (in alphabetical order) France, India, Italy, Japan, the United Kingdom and Country B. Only Brazil and Canada appear to show worsening safety trends. Rankings appear to be unchanged for the "top five".

The Author's method of ranking has been the subject of further statistical analysis by C. W. Smith and J. Taylor. Smith and Taylor, using the same figures, demonstrate statistically that for the small samples involved (Poissons' formula) the number of fatal crashes for eight of the 15 countries examined is "within the limits of variability arising from the play of chance," taking into account each country's exposure related to its volume of activity.

According to Smith and Taylor the eight countries which had no more crashes than might statistically be expected from the play of chance in relation to their activity were: Australia, Belgium, Canada, Italy, Japan, Scandinavia, West Germany and the United Kingdom.

Five countries had more crashes than might statistically be expected from the play of chance in relation to their activity: Country B, Brazil, Country A, France and India (the latter's domestic operations almost entirely). Only two countries had records which were better than might statistically be expected. Paradoxically, those were the two countries with the least and the most crashes: The Netherlands, with no crashes, and the United States, with 91 crashes.

	"Expected" number based on			N = Number of fatal crashes actually experienced	A Probability of experiencing	B	C Probability of achieving better than N 100–B%
	Capacity tonne-kilo-metres	Sectors	Cols 1 & 2 merged		N or fewer %	N or more %	
Australia	4.33	6.42	5.37	2	9.68	97.05	2.95
Belgium	1.97	1.11	1.54	3	92.92	20.13	79.87
Brazil	2.05	3.96	3.01	12	99.998	00.007	99.993
Canada	7.56	6.88	7.22	11	93.61	11.49	88.51
France	6.90	4.62	5.76	13	99.75	0.64	99.36
West Germany	5.69	3.46	4.57	3	33.06	83.41	16.59
India*	1.67	1.86	1.77	12	99.999948	0.00004	99.99996
Italy	3.93	3.74	3.83	7	95.83	9.37	90.63
Japan	5.27	5.60	5.43	10	97.67	5.02	94.98
Netherlands	4.55	2.25	3.40	Nil	3.34	100.0	Nil
Scandinavia	4.44	5.60	5.02	3	26.22	87.70	12.30
UK	12.42	11.11	11.77	16	91.07	13.94	86.06
USA	132.60	136.22	134.41	91	0.0045	99.997	0.003
Country A†	0.50	0.46	0.48	7	99.999954	0.00008	99.99992
Country B**	1.11	1.71	1.41	5	99.67	1.47	98.53

Notes: *Almost entirely domestic operations: †A Middle East country; **A South American country. Source: "Flight," May 17, 1973.

The Smith and Taylor approach to an Overall Safety Index, using the same data, is different. The authors calculate the "expected" number of crashes on the basis of capacity tonne-km (CTK) and sectors (= flights or departures). The expected number of crashes is related to the 15-country averages, which are 2.5 crashes per million flights and 2.64 crashes per 10 million CTK. This method gives a common measure — the expected number of accidents — for each accident index, whether it be sectors, aircraft miles, aircraft hours or whatever. These can then be combined to form a single joint expectation.

Smith and Taylor statistically examine the probabilities of each country experiencing the number of crashes it actually sustained. The authors employ Poissons' Distribution as an appropriate statistical law representative of situations like air safety, where risk exposure is high but the number of events is low. A computer calculates the probability of each country experiencing the actual number of crashes sustained in relation to its volume of activity. The results are shown in the table.

Two countries emerge with probabilities below 5 per cent — in other words, countries which had improbably few crashes in relation to their activity. These are the USA with 0.0045 per cent and the Netherlands with 3.34 per cent.

Five countries experienced more accidents than could reasonably be attributed to chance: Country B, Brazil, Country A, France and India.

Either Column A or Column B in the table can be used for ranking, according to Smith and Taylor. They select Column B purely on common sense, otherwise the Netherlands with zero accidents would come second to the USA — which it would not have done, according to this method, if it had one accident or more. Column B is shown in column C according to its complements — that is to say subtracted from 100. This determines the probability that the country concerned might have had fewer accidents than it actually did. This removes subjective judgement from the ranking, giving it more scientific validity than the Author's method does, though the conclusions are not in fact very different.

INDIVIDUAL RISK OF DEATH The proportion of passengers on board who perish in an air crash was between 80 and 90 per cent in the mid-1960s, falling to between 70 and 80 per cent in the late 1960s as the first generation (narrow-body) jets like the 707 and DC-8, DC-9 and 727 became established in service. These percentages relate to scheduled services only. The same pattern might be expected in charter services. The percentage began to rise again in the 1970s, but this trend could not be attributed to the 300-plus-seat jumbo jets introduced in 1970-1974 (Boeing 747, DC-10, TriStar, A300). Until an accident on November 20, 1974, in which 38 per cent of those on board were killed, there were no fatal accidents to the 747 in its first five years; one to the TriStar in which 56 per cent of those on board died; and one to a DC-10 in which all 346 occupants were killed.

A totally catastrophic crash, for example to the DC-10 near Paris in March 1974, appears less likely to befall the jumbo jets, which benefit from nearly two decades of safety experience with the original subsonic jets, and which have bigger structures to cushion the loads in a survivable crash. The proportion of passengers who survive an airliner accident appears likely to remain, on average, between 10 and 30 per cent.

For the record, the average number of passengers carried in an airliner was between 40 and 50 in the early 1960s, and between 70 and 80 in the early 1970s. International airlines carry almost 10 more than the average, and domestic services about five fewer.

SUMMARY The answer to the passenger's question *what are my chances of being killed before I get to my destination?* is three in a million. This is worked out as follows. Assuming that there are two fatal crashes per million flights (sectors) and that in these crashes 25 per cent of the occupants survive on average, then, assuming two sectors per journey, the chances of "not getting there alive" are three in a million, or .0003 per cent.

Definition of an air-safety statistician: A man who looks at a tadpole today and tomorrow and forecasts a whale in six months time.

---

4 The Government Regulator

Where does safety begin? With well trained pilots and engineers? With aircraft designers? With government regulators? There is no doubt about the answer in the opinion of Mr C. O. Miller, former director of aviation safety, US National Transportation Safety Board. Miller was a Second World War Marine Corps fighter pilot, an engineering test pilot with LTV, a teacher in the Faculty of Flight Safety at the University of Southern California, and Director of the Bureau of Aviation Safety in the National Transportation Safety Board. He is now with the US Flight Safety Foundation.

Miller does not start in the operating field, important though it is: "I start in the design field. Safety begins with the design of an overall system to encompass an overall requirement." He believes that the safety of an aircraft cannot be better than it was designed to be before it goes into operation.

He will then agree on the importance of operational safety, in particular on good defect and incident reporting. "The operating world has a unique capacity to make mistakes that no designer ever thought could be made. The complexity of modern technology is such that I defy anybody — anybody, however good he is — to predict all operating errors. The role of incident and defect reporting is to find those errors before they become accidents." Miller draws a distinction between what operations people are capable of doing, as judged by designers, and what they actually do. "The fundamental mission of incident and defect reporting," he says, "is to measure that difference."

The problem of how to get pilots and engineers to report the really significant "occurrences," to use the British generic term for incidents and defects, is at the heart of air safety. The fear of legal or disciplinary consequences can seriously inhibit such reporting. The best system, in Miller's opinion, is Australia's, where the authorities accept that it is more important to encourage pilots and engineers to relate their experiences than it is to punish them. The law stands, obviously; but it is enforced with what appears to be commonsense and discretion. "Clearly, if there has been gross negligence, the authorities cannot close their ears any more than a priest can to the confessions of an axe murderer."

Federal Aviation Administration inspectors will turn a blind eye when safety appears to be more desirable than a prosecution, but "I have heard others say 'sure I'd like to help you, but I have to write this up as a violation'." This attitude does not always beget air safety.

It is for this reason that the Federal Aviation Administration has introduced a "middleman" — the National Aeronautics and Space Administration — into the US incident-reporting system. Nasa investigates and interrogates, and passes the processed incident reports along to the FAA with names deleted (see below).

More important than the fear of the law to most employees — pilots and engineers — is the fear of being fired. To get round this, airlines have tried to exchange safety information, with no names revealed. "There have been many meetings but you would be surprised how fast people lose touch afterwards. The idea falls down a crack somewhere, perhaps because it doesn't show a direct benefit. In the USA the legal problem is very real. You hear people say 'yes, we would like to participate, but our legal people won't support us'."

Nevertheless, he agrees that it is the role of the regulatory agency to make sure that there is a reporting system operated by somebody, but "just making a voluntary system mandatory does not automatically ensure that the real hazards are reported. You'd be surprised what comes out of the woodwork whenever there is an accident. You tell me of any accident and I will buy you a beer if I can't think of a precedent incident. It was only when we investigated the Miami TriStar crash that we discovered how many pilots had experienced premature autopilot disconnect."

Given a mandatory reporting system, how does the safety regulator separate the wheat from the chaff? Miller maintains that there must be somebody in the airline keeping an eye on air safety. "You have to have a man like Sonderlund of Northwest who will set up a movie camera and take photographs of V + 10 and V + 20kt take-offs and show the guys the experience he himself had."

The safety office — or "safety activity," as Miller prefers to call it — might be an operations executive, such as the vice-president operations or the chief pilot. But such executives have too much else to think about in the day-to-day administration of the airline. The specific safety activity might be one man or five, depending on the size of the airline. The philosophy that safety is everybody's problem still holds good; but there has to be, in Miller's view, a safety activity as well.

"The executive running it will probably have access direct to the president, though it is more important for everyone to know that the access exists than for it to be implemented. The man concerned will be smart enough, too, to let his line-manager colleagues know what he is doing except where there is a family-doctor or chaplain-confessor relationship involved." He will be a man to whom pilots with personal problems can turn. In some cases he may even have to "get to the guy's wife". Men with severe personal problems can, Miller says, be dangerous. He would have no hesitation in advising any airline to set up a safety activity — "no hesitation."

A lot of safety can also be achieved at social functions, perhaps in the cocktail bar after a convention or a manufacturers' meeting. "Any function which gets the professionals together is to be encouraged. Somebody says: 'we keep getting our pilots reporting that it is hard to get the autopilot to level off on the approach', or something, and somebody else asks 'you have that problem too?'

"The main thing is to get people together talking. It doesn't matter who sponsors the meeting, whether it's a government regulator, the Flight Safety Foundation, a manufacturer or whatever — just so long as somebody is doing it. What we have to generate is a co-operative attitude — and this is why I think we have such a good system and safety record in the USA. You won't find it as good in any other form of transportation."

The sort of man who fits into a "safety activity" is in Miller's experience the pilot who has perhaps made a point of working on the union safety committee, who keeps cuttings of accident reports, and reads all the journals. "He is a man with polite curiosity. If he goes around acting aggressively he will get nowhere. He's a man with a 'what happens if?' mentality."

Yet while everyone is advocating a co-operative attitude, there might be a cabin-blower failure somewhere in the world exactly the same as one that previously took place somewhere else. What, the passenger might ask, is Miller doing about this?

He agrees that there is nothing in any national law to co-ordinate accident-prevention activity internationally. The US National Transportation Safety Board publishes a great deal of information and circulates it to all interested foreign Governments, airlines, and technical press. But there is no formal international mechanism for exchanging incident reports. International safety appears to depend to a large degree on individuals. Miller's list of these includes men like George Wansbeek of KLM, the late Hugh Gordon-Burge of BEA, Bob Belton of British Airways, Mack Eastburn of American, Jerry Lederer, formerly of the Flight Safety Foundation, Karl Christiansen of United, Dan Beard of American, and others — "many of whom work through the International Air Transport Association's technical committees."

While airlines have a moral commitment not to kill people, the lives of the public are not, in Miller's opinion, the only safety motivation. "In the hard day-to-day business of accident prevention, killing 200 passengers a year or 350 in the bad years doesn't sell compared with the numbers killed on the roads, though it might do if this number were killed in one crash."

The military have a great deal to contribute to air safety, says Miller. Wiping out expensive materials and men hits the military hard and has led them to develop a special approach to air safety. "If somebody challenges their secrecy often enough this safety will come out."

US FEDERAL AVIATION ADMINISTRATION The US National Transportation Safety Board (NTSB) is primarily an accident investigator. It does not make or enforce air-safety rules. This is the job of the Federal Aviation Administration (FAA). The NTSB acts independently as a check-and-balance, making safety studies and publishing recommendations as well as investigating accidents. Its recommendations impose a professional rather than legal obligation on the FAA to comply. But the FAA is the US authority with the day-to-day executive responsibility for public air safety. To it the American airlines have to report certain specified airworthiness defects (not operating incidents, as in the Australian and British systems) within 24 hours. These are defined in US Federal Aviation Regulations Part 121.703 as follows:

SERVICE DIFFICULTY REPORTS
(a) Each certificate holder shall report the occurrence or detection of each failure, malfunction, or defect concerning:—
(1) Fires during flight and whether the related fire-warning system functioned properly
(2) Fires during flight not protected by a related fire-warning system
(3) False fire warning during flight
(4) An engine exhaust system that causes damage during flight to the engine, adjacent structure, equipment, or components
(5) An aircraft component that causes accumulation or circulation of

smoke, vapour, or toxic or noxious fumes in the crew compartment or passenger cabin during flight

(6) *Engine shutdown during flight because of flameout*

(7) *Engine shutdown during flight when external damage to the engine or airplane structure occurs*

(8) *Engine shutdown during flight due to foreign object ingestion or icing*

(9) *Engine shutdown during flight of more than one engine*

(10) *A propeller feathering system or ability of the system to control overspeed during flight*

(11) *A fuel or fuel-dumping system that affects fuel flow or causes hazardous leakage during flight*

(12) *A landing gear extension or retraction or opening or closing of landing gear doors during flight*

(13) *Brake system components that result in loss of brake actuating force when the airplane is in motion on the ground*

(14) *Aircraft structure that requires major repair*

(15) *Cracks, permanent deformation, or corrosion of aircraft structures, if more than the maximum acceptable to the manufacturer or the FAA*

(16) *Aircraft components or system that result in taking emergency actions during flight (except action to shut down an engine).*

All these reports are fed into the FAA's Maintenance Analysis Centre (MAC) based in Oklahoma City, approximately in the centre of the USA. Each report comes via the FAA maintenance or flight-operations inspector resident with the airline concerned, or from the regional FAA office. MAC is a support group, employing 17 operations and maintenance experts, including mathematics and scientific specialists. All staff have had at least 20 years in the airline or manufacturing industries.

Reports are edited and published daily in summary form as the Service Difficulty Report (SDR). This bright yellow document goes daily to all US airlines, manufacturers, repair bases, insurers, and others, including most foreign airworthiness authorities and all foreign manufacturers with US-certificated products. These daily SDRs form the bedrock of FAA safety policy and rule-making. They help to decide the ultimate FAA safety action — namely the issue of an Airworthiness Directive (AD). ADs can be issued by any of the 12 regional FAA offices with the exception of the European office, which has no legal authority. (The equivalent British document is called the *Mandatory Aircraft Modfications and Inspections Summary* and is published by the Civil Aviation Authority.)

Even under a mandatory reporting system incidents and defects can still become accidents — even though they may have been reported several times, as in the case of the Western Airlines Boeing 720B training accident in March 1971 in California.

There had been four previous failures of 707/720 rudder-actuator support brackets, going back to a KC-135 in 1967. No fewer than 28 cracked fittings had been reported between May 1969 and March 1971, it subsequently transpired. The FAA's view is that the training accident was not a previous defect because it was a bracket failure which occurred uniquely during asymmetric training.

There is also the view, held by the UK Flight Safety Committee, that somebody somewhere in the safety system should connect the combination of such events before chance does. But, as an FAA official says, any reporting system which involves human beings is vulnerable to failure; the argument for mandatory rather than voluntary reporting is that it diminishes the possible human failures.

The FAA's Oklahoma MAC computer can quickly recall case histories to help determine policy. If an incident appears to be unique to a particular carrier it may be a maintenance practice or a training fault, and the appropriate FAA regional action will be taken. But if the record shows a more general trend, other operators of the aircraft type — and the manufacturers — will be alerted.

According to Mr Tex Melugin, Deputy Director of the FAA Flight Standards Service, the relationship with the NTSB works and is good for air safety. The relationship is not as strained as has been suggested in Congress or in the news media, according to Melugin. Congress "leans" on the FAA very much, and he thinks this is healthy, though in his opinion it seldom affects the FAA's judgement on technical matters. Where Congress helps is with legislation and finance. "We have to go before the Congress to justify safety expenditure. Its view, incidentally, is that safety, the end product, should be an industry cost item."

Does the FAA, like the NTSB, believe that openness helps air safety? Melugin replies: "Yes, it helps us to do the job better. This industry cannot be operated in a vacuum."

The need for confidentiality can be a problem, however. According to Melugin, "We are being challenged by consumer groups to publish more and more under the Freedom of Information Act. The SDRs are now in the public domain, which they were not before." But Melugin says this has not greatly affected the preparation or content of the SDRs. "From the strict rule-making point of view they are much the same as when they were confidential."

US law empowers the FAA to punish offenders. Such powers would not be given to a Government agency by, for example, the Westminster Parliament, which allows only the courts to administer justice. But the FAA's right to reprimand or fine pilots and engineers up to $1,000 and to revoke their licences does, in the opinion of the FAA and Congress, produce a discipline which improves air safety.

Airlines vary greatly in their handling of incident and defect information, according to Mr David D. Thomas, past deputy administrator of the Federal Aviation Administration. Mr Thomas is of the opinion that wide dissemination of incident information is essential to air safety. Safety, he says "is in the warp and woof of an airline." He is convinced that a safety officer — what Miller calls a safety activity — is essential. There must, he believes, be an "air-safety record-keeper and gadfly" in every airline.

He respects the doctrine of Juan Trippe, past president of Pan American, that safety is everybody's business and that responsibility for it should not be shuffled off on to a safety department. "But it is better to have as well somebody focusing all this safety activity, somebody who isn't responsible for day-to-day operations. You can get so immersed in operating detail, staff problems and meetings that you don't have time to stand back and take a long hard look at the safety things that really matter."

On the relationship between safety and profitability, Thomas says: "A safe airline isn't necessarily profitable but an unsafe one cannot be."

Mandatory incident and defect reporting, in his view, is like any law — "for the small percentage of people who won't do the correct thing anyway." He quotes the English judge Lord Moulton who said in 1912 that the law cannot expect obedience to the unenforceable. "Passing a regulation," says Thomas, "can be just self-protection." In his opinion the spirit accomplishes more than the letter of the law. Mandatory reporting of the really "useful" incidents is in fact unenforceable. "You ran off the runway? That's easy to report. In any case, if you don't report it one of the passengers will. But you almost ran off the runway? Well, maybe you'll report it tomorrow."

There are a number of reasons why many incidents are in fact not reported tomorrow — inertia, fear of disciplinary reprisals, and perhaps above all the feeling that what happened was isolated, forgetting the Thomas dictum that "an accident is what happens after a series of isolated incidents." Thomas cites the Western 720B rudder-actuator bracket failure as an example. Each of the previous failures had been considered isolated. Everyone thought it had just happened to him, and that he had got away with it.

The important thing is to make incidents and defects easy to report. "Even an answerphone service helps. Above all, never use incident and defect reports for the purposes of disciplinary action." This again is where a safety officer is valuable. He will have a reputation for impartiality and discretion — "and this takes a lot of building up to the point where he has the complete confidence of both management and staff, and especially of the pilots."

How would Thomas ensure that incident and defect information reaches other airlines? "In the case of a new aircraft you can almost see that the job is done on the basis of personal contact," he says. "The obstacle to a completely free flow of information in the USA is the hoard of lawyers who can subpoena information. They are always at the back of everyone's mind and in my opinion they inhibit air safety."

But ways can be found to get information around. For example, the US military have two investigations, one private and the other public with everything on the record. The first is informal "and all concerned can bare their souls." How many times, for example, was recovery effected when the spoilers were pulled inadvertently almost too late for recovery before landing? A hundred times? Never? "The US Air Force says there are 300 incidents for every accident, though I don't know how they know."

What is a trend? Is it, in air safety, a single incident? "It could be, but look at one month's FAA Service Difficulty Reports. Almost every one contains an incident which, given the right set of circumstances, could be dangerous, but you act on them all."

Thomas advocates no-fault liability — "it happened, therefore I am liable." The priority must, he says, be to get the claimants recompensed fully and without delay. If an accident happens there should be prompt payment and the sole objective of the investigation should be to prevent further accidents, not to find who is the most liable. "If the law deters a manufacturer from changing his design for fear of the lawyers then the law is unsafe."

Thomas is aware of the lawyers' argument that, on the contrary, the prospect of huge damages encourages safety, but disagrees with it: "Even if there were no liability laws a manufacturer would not stay in business if he designed unsafe aircraft." He agrees, nevertheless, that manufacturers do make improvements despite the liability laws.

INDIVIDUAL RESPONSIBILITY Although automation can increase safety by narrowing the margins for human error, there remains a psychological danger. A man who feels he is no more than part of a machine can tend to act like one. Human beings respond to challenge. Without it they are vulnerable to monotony and boredom, and may make mistakes — not only in the handling of machines, but in taking over from the machine when it fails. Management and training must therefore encourage individuals, as machine and State tend to dominate, to ask themselves what they are personally doing to make flying safer. Government regulators, machines and laws can never replace human responsibility.

PILOT PSYCHOLOGY Human beings have so many advantages over machines that they have to be kept "in the system." But, unlike machines, they cannot be tested to destruction. Air-safety experts know more about, say, the corrosion of titanium or the surfacing of runways than they do about pilot psychology. Yet half of all accidents are caused by crew failure or error of some kinds. The next major development in air safety must therefore be to motivate pilots to confess their incidents. The fear of what management or fellow pilots or the authorities will say, even though the urge to tell someone is very great, can be as big a deterrent to confession as fear of dismissal. Clearly neither a penal system nor publicity achieves the desire or motivation to report incidents.

The US National Transportation Board says:

> The Board is aware of the many problems involved in obtaining, analysing and disseminating incident information. The reluctance of crew-members to reveal errors; the difficulty in recognising the importance of vital information; and the legal or other inhibiting influences on prompt dissemination of data. However, practical channels of reporting data can be devised. Some methods are: Anonymous reports; Reports to neutral parties; Guaranteed reasonable immunity.
>
> The International Air Transport Association conducts a safety-information exchange programme, but only 64 of its 107 member airlines participate in the programme. The reluctance of air carriers to participate is because of the legal liability aspects...
>
> The practices of immunity and protection of accident prevention data employed in Australia are highly conducive to continual preventive treatment of air-safety problems. A similar treatment exists in certain European countries.

One of the most important developments has been the American FAA's agreement that all operational incident reports — which are not mandatory, like airworthiness defects — should first be processed by an expert but independent body, Nasa.

The trouble with anonymity in incident-reporting is that pilots and engineers need the help of specialists in making their reports. They do not always anticipate the questions which a safety expert like the FAA would pose, with its wider understanding of trends and patterns. The middleman, Nasa, ensures that the FAA's questions are answered while the anonymity of the reporter is preserved. In this way the FAA can concentrate on safety action rather than on punishment, fear of which is no longer a deterrent to the incident reporter. Nasa has in fact had long experience of incident reporting in the field of test flying, and offers to train people in incident-interviewing techniques.

The United Kingdom Civil Aviation Authority (CAA) requires the reporting of all "occurrences" which might endanger aircraft, whether they arise from operational incidents or airworthiness defects. The system is known as Mandatory Occurrence Reporting (MOR).

Requiring the reporting of occurrences is, in the CAA's view, only the beginning of the problem; even more important is to ensure that the information is co-ordinated, analysed, understood, and made available for use. The CAA chairman has said:

> "It is well known that a number of serious aircraft incidents in different parts of the world involving aircraft of different nationalities have been caused or affected by factors which were present in earlier accidents but of which the crews and the operators of the aircraft involved in the accident were completely unaware.
>
> "We think, therefore, that it is our duty so far as British aircraft are concerned to require all such information to be reported to us. We are setting up an organisation which we hope will, with the aid of modern electronic equipment, enable these incidents to be used for the guidance of all concerned with safe operation — crews, operators, manufacturers and regulatory authorities — so that experience and information of life-saving significance is, so far as human skill and devotion can secure it, not wasted in the future as it may well have been in the past."

The British system meanwhile continues to encourage the voluntary incident-reporting on which it has always depended.

Anxious airline banker "Are you making a profit?"
— Well, our income or should I say operating income, by which of course I mean our revenue, is yielding earnings — or should I say net income — which of course is the same thing as profit provided you remember that net income before taxes is quite different from operating income after taxes, which means FOR HEAVEN'S SAKE lend us $100 million quickly or we're bust.

---

5   The Airline

British Airways gets about 1,500 air-safety reports (ASRs) each year, representing about 2 per cent of routine Technical Log reports. Each ASR is passed to the specialist engineers concerned, to flight operations, and to the airline's group safety office. The latter distributes copies to the Civil Aviation Authority, to the Accidents Investigation Branch, to the manufacturer, and to the editor of the airline's monthly *Air Safety Review*. Copies of this journal are distributed to about 300 other airlines; to the International Air Transport Association (Iata) Safety Exchange; to the UK Flight Safety Committee; and several hundred are distributed inside the airline by the group safety officer.

SAFETY MANAGEMENT As airlines become big business there is a tendency to swamp chief pilots and flight operations managers with administration and paper work. They lose track of how the line crews are performing, and get out of touch with the operations. The best airline top managements ensure that flight-crew management's time is applied actually to working with fellow crew-men, striving for perfection.

A TYPICAL AMERICAN AIRLINE Some of the safest airlines in the United States — itself one of the safest air-transport countries — do not hve specialist safety officers. An example is Northwest, which is also of interest to students of the theory that financially strong airlines are safe airlines. By whatever measure of financial and operating efficency, Northwest comes top or close to it.

Incident reporting is made as easy as possible. To the pilot's Technical Log, which is required by law, Northwest adds its own third "pink" page. On the normal Technical Log the pilot lists mechanical deficiencies and the mechanics record the repairs. The pink copy has, in addition, a section headed "Flight Operations Trip Report," containing the question: *Were the following services entirely satisfactory throughout the route segment just flown?* Then listed are:

Approach control

En-route communications and navaids

Letdown

Tower service

Airports

Aircraft maintenance

Flight dispatch

Ground equipment

Passenger handling

Weather (forecasts)

If the answer to any of the foregoing is "no," concludes this pink form, *"Explain below — be specific... Describe alternatives used to check trouble... and add any details that might assist investigations."*

In this way Northwest encourages its crews to report those incidents which are neither trivial nor yet — like engine failure or fire — mandatory as defined in US Federal Aviation Regulations FAR Part 121.

The pink form is the airline's primary method of achieving voluntary incident reporting. The operations department investigates every pink report and claims to give every pilot a reply.

But how do one airline's incidents reach other airlines, the airworthiness authorities, and the manufacturers? Mandatory incidents — those which have to be reported to the FAA — are published by that authority in the form of bright yellow bulletins entitled Service Difficulty Reports. These yellow SDRs are issued daily. They list, by carrier and aircraft type, summaries of the whole industry's incident reports, and the action taken. Every carrier gets a copy. Example: "Braniff 727 returned after take-off following loss of hydraulic pressure. Normal landing. Hydraulic pump pressure line ruptured. Replaced line."

Northwest feels that the FAA's yellow SDR is becoming a sterile document, and that some of the "spirit of the thing" has been lost since the Air Transport Association's voluntary incident-reporting procedure was replaced by the FAA's mandatory system. An SDR might just say "Power Failure". According to Northwest: "We often get phone calls from other airlines asking us what really happened." But it agrees that this in itself is "communications", and that the general awareness of other airlines' defects has improved. Whether this has improved real knowledge and hence the level of safety is hard to say. The fact that the FAA's yellow SDRs are now public documents under the US Freedom of Information Act, following pressures by Nader consumer groups, may have something to do with what the airline considers to be the sterility of their content — "they have to be lawyer-proof."

How then can the "spirit of the thing" be preserved within a mandatory defect and incident reporting system?

Northwest agrees that the FAA's yellow SDR (which used to be called the Mechanical Reliability Report, or MRR) alerts the hangar to other airlines' problems with similar aircraft. There is enough in the SDR to alert an engineer to somebody else's apparently similar trouble. A DC-10 flap cylinder support-fitting crack reported by, say, American Airlines might be worth a phone call to the airline and a word with the local McDonnell Douglas representative. According to Northwest there is a sort of "old-boy network" in air safety which transcends commercial competition. Whenever this works the mandatory defect-reporting system is working.

At 10.30 every morning Northwest has a meeting at Minneapolis of all the maintenance heads. Telephone speakers are connected to the airline's bases at Miami, Washington, Detroit, Seattle, Chicago and elsewhere. These are essentially reliability meetings but they are where safety problems and trends first emerge. The daily meeting and the pink form are Northwest's primary safety instruments. Both serve operating efficiency as well as safety, but it is often hard to distinguish between the two.

Anything that gets into the FAA's yellow SDR has almost certainly already been dealt with by the airline concerned, and by the manufacturer in his Service Bulletins. But the SDR closes the loop, and contributes to the all-important multiplication of safety communications. And the manufacturers, in addition to their Service Bulletins, issue regular product activity reports — yet another safety communications output.

A textbook test of the safety communications system took place when a Northwest 727, at 2,000ft after taking off from Twin Cities, experienced a sudden complete failure of numbers one and three engines. Quick thinking on the flight deck revealed that the engineer had operated the fuel shut-off cocks instead of the tank selectors. The mistake was realised and power restored just in time, and the aircraft landed safely.

The flight engineer had developed the habit, during pre-flight checks, of running his hands over the levers in a way which involved lifting the fuel shut-off lever guards. Eventually he did this during the after-take-off checks. The way he ran his hands over the panels on the ground, perhaps with his mind for a moment on some other problem, was the way he eventually did it at 2,000ft. Northwest immediately eliminated the pre-flight check to break the habit pattern. The flight engineer knew what he had done, and how fatal his action could have been. He was suspended for six months, although discipline was not the main object of the investigation.

Other airlines would read about the incident in the FAA's yellow SDR, power failure being a "mandatorily reportable" incident. But how would other airlines get to know promptly of the full implications? In one or more of three ways: by the SDR, which would have drawn attention to the human error behind the near-tragedy (though SDRs are in general unimaginatively worded); by asking Northwest for the full background; by the manufacturer's regular Service Bulletin and his other safety publications.

In this case Northwest's maintenance department came up with a solution which was applied to the whole 727 fleet. The fuel shut-off lever guards were drilled and safety-pinned, so that these had to be removed for the pre-flight check. A copy of the appropriate Northwest Engineering Order (EO) was sent to the manufacturer — as all EOs are. This is a sort of Service Bulletin in reverse.

The manufacturer may or may not then recommend the modification to other airlines. The point is that the procedure gives the manufacturer the opportunity to do so. In this case the pre-flight check concerned had been recommended by Boeing — who considered whether to recommend cutting out the check, but decided to retain it. All airlines knew, or had the opportunity to know, about the problem.

A copy of Northwest's EO would also have gone to the FAA, and the modification approved by the local FAA engineer. In this case the change in check procedure and the safety-pin modification remained unique to Northwest — an example of how an airline is sovereign over its own safety standards. It will not do anything of which the airworthiness authority disapproves, but it will not wait for safety modifications to be made mandatory.

In this case safety communications would have been ideally perfect if the flight engineer concerned, having once nearly made the mistake, had alerted his superiors to the possible hazard and this had then been communicated to the airworthiness authority, manufacturer and other airlines. It is almost certain that if there had been a fatal accident, and the habit pattern had come to light during the investigation, that perhaps half-a-dozen flight engineers in other airlines all over the world would have been heard to say in the operations room: "That nearly happened to me, but I thought I was just being stupid, and didn't say anything to anybody."

Northwest's pink form procedure helps to overcome this human communications blockage; and so, claims the airline, does the fact that Northwest has no professional pilot-instructor group.

The Northwest line pilot does not find himself being checked by a stranger, but by one of his colleagues from the line. Northwest instructors have no disciplinary role, and are answerable to the chief pilot. The pilot/instructor relationship is essentially "open-door," achieving an atmosphere in which pilots can talk frankly even about their foolish mistakes without fear of discipline. The instructor also fulfils the role of "chaplain-confessor". Of course gross indiscipline would be reported; but the general manager of flight operations would support a check captain for not reporting to him disciplinary matters which he considered had been worth trading for safety. Thus the fear of being fired or suspended is not in practice a great deterrent to safety reporting and confessing.

Safety comes in many ways — over a beer, in letters — besides in the pink forms, and the airline pilots' union Alpa encourages the reporting of incidents. Every US airline has an Alpa safety rep, and Northwest management policy is to give him every encouragement.

Examples of incident inputs from pilots include an accident nearly caused by the wrong 727 flap setting for a particular airspeed — 25° with an air speed for a 15° setting. The importance of pitch attitude during the initial climb was heightened, and second pilots were briefed to question apparently irregular pitch indications.

In the hangar the "what-would-happen-if" questions come mainly from the maintenance instructors. These personnel are responsible for on-the-job training of the airline's mechanics, and the job of airline mechanic is a profession. Northwest believes that the general intelligence of the airline mechanic is several notches higher than that of any other kind.

Northwest is particularly proud of its Turbulence Plot Programme, claiming to have done more on the subject of turbulence and how to cope with it than any other airline. Northwest is probably the only airline which predicts clear-air turbulence (CAT) and updates it in flight.

In addition to what the captain sees on his radar, he has on his knee a map of the turbulence — including clear-air — ahead, showing its height, direction of movement, and strength. On the unique Northwest-developed map grid he plots and updates the forecasts.

Turbulence Plot messages cover three basic types of weather: thunderstorms, low-level wind shear, and clear-air turbulence. Each TP message gives the type of weather involved, its horizontal and vertical extent and intensity, and a brief short-term forecast. The TP messages are made up from a large-scale master plot in Northwest's central Met office at Minneapolis St Paul International Airport. The master plot is made from radar observations of the US Weather Bureau's national radar network. Information on low-level wind shear and CAT is developed by Northwest and includes pilot reports.

Northwest's concern about turbulence originated from its last fatal passenger-carrying accident. This occurred to a Boeing 720B near Miami in February 1963. The aircraft crashed in the Everglades National Park, killing all 35 passengers and the crew of eight. According to the official report the cause was severe vertical air draughts and large longitudinal control displacements. Northwest devoted much of the next ten years to analysing turbulence, refusing to accept it as "one of those things". The Northwest Turbulence Plot is the result. It gives passengers a pleasanter ride too.

As always, keenness is infectious, and many Northwest pilots have become "weather freaks," photographing curious cloud-occurrences. In the Meteorological Office, where weather talk is part of the day's work, there is a fascinating gallery of Met curiosities. Northwest emphasises that CAT can be forecast, and that there is nowadays no excuse for anyone to fly into it.

Sorry I'm late, captain. I overslept due to human factors.

---

6   The Airliner

Airliners are designed to airworthiness requirements which state that the probability of catastrophe arising from a single technical failure shall be no higher than one in a thousand million — to use the mathematical shorthand, 10^{-9}. Dr Howlett of Hawker Siddeley has vividly illustrated this by saying that pins placed at 1mm intervals for a distance of 1,000km (John O'Groats to Land's End) would all be safe to touch except one. This safety level is equivalent to one single-cause catastrophe to one of 20,000 aircraft operated for 3,000 hours a year for 15 years. Such a design safety level is theoretical because no manufacturer could ever demonstrate it by testing.

The actual does not achieve the theoretical. When jets were in full passenger service by the beginning of the 1960s the loss rate from all causes (not only single technical causes) was 5 per million hours. By the early 1970s this was down to almost 1 in a million hours.

Although 50 per cent of all accidents are attributed to crew error, there is no doubt that design error contributes to crew error in many cases. Thus the engineer contributes to safety not only with improvements to technical integrity, but by the way he displays information to the crew and lays out their working environment.

AIRLINER DESIGN The airliner is as noble a piece of work as anything made by man. Military aircraft may be technically more daring, but the civil airliner is designed and built to much higher standards of quality and integrity. An airliner's airframe has to last for at least 40,000 hours without a serious crack; and this fatigue life has to be demonstrated by a test airframe, and guaranteed. Air forces expect to get no more than 1,000 hours out of a combat aircraft before it starts to weaken with fatigue or corrosion. If an airliner engine or vital system fails, the airworthiness authority requires one, two and sometimes three back-ups. The fighter pilot of a single-engined or single-control-system aircraft uses his ejection seat.

Every component of every part of a civil airliner is designed, made, developed and tested to the most stringent airworthiness standards. These do not tell an aircraft manufacturer how to design an aircraft, but define the safety standards which he must meet.

No airliner can carry a passenger unless it has a Certificate of Airworthiness (Chapter 2). The certificate is awarded to the aircraft type when the manufacturer has demonstrated compliance with the Airworthiness Requirements (ARs). These cover everything from the fatigue life of the structure and the loads which must be simulated on the test rig to stability and performance.

AERODYNAMICS An important aerodynamic characteristic of clean fast aircraft is that Vs (stalling speed) is high and, as the aircraft slows down towards Vs, drag increases more rapidly than lift, causing sink.

Because high-subsonic wings are not at their best at slow speeds, lift devices are necessary to keep stalling speed low. Flaps and leading-edge slats increase wing area and lift. Both types of device increase the wing camber, persuading the air to remain "attached" to the wing at increased angle of attack. Premature retraction of these high-lift devices after take-off can be hazardous. The aircraft is close to its "clean" stalling speed, and is flying also at a "draggy" speed, or at least below that for minimum drag.

A number of accidents have been caused by attempting to take off without proper setting of leading-edge and trailing-edge slats and flaps. The two most serious were to a Trident 2E near Heathrow and a Boeing 747 at Nairobi in, respectively, 1972 and 1974.

Swept wings All high-subsonic airliners have swept wings. Sweep "fools the aeroplane" into believing that it is flying more slowly than it is. This is because the wing responds not to the stream-wise velocity component but to the effective chord-wise velocity component, which by the triangle of velocities is smaller. This means a higher speed before the wing section reaches the critical Mach number or speed at which the air compresses and shock-wave drag builds up. For the same reason a thin wing section "fools the aeroplane" into believing it is flying more slowly than it is because the higher-speed flow over the upper wing becomes sonic at a higher free-stream Mach number.

Yawing a swept-wing aircraft produces a stronger rolling moment compared with straight-winged aircraft. This is because the advancing wing becomes effectively less swept and more squared to the flow, and lifts more strongly, while the retreating wing is effectively more swept and slipped to the flow. The fin and rudder should damp out the resulting wallowing, which is known as dutch roll, but most airliners are fitted with automatic yaw dampers which apply rudder to stop the yaw before it sets off dutch roll. Some airliners have roll dampers also.

The best general technical reference to airliner performance and operation is *Handling the Big Jets* by D.P. Davies, chief test pilot of the UK Civil Aviation Authority, published by the CAA Technical Publications Department at Redhill, Surrey, England.

STRUCTURAL TESTS Complete airframes are built for testing to destruction. Separate airframes are made for fatigue-testing, the test rig continuing after certification and always having to be ahead of the hardest-flown aircraft in service. In a few minutes in the test rig all the loads experienced by an airframe in a typical flight — including pressurisation, turbulence, heavy landings, gusts and so on — are simulated.

A duplicate of the wing which a passenger may watch flexing for hour after hour has done the equivalent of at least 40,000 hours of bending on the test rig, with cracks deliberately sawn in the highly stressed critical parts of the structure. The test rig is required to "fly" more than that number of hours depending on the "scatter factor" specified in the airworthiness regulations. A scatter factor has to be applied because identical wings can fail at different ages. One wing may fail after only, say, a third the number of fatigue cycles of another wing made from identical materials on the same jigs. Similar structural tests are applied to components — undercarriages, flaps and flying controls — and to every part of the aircraft and its engines that functions repeatedly throughout its life.

The high cost of civil airliners is attributable not only to the cost of meeting the safety requirements but also of producing an aircraft that will make money for its operators. A fatigue test may easily be passed by increasing the gauge of the skin in a certain area, or by adding frames or stringers. But aircraft designers, and particularly airliner designers, cannot, like bridge-builders or shipbuilders, apply a factor of two or three or more for good measure. An aircraft designer who did that would be mocked by g, that property of our planet which only lift, engine power and lightness can defy successfully, and which makes every gram of structure a gram of commercial payload or fuel lost. A mere 100kg of excess structure weight can cost an airline the equivalent of one passenger, or £100,000, a year.

FLIGHT DATA RECORDERS (FDRs) Many airlines use FDRs to monitor all flights. Investigations are initiated if, for example, approach speeds are too low in more than 10 in 1,000 flights, if normal cruising speed V_{MO} is outside limits, touchdown speed too high, descent rate

43

below 400ft greater than 1,200ft per minute, or if there are excessive "g occurrences". All kinds of trends are detectable from FDRs, even such minor but potentially hazardous pilot habits like lowering the flaps too late or too early. Airlines make sure that pilots are kept informed about FDR and how it is used. Pilots do not like to feel that there is an electronic Big Brother watching their every movement. They have to be convinced that FDR is their friend and protector, not a management snooper.

FDRs were originally "black boxes" intended to help accident investigators and airworthiness authorities, but they are now proving most useful as a flight inspector, incident reporter and training tool.

Some FDRs select data according to the stage of flight. This avoids saturating the operations department with data. Selective FDR is coming close to a system which can warn the pilot of operational anomalies as they actually happen — "in real time", to use the computer jargon. FDR has a potentially most useful role in incident-reporting, but the difficulty is to know what not to report. For example, a puncture can throw tyre debris into the flap transmission, causing flap failure. Should FDR record punctures?

In the 1950s British Airways had a small drawer for incident reports; by the 1970s it was a filing cabinet.

STRUCTURE LIMITS The speed limits of an airliner are set out in the familiar "flight envelope", named after the appearance of the altitude versus speed graph. The left-hand edge of the envelope defines the stalling speed. This is typically, for a subsonic transport such as the 707 or 747, between 120 and 150kt, increasing slightly with altitude. Parallel and close to it (within 15kt) is the "stick-shake boundary" at which the pilot is warned of an impending stall by the shaking of his control column.

The maximum permitted operating indicated airspeed or V_{MO} is typically 380kt up to about 24,000ft. At around this height and at this indicated airspeed the aircraft runs into Mach, or speed-of-sound, limits. The speed limit is now governed by the maximum permitted Mach Number, known as M_{MO}. This is typically 0.88 At lower speeds the M_{MO} of 0.88 is reached at higher altitudes. There comes an altitude at which the aircraft is in both low-speed and high-speed (compressibility) buffet. This altitude is typically well above the performance or permitted ceiling of modern jet transports.

All the foregoing is for normal flying including load factors up to $2\frac{1}{2}$g — proof load, at which the aircraft may bend but does not break. The ultimate load, where the aircraft should theoretically break, is $1\frac{1}{2}$ times the proof load, or $3\frac{3}{4}$g.

The maximum Mach number and indicated airspeeds are respectively known as M_{DF} and V_{DF}. They are typically 0.95 and 440kt respectively and the two meet at about 19,000ft. These speeds are not normally experienced by airline pilots, though a speed half way between V_{MO}/M_{DF} is sometimes demonstrated during training to show pilots the overspeed handling characteristics. This is loosely known in the UK as crew-training V_{MO}/M_{MO} and in the USA as V_{FC}/M_{FG}. Flutter can be expected at about $1.2V_{DF}$.

There are other operating speeds, for example with undercarriage or flaps down. There is not usually any great risk attached to exceeding the undercarriage limiting speed; the worst that is likely to happen is a strong pitch change or blown-off fairings. But the flap limiting speed — say 230kt for the first increment — has to be carefully observed, because the loss of a flap, especially asymmetrically, can be disastrous.

Speed limits can be exceeded in level flight and even in a climb, so great is the power available on most modern transport aircraft, especially in the thicker air of lower altitudes. According to aerodynamic law, drag increases as the square of the speed. Control forces have to be increased accordingly. Power-controls are necessary, and care has to be taken by the designer to ensure that the pilot cannot over-stress the aircraft.

STALLING Every pilot is trained to recognise and recover from a stall. This occurs when the aircraft is flying too slowly for the particular flap and leading-edge settings and aircraft weight. Stalling speed V_s is the baseline for all take-off and landing speeds, and it increases with aircraft weight and manoeuvring. Generally speaking, the lowest take-off speed would be 20 per cent above the stalling speed and the lowest approach speed 30 per cent above. The onset to the stall V_s should be apparent to the pilot from the buffeting of the airframe or shaking of the control yoke at a speed about 10 per cent above the stall to give the pilot ample warning. The stall should ideally be no more than a gentle pitch-down with no sudden wing-drop or other out-of-control manoeuvre. No excessive forces should be required to maintain control even after failure of the most asymmetric engine.

The airworthiness authority's pilots decide what is acceptable in terms of average skill and strength, bearing in mind that the airline captain is not a test pilot and may experience the remote event of a stall once in his life in difficult conditions near the ground at night in bad weather. In general, a maximum elevator stick-force of about 20kg is acceptable. A rudder-pedal force of about three times that is reasonable, though an aeroplane which requires more than about 15kg to achieve full aileron control is likely to be rejected by the airworthiness pilots.

The chance of stalling an airliner in normal operations (as opposed to training) has been estimated by Davies to occur once in 100,000 flights — at least ten times the number ever likely to be flown by most pilots. But the chance of experiencing a stall-warning (say 1.1 x Vs) on normal operations occurs once in 1,000 flights — which is well within the early part of a senior pilot's 30-year career.

The stall should be "docile", and airworthiness authority test pilots expect designers to provide natural or artificial warning, usually in the form of buffet or stick-shake, and a natural recovery. In other words, there must be no violent banking, rolling or pitch-up. The aircraft should of its own accord pitch nosedown, wings remaining level, gathering speed until after a reasonable loss of height level flight is regained.

There is one exception to the requirement for stall-recovery to be natural. The British airworthiness authority, the CAA, requires a stick-pusher to be fitted to airliners with T tails and rear-mounted engines. Test-flying and military experience revealed a superstall or deep-stall phenomenon. At high angles of attack the wing of a high-tailplane ("T-tail") aircraft can blanket clean flow to the tailplane so that it is stalled too, together with the elevators, providing no natural correcting pitching moment. The intakes of rear-mounted engines may be blanketed also. At the same time aircraft drag has increased. The pilot has no way of recovery.

The CAA therefore required a stick-pusher to come into effect after the stick-shaker. The stick pusher is a simple pneumatic actuator which pushes the stick forward automatically before the stall deepens irretrievably.

SPEEDS The various speeds used in airliner operations and performance calculations may be defined as follows:—

V_S is the indicated airspeed (IAS) at which the airliner exhibits the characteristics accepted as defining the stall — severe buffet or nose-down pitch. Subvariants are V_{S1} and V_{S0}.

V_{MS} is the minimum stalling speed in IAS corrected for instrument error (EAS, or equivalent airspeed) and is the minimum speed observed during the stall. V_{MS} may be used in calculating such critical performance as take-off and landing speeds instead of Vs — provided that it is not less than 94 per cent of the so-called "1g stalling speed" or V_{S1g}. Subvariants are V_{MS} and V_{MS0}.

V_{S1g} is the speed in EAS at which the aircraft develops lift equal to its weight. The lift is assumed to be perpendicular to the flight path, and V_{S1g} is calculated by correcting V_s for the acceleration perpendicular to the flight path. V_{S1g} is the "normal gentle stall" speed.

V_{MCA} is the minimum control speed (directional and lateral) in the air. It is the speed at which, when the critical engine is suddenly made inoperative, the pilot can recover control with the engine still inoperative and maintain it in straight flight at that speed — either with zero bank or with an angle of bank not exceeding 5°. Rudder force required to maintain control should be not greater than about 70kg.

V_{MCG} is the minimum control speed on the ground, the minimum speed at which, when the critical engine has been made suddenly inoperative, the pilot can maintain directional control without applying a rudder force of more than 70kg and without reducing power on the other engines — and without the aircraft swerving about the runway, which should be wet and exposed to a crosswind of not less than 7kt. Below these speeds the flying controls, notably the rudder, do not have sufficient bite on the air to counteract the asymmetric thrust due to the suddenly failed engine. In such a case the pilot would not be able to prevent the aircraft from yawing or rolling into the ground, or swerving off the runway.

V_{MCL} is the minimum control speed in the landing configuration with the critical engine out.

V_1 is the Take-off Decision Speed. It should not be less than V_{MCG} as defined above. V_1 is the speed at which, should an engine fail, the pilot can either abandon the take-off and stop within the remaining length of the runway, or continue the take-off safely. V_1 is calculated for each take-off according to weight, airport altitude, temperature, and runway length. It might typically be 120kt.

If the pilot continues the take-off after an engine failure below V_1 he risks losing control because the speed of the aircraft will not have reached V_{MCG} If the brakes are not powerful enough for the V_1 speed, or effective enough on a wet runway, weight restrictions will be necessary to prevent the aircraft overrunning its scheduled Accelerate-Stop Distance.

Take-off Distance should be measured from the start of the take-off run to the point where the airliner clears an imaginary screen of about 10m above the runway, assuming engine failure at V_1.

V_{MU} is the minimum "unstick" speed — the speed at which the aircraft can be made to lift safely off the ground. The actual speed at which the pilot pulls back the control yoke, V_R (see below), is up to ten per cent higher.

V_R, Rotation Speed, is the speed at which the pilot pulls back the yoke and the aircraft "rotates" about its lateral or wing axis, and is ready to lift off (V_{LOF}, see below). V_R should not be less than V_1, not less than $1.05V_{MCA}$ and not less than 1.05-1.1 V_{MU}.

V_R was introduced after a series of ground-stall accidents to Comet 1s in 1952 and 1953. The Comet 1, the world's first jet airliner, had a symmetrical aerofoil for best cruising performance. There were no leading-edge slats and the achievable ground angle on take-off exceeded the stalling angle. Thus the aircraft could be so angled that it stalled on the ground, staggering along the runway at full power unable to gain height. The aircraft overran and crashed on one delivery flight killing all the 11 occupants.

V_{LOF}, the lift-off speed, is the point at which the aeroplane becomes airborne.

V_2 is the one-engine-out take-off safety speed. The aircraft should attain V_2 after a continued engine-out take-off before clearing a 10m screen, and should continue at not less than V_2 untl 120m. Changes to the aircraft configuration, except for retracting the undercarriage or feathering a propeller, should not be made until above this height. Engine-out climb gradient above 120m should be not less than 1.5 per cent for four-engined airliners, 1.4 per cent for those with three engines, and 1.2 per cent for twins.

V_3 is the normal 10m screen speed with all engines operating. It is usually about $V_2 + 10$kt. It is sometimes referred to as V_4 for a four-engined aircraft.

V_A is the design manoeuvring speed.

V_B is the design gust speed.

V_C and M_C are the design cruising speeds.

V_D and M_S are the design diving speed and Mach number.

V_F is the design speed with full flap.

V_{FE} is the maximum speed with wing flaps extended in a given position.

V_{LE} is the maximum speed at which the aircraft can be flown safely with the landing gear extended. (V_{LO} is the speed at which it is safe to extend the undercarriage.)

V_{MO} and M_{MO} are the maximum permissible operating speeds (replacing the old V_{NO} and $M_{NO})$.

V_{NF} is the never-exceed, "red-line" speed.

V_{RA} and M_{RA} are the rough-air or turbulence speeds.

V_T is the target threshold speed. It is the speed obtained at the screen height of 10m above the runway after a steady, stable approach at an angle of descent of not less than 3°. The target threshold speed V_{AT} lies between the minimum threshold speed, V_T min, and the maximum threshold speed, V_T max.

V_T**min** is typically V_{AT} - 5kt and V_T**max** not less than V_{AT} plus 15kt.

Landing distances are calculated for airworthiness purposes on the basis of V_T max, a wet runway, and the application of air brakes, spoilers, reverse thrust and wheel brakes according to the type of aircraft. Excessive braking, causing tyre or brake-pad wear, is not permitted in calculating the scheduled landing distance.

DUTCH ROLL Because of their highspeed aerodynamic design modern airliners are not inherently stable. They require yaw dampers, without which a wallowing motion can develop. If this is divergent and is not constrained, eventual structural failure could occur. Some airliners are less naturally stable than others, one of the "worst" Dutch-rollers being the VC10. This aircraft has a three-section rudder, each section with a yaw damper. Without yaw dampers at cruising speed a VC10 would be up to a bank angle of 20° each way within about 6 sec. By 12 sec the amplitude would be up to double that — 45° bank each way.

Yaw dampers automatically correct any directionally unstable tendency without the pilot or passengers being aware of the slight trimming corrections.

APPROACH AND LANDING The speed for the approach and landing, at least 1.3Vs, must not be less than V_{MCL}, or "minimum control speed, landng". The minimum threshold speed — the speed over the threshold of the runway — must be enough for elevator bite and for a sink rate not greater than 4ft/sec. The target threshold speed must be at least 5kt faster than the minimum threshold speed. Touchdown speed is typically 1.25Vs.

A graph of drag plotted against airspeed shows a U-shaped curve. The bottom of the U is known as the minimum-drag speed or V_{MD}. There is a steep increase in drag as speed falls towards the stalling speed Vs. Care must be taken during the approach to avoid letting drag increase above the available thrust — "getting on the back side of the drag curve" — especially in the case of an approach with a failed engine.

The airliner approaches at a speed safely above Vs, typically 1.3Vs plus 10kt. The closer the speed to the stalling speed the poorer the speed stability of the approach. Weak speed stability makes the aircraft particularly vulnerable to windshear, that is to say to any changes in speed and direction of the wind, or turbulence. Pitch-up, because it increases the angle of attack, will increase the rate of descent, unless the extra drag is compensated by more thrust.

The jet engine responds more slowly than the propeller engine does; the acceleration time for a typical high bypass-ratio turbofan from idle to full thrust is up to eight seconds. There is none of the slipstream effect of the propeller-driven aeroplane, when an increase in power immediately produces an improvement in both control and lift. Opening jet throttles to correct a sink, on a low or slow approach, can involve considerable height loss before the required effect is achieved.

The importance of speed stability on the approach is paramount. Critical to the assessment of approach speed is the basic stalling speed, Vs. The normal gentle stall, the so-called 1g stall or V_{S1g} (defined above), is the basis on which the approach speed may be calculated. An approach speed of 1.3 times the 1g stalling speed theoretically gives a speed margin 30 per cent over the stall. But in practice this margin is eroded by different computations of Vs. Instead of the 1g stalling speed (that is to say the minimum speed at which the lift is equal to the weight in level flight) pressures for better load-carrying performance led to the acceptance of VMS, below the 1g stalling speed. Because of this many pilots add five or ten knots to the recommended threshold speed, even though this will result in increased landing distance. Some authorities maintan that the use of V MS for calculating performance is at the root of many landing accidents.

ANGLE OF ATTACK Another approach technique, as yet unadopted, is to "fly alpha", the Angle of Attack. This is the angle between the chord line of the wing and the airflow. It is not to be confused with pitch attitude, which is the angle between the chord line of the wing and the earth's horizon.

At low speeds, that is to say during the approach or climb-out, angle of attack can be flown precisely, airspeed being accurately controlled for a given weight. Flying angle of attack, or alpha, eliminates the need in theory for both airspeed indicator and artificial horizon, or attitude director indicator (ADI). On the approach, for example, the descent path of the aircraft will be at an angle of alpha minus the pitch attitude angle. This is sometimes known as the Velocity Vector. This velocity vector can be shown electro-optically "in the windscreen" by a head-up display (HUD) (Chapter 20). The horizon line on the HUD is aligned with the true horizon, and the velocity vector line below it with the aiming point on the runway. Electronics can then provide a small reference triangle on the display which, if kept on the velocity vector, ensures that the correct alpha and hence airspeed are flown.

Electronics can provide another symbol to denote power. When thrust is the same as drag, this symbol would appear on the velocity vector line of the display. If it moves above, the pilot knows that he must reduce power, and vice versa. Thus the pilot could, in theory, as proposed by the electronics experts, fly the approach without looking down at either his airspeed indicator or ADI or power settings. He would simply look ahead through his windscreen and fly the angle-of-attack and power symbols electro-optically projected by the HUD. This system could be useful during an overshoot or an engine failure on climb-out, when the pilot would have an instant read-out of his situation, and in particular his angle of attack.

The angle-of-attack or alpha HUD display could be useful also for showing pilots the effects of wind-shear (Chapter 20). Any sudden change of wind velocity or wind direction changes the angle of attack and this would be immediately apparent to the pilot as a change in his velocity vector. He would apply power to move the power symbol up to the runway aiming point, at the same time pulling back the stick to raise the velocity vector to coincide with it.

"Flying alpha" is a subject for debate among practical and theoretical pilots, and it is not operational. Even pilots of Concorde, which uses unusually high angles of attack, still fly "airspeed and attitude".

SUPERSONIC SAFETY When a new airliner like Concorde is launched the airworthiness authority has to frame requirements to cover the new technical problems.

"Concorde TSS Standards" is the supersonic airworthiness code drawn up by the British and French authorities outlining the requirements Concorde must meet. This document is the supersonic passenger's assurance that the Concorde is as safe as the airliners before it. Concorde had to undergo something like 6,000 hours of testing to qualify for its certificate of airworthiness, including flying down the routes for 1,500 hours in typical airline conditions. Total test time of the Boeing 747 was only about 1,500 hours, but it had ten years of Boeing 707 experience behind it.

SUPERSONIC HEALTH ASPECTS The medical problems of supersonic flight have been engaging the attention of a joint Anglo-French aeromedical group since 1963, the year after the Concorde project was launched. The British and French aviation doctors, and the national research and scientific facilities on which they can draw, have studied two problems especially: cosmic radiation and ozone.

Radiation increases with altitude, and the expected Concorde dose for passengers and crew will be a small percentage greater than in a subsonic type like the Boeing 707. But the exposure time will be halved, and the dose will be several times less than that of a routine chest X-ray, even under the worst solar-flare conditions. In the event of high solar-flare activity, which increases the ambient level rapidly, Concorde's radiation meter warns the crew to descend to a safer altitude. Typical ambient background radiation is 1.5 mrem/hr (1 mrem = 1,000th of a rem, the unit of radiation). The more northerly the latitude the higher the ambient radiation. The maximum allowable radiation dose as specified for industrial workers is 5 rem a year. A pilot flying 160 Concorde round-trips in one year on the North Atlantic might receive a total dose of 1.3 rem. Workers must not be exposed to more than 5 rem in one year or to more than 1.3 rem in any quarter.

Ozone, O_3, is a toxic gas more prevalent at Concorde cruising altitudes than at subsonic levels, but it is broken down by heat and by the nickel brazing of Concorde's air-conditioning heat exchangers. The breakdown is in fact nearly 100 per cent, and Concorde passengers and

51

crew will not inhale any significant quantities of ozone.

AIRLINER DEVELOPMENT Airliner development appears to progress in 20-year plateaux, with smaller steps in between. With a little rounding off of dates, the major plateaux look something like this:

1900 Man's first powered flight (Wright Brothers, 1903).

1920 Converted 100 m.p.h. 1914-1918 wartime bomber biplanes started carrying passengers. By 1925 the first regular, scheduled passenger-carrying international services began with a two-passenger de Havilland D.H. 4A between London and Paris. By 1930 aircraft worthy of the name airliner, with 10 passengers or more and two or three engines, were in operation.

1940 The first long-range 200 m.p.h. all-metal monoplane airliners, with four engines, retractable undercarriages, flaps and variable-pitch propellers, appeared in America. The classic was the Douglas DC-4. The twin-engined DC-3 with these new features had entered service in the second half of the 1930s (and was still in service in the 1970s). The DC-4 set the pattern for a long line of fast (300 m.p.h.) propeller-driven, four-engined transports such as the pressurised DC-6 and DC-7, the Lockheed Constellation, and — linking the propeller age with the jet age — the 400 m.p.h. turboprop airliners of which the Viscount was the first and most successful.

1960 The jet age was established. The world's first pure jet airliner, Britain's de Havilland Comet 1, had entered passenger service in 1952. In 1954, after two accidents, the aircraft was withdrawn from service. Towards the end of 1958 the Comet 4, closely followed by the Boeing 707 and later the Douglas DC-8, entered service on the North Atlantic. By 1960 the propeller-driven airliner had been ousted by the jet from the main long-haul routes. By 1970 double-size subsonic jets such as the Boeing 747 were in service.

1980 The supersonic airliner should be established on the main long-haul routes. The Concorde entered service on January 21, 1976, heralding the supersonic plateau which will eventually take over the traffic of the jumbo subsonic airliners on the longer-haul routes.

		Maximum seats	*Take-off weight (lb)*	*Cruising speed (m.p.h.)*
1920	Junkers F.13	4	3,850	85
1929	Ford Trimotor	14	13,500	120
1935	DC-3	28	25,200	180
1949	Boeing 377 Stratocruiser	60	145,800	300
1959	Boeing 707-320	144	311,000	545
1969	DC-8-60	257	353,000	555
1970	Boeing 747	490	713,000	585
1976	Concorde	120	400,000	1,300

AIRLINER PRODUCTIVITY is the payload capacity multiplied by block-to-block speed. It is usually measured in seat-miles (or capacity ton-miles) per hour. The progression has been from 3,500 seat-m.p.h. by the DC-3 to 15,000 by the DC-6, 100,000 by the DC-8-60, 210,000 by the Boeing 747 and 156,000 by Concorde.

AERODYNAMIC EFFICIENCY has also steadily improved and may be expressed as the product of cruising Mach number M and lift-drag ratio, L/D. It has increased from 3 for the DC-3, 6 for the DC-6B, 12 for the 707 and 14 for the 747. It is further increased by developments such as the supercritical wing, which is shaped to allow a lower drag for a given Mach number.

FUEL EFFICENCY Specific fuel consumption (SFC) in the 1950s piston era was just under 0.9kg/kg/hr*. By the 1960s the first fan jets had got this down to below 0.8. By the 1970s the SFC of the second-generation turbofans was below 0.6.

THE MANUFACTURER "Safety shall be given priority in all design decisions." There are other design precepts, including performance, economy, price, and reliability. But all these can be compromised. Success in the making of an airliner must be built on uncompromised safety. Design for safety calls for more than technical ability, money, and experience. The prerequisite, in the opinion of Boeing, is management. "You have to manage safety into the design," asserts the 747 chief safety engineer.

Not the least important management input is experience. Boeing's customers have flown 2,500 aircraft ranging from the local-service 737 to the 7,000 mile, 490-passenger 747. Boeing 707s, 727s, 737s, and 747s are flying just over six million hours a year, or 52 per cent of the total Western airline jet experience. Between each morning's meeting of the customer support department Boeing aircraft have flown about 17,000 hours and made at least 10,000 landings.

The 747 was the first Boeing airliner to have its own safety engineering group. Whatever the product — can-opener or airliner — the hazards first have to be identified, measures taken to guard against them or minimise their consequences, and tests carried out to verify the measures. The team was concerned with almost every one of the 18 million man-hours put into the 747 by up to 5,000 engineers.

All Boeing drawings are subject to the usual departmental inspection. In addition, before being issued to the shops, they have to pass the scrutiny of the company's own central engineering organisation, which

*Kg of fuel consumed per kg of engine thrust per hour.

makes its own independent safety checks — a sort of internal airworthiness discipline. The requirements of the external airworthiness authorities have resulted in safety engineering teams specially assigned to co-operation with the FAA, CAA and other government agencies. In the case of the 747 nearly 200 documents were involved.

The discipline of satisfying the customer — the feedback of 50 million flying hours — is in practice the toughest of all. The resulting "failure-tolerance" principles and practices managed into the 747 appear in the safety record of this aircraft. Failure-tolerance of the 747 extends, for example, to four main-undercarriage struts, any opposite combinations of which will permit a safe landing in the event of a gear failure; four independent hydraulic sources and systems, any one of which will power essential services; more than 50 structurally independent control surfaces, including four ailerons, two rudders and four elevators; three wing and two tailplane spars; strengthened structure in the way of compressor/turbine-burst trajectories, and no critical systems in these areas; smooth-surfaced pulleys with covered and chamfered cable ends to eliminate foreign-body jamming; landing gear fused to tear out in a crash landing without rupturing fuel tanks; and exits and slides for the evacuation of 500 passengers in 90 seconds using only half the available exits.

In the first five years of 747 operation there were 22 precautionary evacuations, in the course of which 3,526 people were got out with an injury factor of 0.7 per cent. The 747 chief safety engineer believes that this says a lot for the aviation industry — "test your local theatres some time."

A 747 taking off from San Francisco failed to unstick properly and the landing gear struck the approach-light pier. Three of the four hydraulic systems were disabled, two of the four main undercarriage trucks were written off, and one of the two starboard-side tailplane spars was severed. Steel girders penetrated the cabin (seriously injuring two passengers), one 17ft section lodging up in the fin. The aircraft was fully controllable for 90 minutes while 300,000lb of fuel was jettisoned and the damage assessed by a Coast Guard aircraft. Two surviving main undercarriage trucks withstood the subsequent very heavy landing, and a brake fire was extinguished by the internal system.

Another 747 on a test flight hit a bank on the approach to Renton. One main landing gear structure fused; the remaining gear prevented destruction of the engines and there was no fuel leakage.

There have also been examples, in the early days of the JT9D-3, of turbine bursts contained without damage to vital aircraft organs.

Customer support is considered to be a prime safety tool, more so than an instrument of goodwill or good business.

THE SERVICE BULLETIN (SB) is the main safety communication between manufacturer and customer. The Service Bulletin is a private communication, and is concerned with product improvement or reliability as well as with safety. Special attention is given to the editorial presentation of Safety Service Bulletins. Busy operators can sometimes fail to appreciate the reasons for a modification. Boeing therefore issues two types of Service Bulletin, Alert and Routine.

The ALERT Service Bulletin, the main safety control, is first communicated by telegram or telephone. The Alert SB is on blue paper with a bold Alert flag in the heading. A section headed REASONS gives the background history of the problem and its possible consequences. ACTION to be taken is described, with drawings. In addition there is a one-page summary sheet giving a quick "overview" to guard further against the possibility of a busy operator not reacting.

For example, under the heading BACKGROUND, it is stated: *"One 747 operator reported that on one airplane the 0.16in thick detent pin of the flap handle had worn approximately half way through... if the pin should break, the flap control unit's bias spring would tend to move the handle and the flaps to the retracted position. During a critical flight phase, control of the airplane would depend on early recognition of the problem and correct pilot reaction."*

Under the heading ACTION this Alert SB outlines the required inspection and modification (in this case a chrome-plated pin). A drawing appears on the first page. Under the heading REASONS the implications of what might happen if the pin were broken are amplified.

A telex alert went out when cracks were found in a Boeing 707 upper-wing skin:

"A second operator has now reported finding cracks in two 707-320C airplanes of approximately sixty-seven inches (repeat 67in) and fourteen inches (14in) in length at wing station 360 upper-surface splice. Both airplanes have accumulated approximately 15,000 flights. The 67in crack was found after tank entry to investigate a fuel leak... preliminary stress analysis indicates that structure with crack sizes reported above may not be capable of withstanding ultimate design loads." In this particular case, an AD was issued on the same day by the FAA.

The legal and warranty implications of Service Bulletin alerts can be troublesome. There is at least one well documented case (involving a light-aircraft manufacturer) in which a safety problem was presented in a Service Bulletin as a product improvement. Boeing maintains that it has never suffered from being frank about problems. "Quite the opposite is true," says the director of customer support. "We call a spade a spade. It is in our interests."

AIRWORTHINESS DIRECTIVES The relationship between a manufacturer's Service Bulletin and a Government Airworthiness Directive (AD) or equivalent is a sensitive subject. A Service Bulletin issued by one manufacturer recommended modifications after a serious incident, but did not emphasise the reasons and possible consequences. When a fatal accident occurred subsequently the US Federal Aviation Administration (FAA) came under fire for not having made the Service Bulletin the subject of an Airworthiness Directive.

An AD is issued when, in the judgement of the parent certification authority, emergency action is essential in the interests of public safety. Naturally, no manufacturer likes his product to amass a high AD score, and there can be pressure on the airworthiness authority to "leave it to our Service Bulletin". There are no hard and fast rules; each case has to be judged on its merits. One extreme is the airworthiness authority which slaps an AD on every modification affecting safety, grounding aircraft and disrupting services as a result. The other extreme is the airworthiness authority which is persuaded by the manufacturer to leave everything to the Service Bulletin.

Boeing's attitude towards ADs is: "Don't solicit them; don't fight them; but do attempt to influence the FAA to make them reasonable." Almost invariably the Service Bulletin will have been issued before an AD, of which the Service Bulletin is in any case nearly always the instrument. AD or not, Boeing send copies of Alert Service Bulletins to all foreign airworthiness authorities, though there is no international law obliging them to do this.

Boeing takes care to keep its own airworthiness authority fully informed of the action it is taking on safety problems — "It would be very unsmart of us not to do so." Consultation is the basis of the confidence which puts safety where it belongs, with the manufacturer.

Boeing's emphasis on strong wording in Alert Service Bulletins may date in some degree from the fatal training crash of a Western 720B in March 1971 in California. There had been four previous failures of 707/720 rudder-actuator support brackets, going back to a KC-135 in 1967. No fewer than 28 cracked fittings had been reported between May 1969 and March 1971, it transpired subsequently. A bracket failure would be survivable in normal passenger service, but nobody had appreciated the consequences of the heavy rudder demand of asymmetric training. This was a textbook case of how incidents — even those that are thoroughly reported and followed up — can still become accidents.

MAKERS' ACCIDENT INVESTIGATIONS Manufacturers also have to be in the accident-investigation business. International law now recommends that the manufacturer be given official observer status. Boeing's customer support department has a senior accident investigation co-ordinator whose sole job is to assist the national accident investigation authorities, at the scene and afterwards. Boeing considers that this staff post improves product quality because it avoids "it crashed" or "pilot-error" accident reports. In one case a national authority was reluctant even to go to the scene of the accident and knew nothing about the existence of flight data recorders.

Even with well investigated incidents a manufacturer's expert might perceive something the authorities missed. For example, a 747 overrun at Miami showed that if the landing gear had been pushed just a little further back it could have hit some oxygen lines. These were repositioned.

The Boeing accident officer is the focus of all accident investigation work, becoming automatically the official designated as the manufacturer's representative. He is the co-ordinator of all specialised support in the company. "The report might still come out with pilot error but," says Boeing's chief accident investigator, "we see other things, build up the file, and keep records."

Boeing policy towards vendors, the suppliers of spares and equipment, is that they are responsible to Boeing. The vendors' warranty to Boeing is the same as it is to the customers. In addition, the contract between Boeing and the vendor provides for Boeing to direct specific action where safety is involved. In practice such directions are rare and relations with suppliers good, probably thanks to the existence of the contractual framework.

Customers can deal direct with vendors but they expect the prime aircraft contractor to take overall responsibility. Boeing releases Service Bulletins on vendor matters, perhaps endorsing vendor SBs. The director of 747 customer support says: "The customer has a right to a safe product and should not be stuck on the ground while we are having a fight with the vendor. We are in the middle of it and if the vendor is not performing we get in there with both feet. The criterion for selection is whether a component meets the engineering requirements — the cost and other responses come second."

The technical solution goes forward, and the legal and financial implications are sorted out later. The contract with vendors provides for arbitration by a Government agency. Boeing's relationship with vendors is, in effect, that of an airworthiness authority.

RESPONSIBILITY FOR OLDER AIRLINERS The record of hulls lost per million departures is completely indifferent to whether the aircraft concerned is one that has been resold. As soon as one of the seven Boeing regional directors hears of a "second-tier" Boeing product in his area he advises the Seattle customer support office which immediately despatches a personally addressed letter offering support services including Service Bulletins free of charge, and giving the names, addresses and telephone numbers (including home) of all Boeing engineering and support personnel, headquarters and local. A letter addressed to a new European charter operator of a used Boeing 720 runs to four pages and lists seven Boeing engineers who will deal with "all enquiries concerning maintenance, operation, repair, training, publications and spare parts."

TRAINING CUSTOMERS A series of "pilot-error" accidents and incidents in the mid-1960s, mainly to 727s, forced Boeing to care as much about the flying as the engineering of the product. The record of hull losses per million departures is indifferent also to whether the crash was caused by piloting or a design error.

Boeing has a flying and simulator staff of 50 full-time pilots, each with not less than 10,000 flying hours on the line. The training school at Seattle has a simulator for each model, with computer-generated colour visual attachments. There are also procedures trainers on which customer pilots can learn basics such as the flight director so that the more expensive simulators — some of which are flown 16 hours a day — are not wasted on elementary work.

Customer pilots get from ten to 25 simulator hours, depending on experience. After a spell in ground school they go to a nearby base, clear of traffic, to complete training on their own aircraft. Pilot training is included in the contract price of the aircraft. There is no refund if the customer opts out. The result is that 99 per cent of customer pilots are trained to fly Boeing's way. So far nearly 4,500 pilots and 2,000 flight engineers have been trained.

Before delivery a manufacturer's pilot flies the customer's routes in case the standard training course has to be adapted to particular needs — for example, take-offs with reduced thrust to simulate 110°F days or short fields. The customer's pilots arrive at Seattle about four weeks before aircraft delivery, typically spending three weeks in ground school, two in the simulator and two in the air. The philosophy is to cut out all non-safety items and concentrate on the procedures pilots must know. According to Boeing's chief of operational engineering, the training programme is highly standardised.

The manufacturer is brutal about failing customer pilots who do not make the grade, including, in one case, the chief pilot (he had been flying a desk too long and was "behind the aeroplane" too much of the time).

Contracts provide for a Boeing pilot to accompany every revenue flight for 30 days after delivery. Initial rides are made in the right-hand seat, then in the jump seat. Thereafter, every six months or so, a Boeing pilot and engineer will spend a week or ten days with the airline, exchanging information and checking that procedures have not diluted. This Flight Operations Support Programme is very much, according to Boeing, a two-way street.

Boeing is licensed by the FAA under Part 121 of the Federal Airworthiness Regulations as a certificated air carrier. This means that all its operating standards are those of the US airlines. A course in Boeing's 747 simulator is interchangeable with one in American Airlines'. Boeing cannot dictate procedures to foreign customers, but its recommendations carry weight. A customer airline which gave flight engineers control of the throttles changed on Boeing's advice that thrust management must always be the responsibility of the pilot.

Boeing pilots advise strongly against the transfer of control from one pilot to another during ILS transitions. They recommend the use of preset speed bugs on the ASI so that pilots are not number-watching, and advocate the appointment of specialist safety officers in every airline, detached from day-to-day admin work and discipline problems. They advise adding half the wind and all the gust increment to the approach speed up to 20kt. Check lists, Boeing pilots believe, should be used as check lists rather than "do" lists — "do first then check".

No manufacturer can ever be sure of getting a 100 per cent feedback of operational incidents. However good the communications system, however many of the manufacturer's pilots and engineers are in touch with the airlines, there are still problems which, though known to an airline, escape the safety net and do not become generally known before they hit another. Boeing try to stop these cracks with In Service Activity Reports, listing the main incidents of the week, type by type (without identifying customers), together with causes and corrective action. A typical one: *"An operator experienced a fire on a Number 4 engine 18min after take-off. The centrifugal oil-filter element had come adrift, cutting through the housing cover and spilling oil into the cowling... the oil filter uses a snap ring to retain the element. The snap ring has been subject to incorrect installation..."* The appropriate Service Bulletin is then cited.

These weekly product-activity reports have a more readable editorial style than Service Bulletins and stimulate "Yes, and I'll tell you what nearly happened to me" feedback. Boeing also publishes a flight-crew bulletin in the same vein. Meanwhile pilots and engineers visit all customers every six months and sometimes every two or three. They aim to build up a rapport with operators, making a point of talking to the same people and developing the personal contacts which will often open up on matters not reported to their own mangements or airworthiness authorities.

In Boeing's view the question of whether incident-reporting should be mandatory or voluntary does not really effect the origin of safety. Most manufacturers have informal arrangements with operators for the supply of accident and air-safety information. The voluntary reports of flight crews are particularly helpful. But Governments which require mandatory reporting help to ensure that as much safety information as possible stays in the net. Mandatory reporting also helps to make sure that not only the Government's authority knows what goes on but that other operators, airworthiness authorities and — perhaps most important — manufacturers know what goes on too.

Safety in the case of the 747 flap detent pin did not begin with Boeing or with the safety authority. It started with a well trained, intelligent airline employee spotting a tiny bit of wear on a very small pin, asking himself "what would happen if," and alerting somebody.

If you listened to the airworthiness authority you would use an iron bar to hang your ties on.

---

7 Crimes against aircraft

From 1945 to 1975 there were just over 20 fatal airliner accidents attributed to criminal causes such as sabotage and hijacking. The majority, 17, were caused by sabotage. Only four or five accidents killing passengers were caused by hijackers — involving the loss of 132 passengers.

The number of hijackings has fallen dramatically since the peaks of 1968, 1969 and 1970, as the following table shows:

HIJACKINGS OF NON-US AIRCRAFT 1930-1974*

	Attempts	Successful
1930-67	66	52
1968	13	11
1969	47	37
1970	57	37
1971	31	10
1972	31	13
1973	20	10
1974	19	5

*Source: US Federal Aviation Administration. Includes air carrier and general-aviation aircraft.

HIJACKINGS OF US AIRCRAFT 1961-1974*

	Attempts		Successful	
	Air carrier	General aviation	Air carrier	General aviation
1961	5	—	3	—
1962	—	1	—	1

61

1963	—	—	—	—
1964	—	—	—	1
1965	4	—	1	—
1966	—	—	—	—
1967	—	1	—	1
1968	17	5	13	5
1969	40	—	33	—
1970	25	2	17	1
1971	25	2	11	1
1972	27	4	8	2
1973	1	1	—	1
1974	3	4	—	3

*Source: US Federal Aviation Administration.

This remarkable achievement sets an example to all air-safety authorities. It may now be reasonable to say that a successful hijacking is attributable to the failure of airport and airline security measures. Responsibility for sabotage is less easily assigned, but measures can be taken, as one Middle Eastern airline's ground security procedures and cargo-hold armour plating demonstrate.

LAW The word hijacking is internationally accepted to describe the crime defined in the 1971 Hague Convention as "the unlawful seizure of aircraft". Hijacker was originally the name given in the United States to the armed criminal who took by force a train or truck and its load. The Academie Francaise, ever vigilant against the encroachment of Anglo-Saxonese, prefers "deroutement," but Air France has adopted "hijacking" as the unique word for a unique crime.

The Hijacking Act of 1971 lends English law's majesty to the word, and gives expression in the Statutes of Westminster to the international convention — signed at The Hague in the same year, and ratified by some 60 States — for the "Suppression of Unlawful Seizure of Aircraft".

Article 1 of The Hague Convention defines an offender as "any person who on board an aircraft in flight... unlawfully, by force or threat thereof, or by any other form of intimidation, seizes or exercises control of that aircraft".

Airliners are peculiarly vulnerable to the criminal, lunatic or fanatic with a gun or bomb. Such people can be determined and desperate, caring little whether they live or die. The one sure way to deter hijackers is for all States to refuse sanctuary to them, or to arrest and return the offender. Some progress has been made in refusing hijackers sanctuary. Cuba, which once fêted fugitives from the USA, has signed an extradition treaty on hijacking. All the traditional Arab country havens have now refused hijackers; civilised Arab States have returned hijackers whence they came, or to the Palestine Liberation Organisation; and the PLO stated after the 1974 Tunis hijacking that it would punish the offenders. But world-wide extradition agreements have so far been politically unattainable.

The Hague Convention does not require extradition. Few countries would bind themselves to return one of their own nationals to an unfriendly State. Instead The Hague Convention says in Article 7 that the State in which

> "the offender is found shall, if it does not extradite him, be obliged, without exception whatsoever and whether or not the offence was committed in its territory, to submit the case to its competent authorities for the purpose of prosecution. Those authorities shall take their decision in the same manner as in the case of any ordinary offence of a serious nature under the law of that State."

Article 8 provides the legal basis for extradition in a case of hijacking where the two countries concerned do not have an extradition treaty. In other words, The Hague Convention makes extradition as easy as possible.

FATAL CRASHES CAUSED BY HIJACKINGS

Date	Aircraft	Carrier	Location	Type of Flight	Fatalities Crew	Fatalities Pass.	Total Occupants Crew	Total Occupants Pass.
July 17, 1948	Catalina PBY-5A (VR-HDT)	Cathay Pacific	Pearl River Estuary	SP	3	22	3	23
December 30, 1952	DC-3 (PI-C-38)	PAL	Formosa	—	2	0	—	—
May 7, 1964	F-27 (N277012)	Pacific Airlines	California	SP	3	41	3	41
March 27, 1966	Il-18 (CU-T-831)	Cubana	Over Cuba	—	2	0	—	—
March 17, 1970	DC-9 (N8925E)	EAL	Boston	SP	1	0	5	72
January 1, 1971	F.27 (HL85212)	Korean Airlines	Kangmung	SP	1	1	1	59
September 15, 1974	B.727 (XV-NJC)	Air Vietnam	Da Nang	SP	8	68	8	68

ULTIMATE HIJACKING DESTINATIONS 1968-74

	Cuba	Europe	Middle East	Far East	Africa	Others	Unknown	Total
1968	32	1	—	2	2	1	—	38
1969	63	7	4	1	2	1	4	82
1970	26	13	14	5	2	2	10	72
1971	20	6	8	6	2	13	7	62
1972	13	13	8	3	1	15*	17	70
1973	3	3	8	3	1	5	5	28
1974	2	3	3	4	—	2	4	18
Total	159	46	45	23	10	39	47	

*USA internal 8; Bahamas 1; South America 5; Canada 1.

HIJACKING TARGETS 1968-74

	USA	South America/ Caribbean	Europe	Middle East	Far East	Africa	Unknown	Total
1968	23	10	1	1	1	1	1	38
1969	40	29	6	1	2	4	—	82
1970	22	15	19	6	5	—	5	72
1971	31	10	7	4	5	2	3	62
1972	31*	9†	17	3	5*	1	4	70
1973	3	6	11	4	3	—	2	29
1974	3	3	3	1	7	1		18

*One military aircraft. †Including Puerto Rico.

Article 12 provides for the arbitration of a dispute between States and for the reference of a dispute to the International Court of Justice. These provisions are not, however, binding on States.

If States cannot agree to extradition then at least, provides The Hague, they should agree to punishment. The 1963 Tokyo Convention on Crime in the Air provided for the immediate return of a seized aircraft, its passengers and crew. Nothing was said about the hijacker (the crime was uncommon at that time). The Hague Convention, in Article 7, follows the principle *aut dedere aut punire*: either return the offender or punish him.

The Convention is remarkably definite about this. The words "without exception whatsoever" are probably the strongest to be found on the international statute book. Whether or not they are obeyed, they provide a standard by which the civilised world may judge a State's behaviour towards those who "unlawfully seize aircraft," and who for political or criminal purposes would murder innocent people.

Some air-law experts believe that the 1944 Chicago Convention on civil aviation, in Article 93, can be used against nations which harbour hijackers. The particular Article gives Icao the power in certain circumstances, and with the consent of the United Nations General Assembly, to bar States from membership of the International Civil Aviation Organisation (Icao). Expulsion of a State from Icao would deprive that State and its aircraft of the benefits of the Chicago Convention, and its airlines would not be eligible for membership of the International Air Transport Association (Iata). Such penalties might thus deprive a State of participation in international air transport.

Some States have proposed a World Hijacking Court to advise on action in a particular case according to circumstances. Others have wanted hijackers to be returned without fail to the State of registry of the aircraft. Others have wanted The Hague actually to be written into the 1946 Chicago Convention, and expulsion from Icao of any State which failed to ratify the amendment. Others have proposed writing The Hague into Chicago and also the Montreal Convention on aerial sabotage and letting sanctions be governed by the existing Article 87 of Chicago.

One by one the various proposals have fallen by the wayside, though the last proposal, Anglo-Swiss but supported by the French, came within two votes of adoption by the Icao assembly. This requires a two-thirds majority for any amendment to the Chicago Convention. It is very difficult to get two-thirds of States to take sanctions against others. Governments which may themselves have gained political ends by violence are not particularly shocked by it.

Should the airlines and their passengers despair at the law's delays?

Laws, however wide the consent to them, do not rid the world of crime. There will always be hijackers. How do you guarantee society's protection against men with guns and bombs? But the civil-aviation industry now has the protection of The Hague Convention, with its agreement to bring hijackers to trial "without exception whatsoever." The civil aviation industry also has the Chicago Convention, with its commitment by all States to "the safety of civil aviation," and its provision for the imposition of sanctions on States which threaten that safety. There is also the United Nations Charter itself, which facilitates the expulsion of States from a UN specialised agency such as Icao, and hence denies them their air-transport rights.

Vigilant security measures by airlines and airports are still the best physical safeguard against hijackers, who must be prevented from boarding the aircraft at the airport.

SECURITY After check-in, passengers pass through the twin poles of a metal detector. Hand-held detectors are also used. The operator, usually an airline employee, watches the control console on which metal objects and their position on the passenger are illuminated. Passengers' hand baggage is searched by hand. Checked-in baggage, for stowage in the holds of the aircraft, is not always put through detectors but instead the crew take-off checks ensure that no unaccompanied baggage — perhaps containing some timed explosive device — is on board. If a passenger who has checked in is not on board, the captain will order the baggage out of the holds and require every passenger to disembark and identify his baggage.

Air transport is inevitably slowed down, and its cost increased, by security arrangements. But they are effective. In the late 1960s and early 1970s the US airlines were suffering successful hijackings at an average rate of nearly 20 a year. By the mid-1970s, after security precautions had been introduced and enforced by the FAA (Federal Aviation Administration) at all US airports, there were none.

There are some 1,200 hand-held detectors in use at all 530 US airports, and approximately the same number of walk-through detectors. There are more than 3,000 security officers on duty at these American airports.

An airliner is particularly vulnerable to saboteurs while it is on the ground being serviced and loaded. The safe airlines keep a careful check on cleaners, loaders and mechanics and all personnel with access to aircraft during turnround. The airline's responsibility is particularly heavy at airports away from base, where security arrangements may be different and fewer staff may be available. One danger is that weapons may be stowed on board for later use in flight by hijackers with accomplices among the airport ground staff. Airport authorities make special remote-parking arrangements for the aircraft of "sensitive" airlines.

The cost of airport security is high — in detection equipment, staff, and the delays which checks cause. Airlines say that the cost of security should be borne wholly by the State, like the cost of protecting society as a whole from crime. Governments reply that public-transport companies should share the duty to protect their customers from criminals. The compromise in many countries has been for the airlines to accept responsiblity for deterring the hijacker from boarding and for the State to make a substantial contribution to the cost. The British Government, for example, claims to have contributed £1 million towards airport security measures.

Armed guards are carried by some airlines, including El Al. They travel incognito as passengers, and are trained to use guns in densely populated and vulnerable airliner cabins. But thin-walled pressurised fuselages, high-pressure hydraulic lines, oxygen and electrical systems make airliner-cabin gunfights highly risky, and in the case of hijackers with bombs, merely reckless. There have been a number of shoot-outs initiated by American "sky marshals", and at least one instance of a grenade detonating in flight and blowing a hole in the pressurised cabin. The aircraft have survived and the hijackers have been overpowered, but the risk was high and sky marshals are no longer routine in the USA.

Various schemes have been proposed for isolating the flight crew in the cockpit by locked and armoured doors and bulkheads. Cutting off communications between cabin and cockpit could, it has been argued prevent the hijacker from seizing control. But the hijacker knows there must be communication between cabin crew and flight crew, and he can take remote control by holding cabin staff and passengers hostage.

Some airlines are especially sensitive to hijacking and sabotage and take extreme precautions. One has armour-plated its baggage holds to withstand bomb blast, and this is believed to have saved at least one aircraft from destruction.

The hijacker is not obtaining his objectives. The airlines' objective is to beat the hijacker out of business by strengthening the international law, and by stricter airport security measures.

SABOTAGE and other violent crimes against airliners (crimes other than hijacking) are regulated by the 1971 Montreal Convention. Like the Hague, this does not provide for the extradition of offenders — a measure on which international agreement is always elusive — but it is strong in its provisions for arrest and punishment. Article 7 is word for word as Article 7 of The Hague Convention on hijacking (above).

Criminal offences committed on board aircraft, whether or not they hazard safety, are regulated internationally by the Tokyo Convention.

SABOTAGE (PROVED OR STRONGLY SUSPECTED)

Date	Aircraft	Carrier	Location	Type of Flight	Fatalities Crew	Fatalities Pass.	Total Occupants Crew	Total Occupants Pass.
May 5, 1949	DC-3 (PI-C-98)	PAL	Manila	SP	3	10	3	10
September 9, 1949	DC-3 (CF-CUA)	CPA	Nr Quebec	SP	4	19	4	19
April 11, 1955	L.749A (VT-DEP)	Air-India	S China Sea	NSP	5	11	8	11
November 1, 1955	DC-6B (N37559)	UAL	Longmoat, Col	SP	5	39	5	39
July 25, 1957	CV-240 (N8406H)	Western	Daggett, Cal	SP	0	1	3	13
January 6, 1960	DC-6B (N225H)	National	Bolivia	SP	5	29	5	29
April 28, 1960	DC-3 (MV-C-AFE)	LAV	Nr Calabozo, Venezuela	SP	3	10	3	10
May 22, 1962	B707 (N70775)	Continental	Unionville, Miss	SP	8	37	8	37
December 8, 1964	C-47 (CP-649)	Aerolineas Abaroa	Nr Millumi, Bolivia	SP	4	13	4	13
July 8, 1965	DC-6B (CF-CUQ)	CPA	100 Miles House, B.C.	SP	6	46	6	46
November 22, 1966	DC-3 (VR-AAN)	Aden Airways	Meifah/ Aden en route	SP	3	27	3	27
October 12, 1967	Comet (G-ARCO)	BEA	100 miles E of Rhodes	SP	7	59	7	59
February 21, 1970	CV-990 (HB-ICD)	Swissair	Frankfurt	SP	8	39	8	39
April 21, 1970	HS.748 (PI-C-1022)	PAL	Manila	SP	4	32	4	32
June 2, 1970	F.27 (PI-C-507)	PAL	Between Romblon & Roxas	SP	0	1	4	40
November 20, 1971	Caravelle (B-1852)	China Airlines	Formosa Strait	SP	8	17	8	17
September 8, 1974	B707	TWA	Mediter- ranean	SP	9	79	9	79
January 1, 1976	B.720B (OD-AFT)	MEA	Saudi Arabia	SP	15	67	15	67

INTERCEPTIONS Civil or military aircraft may be intercepted if they infringe a State's sovereign air space. In 1973 an airliner which had strayed into a Middle East war zone was shot down by fighters after a tragic misunderstanding. Interceptions are severely discouraged by the International Civil Aviation Organisation; but the procedures are clearly set forth in Annex 2 to the Chicago Convention.

If, following the identification manouvres, it is considered necessary "to intervene in the navigation of the intercepted aircraft", the intercepter leader should take a position slightly forward of, and on the left side of, the intercepted aircraft so that its captain can clearly see the signals which the interceptor is about to make. They include wing rocking and the lowering of flaps and undercarriage, as defined below. The two commanders should try to achieve direct voice communication using the international VHF distress frequency of 121.5MHz.

The signals to be used during an interception, by the intercepter and by the "target", are as follows:

INTERCEPTING aircraft signals	Meaning	INTERCEPTED aircraft responds	Meaning
DAY Rocking wings from a position in front and, normally, to the left of intercepted aircraft and, after acknowledgement, a slow level turn, normally to the left, on to the desired course	You have been intercepted. Follow me	**Day** Rocking winds and following	Understood. will comply
NIGHT Same and, in addition, flashing navigational and, if available, landing lights at irregular intervals		**NIGHT** Same and, in addition, flashing navigational and, if available, landing lights at irregular intervals	
Note *Weather or terrain may require the intercepting aircraft to take up a position in front and to the right of the intercepted aircraft and to make the subsequent turn to the right*		**Note** *Additional action by intercepted aircraft is prescribed in Chapter 3, 3.7*	
DAY OR NIGHT An abrupt breakaway manoeuvre from the intercepted aircraft consisting of a climbing turn of 90 degrees or more without crossing the line of flight of the intercepted aircraft	You may proceed	**DAY OR NIGHT** Rocking wings	Understood, will comply
DAY Circling aerodrome, lowering landing gear and overflying runway in direction of landing	Land at this aerodrome	**DAY** Lowering landing gear, following the intercepting aircraft and, if after overflying the runway landing is considered safe, proceeding to land	Understood, will comply
NIGHT Same and, in addition, showing steady landing lights		**NIGHT** Same and, in addition, showing steady landing lights (if carried)	

INTERCEPTED aircraft signals	Meaning	INTERCEPTING aircraft responds	Meaning
DAY Raising landing gear while passing over landing runway at a height exceeding 300 m (1,000 ft) but not exceeding 600 m (2,000 ft) above the aerodrome level, and continuing to circle the aerodrome	Aerodrome you have designated is inadequate	**DAY or NIGHT** If it is desired that the intercepted aircraft follow the intercepting aircraft to an alternate aerodrome, the intercepting aircraft raises its landing gear and uses the Series 1 signals prescribed for intercepting aircraft	Understood follow me
NIGHT Flashing landing lights while passing over landing runway at a height exceeding 300 m (1,000 ft) but not exceeding 600 m (2,000 ft) above the aerodrome level, and continuing to circle the aerodrome. If unable to flash landing lights, flash any other lights available		If it is decided to release the intercepted aircraft, the intercepting aircraft uses the Series 2 signals prescribed for intercepting aircraft.	Understood. you may proceed

---

Airline passenger Can't you start flying earlier in the day?
Airline clerk Good heavens no — it would interfere with our captains' paper rounds.

---

8 The Survivable Accident

"If it happens it happens, and anyway there won't be much I can do about it" might be the typical passenger's attitude to flying. But 30 out of 100 passengers survive the average fatal crash, and there are accidents in which the passenger has at least some control over his destiny — in a fire after a landing crash, after ditching, and in turbulence.

EMERGENCY EVACUATION Getting out of a crashed airliner is an exercise that is difficult to simulate realistically. A study of three crashes has shown how passengers behave differently from test personnel in evacuation experiments. The test passengers do not panic, or rush desperately through fire and smoke and explosions from their nearest exit queue to another and back again, frantically looking for their children or trying to help elderly and disabled people. Everyone, including the cabin staff, has been briefed and knows what to do. Simulated evacuations are valuable and necessary, and improve the design and crashworthiness of an airliner. But only real-life lessons are truly valid.

Three crashes have been studied by the US Federal Aviation Administration:

(1) A DC-8 with a hydraulic-system failure at Denver in 1961, in which 27 of 114 passengers died in a fire following an undercarriage collapse and belly slide;

(2) A Boeing 727 at Salt Lake City in 1965, in which 43 of 85 passengers died in a fire following a 4.7g landing, undercarriage collapse and belly slide;

(3) A Boeing 707 at Rome in 1962, in which 45 out of 62 passengers died in the blast of a JP4 gasoline fire which followed a pod's impact with a roller during take-off.

In all these accidents the deceleration forces were survivable. The obvious conclusion, deduced from the positions of the seats of those who survived, is that it is better to sit near an emergency exit. Less obvious is that many passengers sacrifice this initial advantage by switching to more distant exits in panic — and without knowing where other exits are.

The main conclusion is the need for more thorough pre-flight briefings on emergency drill by cabin staff. When a crash is expected, as in the Denver accident, repeat briefings — not given in that case — are recommended.

FUEL SPILLAGE Everyone knows that a match thrown into a pool of gasoline will ignite it, while kerosene takes more persuasion and heat. The flash-points or. volatilities (vapour pressures) of the two fuels are very different.

Ever since the jet age began in the early 1950s, there has been controversy about the relative safety of JP1 kerosene (paraffin) and JP4 "wide-cut" gasoline (in effect petrol). Piston engines require the higher-volatility gasoline. Turbine engines run on lower-volatility, and therefore less flammable, kerosene fuel.

Thus the jet offers improved safety, especially after a crash-landing in which fuel tanks are ruptured and fuel spilled out and exposed to fire. Many people owe their lives to the fact that kerosene ignites less readily than gasoline. But JP4 gasoline has usually been either cheaper, with its higher heat content per kg, or more available. Some airlines have therefore used JP4 instead of JP1 for commercial reasons. Airlines which put economics before safety, and use JP4 instead of JP1, are in the minority. Two governments, those of the United States and the United Kingdom, have advised their airlines to use the safer fuel.

JP4 gasoline has a flash-point of about -20°C. JP1 kerosene has a flash-point of +40°C. The Reid vapour pressures are between 2 and 3lb/sq in for JP4 and 0.125lb/sq in for JP1. The rate of flame propagation depends on temperature but on a "standard" 15°C day is measured in seconds for JP4 compared with minutes for JP1. What this means to most passengers is that if kerosene is spilt in a crash landing and a flame is applied, the probability of having enough time to escape is much greater than in the case of JP4 gasoline.

Some airlines still use JP4 for economic reasons, but will not readily admit in public to doing so. Airlines which use JP1 exclusively never hesitate to confirm that they do.

A Cranfield Institute of Technology study of 176 survivable airliner accidents involving post-impact fire shows that "the advantage of kerosene over wide-cut gasoline is again confirmed." The study, by A. F.

Taylor and Lin Beow Hong, shows also that the majority of people who died by fire could have survived the impact if JP1 kerosene rather than JP4 wide-cut gasoline had been aboard.

In 130 JP1 accidents, just under 30 per cent of those on board died, of whom just over 10 per cent were the victims of fire rather than impact. Of 28 JP4 accidents, nearly 40 per cent of those on board died, of whom over half were burnt to death before they could escape.

"The advantage of kerosene over wide-cut gasoline is confirmed," says the study, "and is found to be similar for turboprops and for jets. With either fuel it is found that the majority of people who have died as a direct result of fire have done so in accidents where few if any have died as a result of the impact."

PASSENGER EMERGENCY EXITS There are four types of emergency exit in addition to normal doors; Types I, II, III, IV, and Type A.

A **Type A exit** would normally be a door. It must measure not less than 6ft (182cm) x 3½ft (106cm). It must be at floor level, and located so that there is unimpeded passenger flow to it along the main aisle from both the forward and aft directions. There should be an unobstructed passageway of at least 3ft, 91cm, leading from each Type A exit to the nearest aisle. There must be space for a seat by the door, and space for attendants to assist the exit of passengers in an emergency. If the door is not over a wing, a chute capable of carrying simultaneously two parallel lines of evacuees must be available, capable of automatic deployment and erection within 10 seconds of opening the exit door Type A.

A **Type I exit** should measure 4ft, 122cm, x 2ft, 61cm. It should be at floor level.

A **Type II exit** should measure not less than 112cm x 51cm, and should be at floor level unless it is over the wing, in which case the step-up inside the cabin must not be more than 25cm, and the step-down outside the aeroplane not more than 43cm.

A **Type III exit** should measure not less than 91cm x 51cm, with the same step-up as a Type II and a step-down onto the wing not exceeding 9cm.

A **Type IV exit** should be not less than 66cm x 48cm; the step-up inside the aeroplane should be not more than 74cm, and the step-down onto the wing not more than 21cm.

In addition, a ventral type of exit, from the cabin through the lower fuselage, should be as Type I in dimensions and rate of egress, with the aeroplane on its landing gear.

An aircraft must have a minimum number of exits according to its seating capacity. For example, an aircraft seating 140-179 passengers must have on each side of the fuselage at least two Type III and two Type I exits; an aircraft seating 110-139 passengers must have at least two Type Is and one Type III; and so on down to an aircraft of up to 9 passengers, which can get by with one Type IV.

For more than 175 passengers and up to 299, each additional 100 passengers requires an additional pair of Type A exits; 45 more passengers require two more Type Is; 40 more passengers must have two more Types IIs; 35 passengers must have two more Type IIIs on each side of the fuselage.

For more than 299 passengers, and passenger capacities in excess of 299, all exits must be either Type A or Type I.

All emergency exits must be distinguishable and openable from both inside and outside the aircraft by unskilled personnel. The location of each emergency exit should be indicated by a sign in the cabin visible to the occupants approaching it along the main aisle. The location of the operating handle and instructions for opening the door from the inside are specified precisely, even down to the initial brightness level of the self-illuminating handle (160 micro-lamberts) and the width of the red arrow showing the direction of opening ("at least 1.9cm") and the size of the letters of the word OPEN (2.5cm high).

The emergency exits must be outlined in a coloured band on the outside of the fuselage. The width of the band must be not less than 5cm, even though this may spoil the aircraft colour-scheme. Similarly, all emergency-exit signs inside the passenger cabin must be of an exactly specified size and brightness.

After a crash, emergency lighting in addition to the main aircraft emergency-lighting system is required. Exterior emergency lighting should be provided, for example, at each emergency exit. Illumination level is precisely specified ("not less than 0.03ft-candle") where an evacuee is likely to step outside the cabin.

Doors must be designed to be easily found and opened in darkness, even though passengers will be crowded against the inside. Design of locking mechanisms must provide for direct visual inspection by crew members.

Airliners having a seating capacity of more than 44 should show, by actual demonstration in darkness, that they can be evacuated, including crew members, in 90 seconds.

EMERGENCY EVACUATION TESTING All occupants should be safely on the ground or in life rafts within 90 seconds from the seated position with seat-belts and shoulder-harness fastened, and after safety drills have been announced in the normal way. The airworthiness authorities require the evacuation to be demonstrated using the emergency exits and equipment on one side of the fuselage only. The evacuation must be conducted in the dark, using emergency lighting only. The passenger load for the demonstration should be persons in normal health, at least a third being female, about five per cent over 16, and 10 per cent children under 12. Trained cabin crew may be used to assist the evacuation.

Markings on the top of the wings, under each overwing emergency exit, should be provided to indicate the escape route, and should be covered with a slip-resistant surface. The specification of this escape route is precisely defined: it should be 106cm wide at a Type A exit, 60cm wide at all other exits, and it should have a reflectance of at least 80 per cent. It should be defined by markings with a surface-to-marking contrast ratio of at least 5 to 1.

There are survivors in six out of ten fatal air crashes, and 30 per cent of occupants survive, because most accidents take place during take-off and landing at relatively low speeds. The commonest unsurvivable accidents are those resulting from collisions with mountains and high ground when the pilot is not where he thinks he is, or has been misdirected.

Chairs and seat-belts must be able to withstand peak dynamic loads of up to 25g, or at least as much as the human body can stand. Cabin furnishings must be non-flammable and smokeproof. Inflatable chutes down which passengers can slide must be designed into the cills of each door. Life-rafts sufficient for all occupants must be stowed on long overwater flights. They should eject from the aircraft and be automatically inflated in the event of ditching. (Usually the escape chutes double as rafts). Life-jackets must be stowed under each seat and cabin staff must demonstrate the life-jacket drill before an overwater flight. All external doors and escape hatches must be clearly outlined to help outside rescuers.

In case of cabin-air failure or decompression at high altitudes emergency oxygen masks must be provided for each passenger. There must be portable fire extinguishers, smoke masks, axes, megaphones, asbestos gloves, nylon rope and flashlights.

In the event of a total electric power failure there must still be an emergency circuit available for use during an evacuation in smoke and darkness. The cabin crew, upon whose coolness and efficiency passengers' lives can depend, must be trained in crash drills as thoroughly as they are in smiling.

For up to 200 passengers there should be at least one cabin attendant trained in emergency-evacuation procedures per 50 passengers. Above 200 passengers there should be one cabin attendant per 25 passengers, and at least half the number of cabin attendants as there are cabin exits.

The US National Transportation Board has made a special study of airliner accidents, including those above, involving emergency evacuation; and recomends that:

1 Airlines must report to the safety authorities all emergency evacuation-slide deployments, failures and malfunctions.
2 Airlines should inspect their aircraft regularly to ensure greater reliability of emergency evacuation slide systems.
3 Slides must be long enough to reach the ground at a safe angle in a landing-gear collapse.
4 Slides on all floor-level exits must inflate automatically on deployment.
5 Exterior emergency lighting must activate automatically when emergency exits are opened.
6 Flight attendants must be responsible for megaphones during evacuation, and such equipment must be within easy reach of the assigned attendant's seat. Consideration should be given to installation of new, compact, lightweight megaphones.
7 Public-address systems must be capable of operating from a power source independent of the main aircraft power supply.
8 Passengers must be warned during pre-take-off briefings how important it is that they understand how to use emergency exits.
9 The airline industry should standardise its presentation of safety information to passengers.

SAFETY AND THE CABIN CREW Passengers are very dependent on flight-attendant leadership during evacuations, and rarely exert authority themselves, according to the safety director of the US Association of Flight Attendants. Reviewing survivable accidents over four years he says: "We know that time is the essence and that approximately one minute can be allowed for evacuation in which fire and smoke occur." Behaviour patterns are predictable, but have contributed to the death and injury of many individuals: passengers are often reluctant to leave their carry-on items behind, and to remove their shoes. There is a tendency among passengers to get out of the aircraft through the door by which they boarded, and they do not know how to operate exits because they did not listen to the pre-take-off announcements. They tend to "follow the crowd", and rarely assist others in critical situations — pushing, shoving or walking over other passengers. Irrational behaviour causes total disorientation, and even "negative panic" or failure to realise the seriousness of the situation. Most passengers are not aware that smoke rises and that their chances of breathing and seeing can be enhanced by momentarily dropping to the floor.

SAS's cabin-crew association urges its management to "build cabin crews into the feedback system; let them conduct workshops or act as guest lecturers at seminars; involve them in the initial design; and ask them for their ideas." As for the stewardesses's view of the captain: "He is accountable for the safety of his crew and his passengers. In effect he is the manager of the aeroplane and ideally he should maintain a positive, management-like attitude towards the crew, including their personal safety. When the employee knows his manager cares, he or she cares too."

SEAT DESIGN The average passenger can tolerate a forward crash acceleration of about 25g for just under ¼ second. This is roughly equivalent to the load experienced by a trapeze artist falling face down from 400ft, hitting the restraining netting at 110 m.p.h. and being brought to a stop in 16ft.

A survivable airliner crash is one in which the aircraft structure absorbs the loads, and the human beings inside are not stretched beyond their g tolerance. A typical survivable accident occurs during a crash landing in which the forces are "straightforward" and the velocity is not much more than 100 m.p.h. Crashes have been survived at higher speeds and in impacts with heavy yaw and pitch. But in such survivable accidents the peak g load can reach 25g for almost ¼ second, averaging something over 10g measured at the floor near the seat.

Typical seat-strength requirements call for static loading of 9g forward, 6g down, 2g up, and 1.5g sideways. For comparison and contrast, an egg well packed in a crate can withstand up to 70g. The passengers must be restrained in order to "ride down" a crash during which the peak g can be fatal.

If a passenger or stewardess is standing when the aircraft hits the water or the earth in a crash landing, he or she will probably finish up somewhere near the cockpit, passing through one or even two bulkheads, at up to 500g "dynamic overshoot". The passengers with tight seat belts, provided their seats hold to the floor attachments, will survive. The need to attach seat belts securely is very great. Metal-to-metal seat belts are safest, much safer than the old-fashioned fabric-to-metal type.

There is scope for much improvement in the restraining of passengers in the event of a crash landing. Ideally they should have, as in cars and military aircraft, shoulder and upper-body restraint as well as a belt simply across the lap. The engineering and mechanical problems would be formidable, and a forest of webbing in every airliner cabin would not be acceptable to passengers.

Another solution would be for all passengers to sit in rearward-facing seats, and to let the seat itself cushion the "dynamic overshoot." Some military transport aircraft, including those of the Royal Air Force, are fitted with rearward-facing seats as a matter of safety routine. There is strong practical and theoretical evidence that rearward-facing seats are safer in a survivable accident. So far no civil safety authority has had the power to overcome the commercial and financial objections (see below).

The main seat-design problem is the absence of experimental data. Aircraft structures can be artificially crashed in all kinds of controlled and measured conditions, but not with humans inside. Corpses and animals have been used to test seat and seat belt designs more scientifically but, as McLay of the University of Vermont has said, "structural analysis of a live, conscious human is a difficult, complex task. A dynamic analysis is virtually impossible. When this multiple-articulated blob of jelly and bones is combined with an elastic-plastic restraint on a rigid-plastic seat in a rigid-plastic vehicle, the analytical problem is beyond the capabilities of men or computers. How the human body will react to an infinite variety of crash impulses is impossible to predict."

REARWARD-FACING SEATS By tradition, airline passengers sit in forward-facing seats. In the event of a crash their bodies are prevented from being hurled forward by seat belts. In a crash of, say, five or six g the passenger will probably be killed by striking the seat in front. At best the passenger is dazed and shocked enough to impede escape. In an aft-facing seat, the passenger is likely to survive a greater acceleration. This is borne out by the limited statistics which have been kept. A crash at Munich in 1958, for example, killed internationally famous footballers who were in forward-facing seats, while those in aft-facing seats survived.

The Royal Air Force, when awarding long-term contracts for trooping flights, has given preference to operators whose seats face aft. The same airlines which would protest to the civil airworthiness authority if it made aft-facing seats mandatory turned their seats round for the RAF without comment or apparently trouble.

The RAF has had no accidents to provide evidence one way or the other. There is little or no evidence to prove whether passengers would be deterred from buying tickets on airlines which fitted aft-facing seats. No airline has ever offered this facility as part of its service (the International Air Transport Association prohibits the advertising of safety). If one airline were required to fit aft-facing seats by its national airworthiness authority it would protest on the grounds that its competitors would be immediately at a commercial advantage.

The issue of rearward-facing seats has never been the subject of a major international controversy, but there is no doubt that such seats are generally likely to be safer in a survivable accident than are the traditional forward-facing seats. This is one of the very few examples in air transport of safety giving precedence to profit.

DITCHING There have been very few cases of airliners being forced to alight on water. A number of accidents in which airliners have crashed into water have occurred, but these were no more survivable than crashes on land. Indeed, water impact can in certain cases be more damaging than land impact.

One notorious ditching has been studied in detail by the US National Transportation Safety Board. A DC-9 operated by a US airline ran out of fuel en route from New York to the West Indies. Of the 63 occupants, 23 were either killed on impact or subsequently drowned. The captain and co-pilot survived.

The captain, obviously shocked at running out of fuel and perhaps believing until the last few minutes that he could redeem his airmanship, failed to order the cabin staff to brief passengers on the ditching drill. Passengers had been briefed before take-off, in accordance with international rules, and shown how to don lifejackets. Most did so in the event, though some had difficulty withdrawing them from under their seats, unpacking and putting them on. Some passengers removed loose articles and bent forwards with arms over their heads against the soft part of the seat in front in accordance with instructions in the safety leaflet in the seat pockets. But most were quite unprepared for the violent crash that followed, and one of the main recommendations — again — is the paramount importance of briefing passengers.

Shortcomings were also found in the training of the flight and cabin crew in ditching procedure. The US National Transportation Safety Board says: "Survivability in emergency landings... is primarily dependent on the proper preparation of the occupants... and knowledgeable, well trained crew members who make authoritative decisions and maintain discipline."

The ditching was violent enough to cause a number of seats to fail. It was estimated that the impact may have caused a deceleration of between 8g and 12g for a half to one second. A fit and healthy adult restrained by a seat belt can withstand up to 25g for ¼ sec without disabling injury. Airline seats are typically stressed to 9g forward, and it was found that more people might have survived if the seats had been more strongly attached, and if they had been rearward-facing. A number of passengers were killed when their seat belts failed.

The aircraft floated for between five and six minutes. Most of the survivors got out through a single aft overwing exit. This had been opened by an experienced passenger who, as was his custom, had made a point of sitting near an exit and making a mental note of its operation. One of the exits, a door, was blocked by a liferaft which inflated while the crew was trying to unpack and launch it. Evacuation was further impeded by the spillage of galley contents — ovens, bins and drawers — when cupboard locks broke on impact.

The captain saved several lives by swimming from the cockpit window to wing exits, one of which he opened from the outside. Once in the water the passengers (all in their lifejackets) swam to a slide which had been ejected from the rear door. None of the five liferafts stowed on board was deployed. The slide — normally intended for passengers to escape from a survivable crash on land — served as a focal point for those in the water.

One lesson of this accident is the value of the combination slide-raft. Other lessons are the need for simpler lifejackets, and for stronger seats, seat belts and galley locks. The most important lesson is the need for the briefing of passengers and the training of cabin crew in emergency procedures and in the control and discipline of passengers.

CABIN UPSETS The "fasten seat belts" sign comes on not just for take-off and landing but whenever the captain's weather-radar scope shows storm clouds ahead, or when clear-air turbulence is predicted. Captains will invariably try to fly round storms; but it is not possible to avoid cloud without detours or changes of height, and air traffic control cannot always grant them. And clear-air turbulence, or CAT, can cause violent and completely unexpected jolts. This is why, as aircraft cabins get bigger and more inviting to promenaders, passengers are increasingly advised to keep their seat belts fastened.

Turbulence — either CAT or storm variety — rarely damages the aircraft structure but it can be distressing and injurious to passengers and crew, especially to flight attendants. Fatalities are uncommon, but perhaps 60 serious injuries a year occur on average. Most turbulence results in the vertical displacement of airliner occupants, with only relatively small lateral displacement. A passenger's trajectory can cause him to hit the cabin roof, baggage lockers, galleys, food-service carts, adjacent seats or other passengers. Injuries have included skull fractures, multiple fractures, internal injuries and lacerations.

Statistics are hard to get because few national authorities call for them and, even when they do, statistically useful incidents involving minor cuts and bruises are not always reported. But figures compiled by the US authorities, and published by the National Transportation Safety Board, might be regarded as representative of the world's air transport industry.

An average of 17 passengers and 13 flight attendants a year are seriously injured in American airliners as a result of turbulence — storm or CAT — or by evasive action and other unknown causes. The corresponding average number of incidents is 20.

It may be assumed that the world figures are at least double these, since US air-transport activity is about half the world total. Thus, in round figures, it is probable that as many as 40 flights a year experience turbulence or violent evasion, causing probably as many as 60 serious injuries a year on average.

The US figures show that the 20 or so American accidents a year result from storm turbulence (eight passengers and six flight attendants) and clear-air turbulence or CAT (four passengers and three flight attendants). Other injuries result from evasive action or unknown causes.

Although the rear of an airliner's cabin is often the safest in a survivable crash, it is not the safest in turbulence because it is the furthest from the aircraft c.g.

The statistically high proportion of injuries to cabin attendants results from their being "loose" rather than seated. The American statistics show that the highest-risk area is the rear galley, where cabin attendants are exposed not only to the biggest jolts but also to sharp projections and flying utensils. The second high-risk area is found to be in and around the rear lavatories. Most turbulence injuries occur to passengers waiting in the lavatory area. The new large "lavatory-occupied" signs, visible from every part of the cabin, are sensible as well as civilised.

As aircraft get bigger the turbulence injury rate increases, not only because passengers tend to walk around more, but because they have further to walk when the "return to seats" announcement is seen or heard. Passenger mobility is actually encouraged by some airline advertising, which depicts passengers congregating in lounge areas and around stand-up bars, occupying lounge sofas with seat belts unfastened, or chatting on staircases. Most airlines avoid this type of advertising, partly too because promenading passengers disrupt cabin service.

Another tendency is for food and beverage carts to become heavier and capable of carrying more serving utensils and bottles. All these can become dangerous projectiles in turbulence.

The US National Transportation Safety Board recommends that furnishings, especially in rear galley and lavatory areas, should be padded and without protuberances. Galley cupboards and ovens should have strong locks, lavatory doors should open outwards; and "lavatory occupied" signs should be visible to everyone in the cabin. Above all, passengers should be briefed, and should understand the importance of being briefed, on safety drills in turbulence as well as safety drills in general.

FLAMMABILITY The flammability of cabin materials is the subject of strict airworthiness and design control. Interior ceiling panels, wall panels, partitions, structural flooring and materials used for stowage compartments must be self-extinguishing. The average burn length should not exceed about 150 mm and the average flame time after removal of the flame source, according to carefully specified tests, should not exceed 15 seconds.

Similarly, materials used for floor carpets, upholstery, curtains, cushions and coated fabrics, and leather, electrical conduits, insulation, air ducts, cargo compartment liners and so on should be self-extinguishing when tested in accordance with carefully specified conditions; the average burn length should not exceed about 200 mm and the average flame time should not exceed 15 seconds.

Similar flammability requirements, though differing in detail, are specified for acrylic windows and signs, elastomeric materials, seat belts, and even knobs, handles, fasteners and rubbing strips. Particular attention is given to receptacles for towels, paper and waste in lavatories, and ashtrays. The average flame time after removal of the flame source must not exceed 15 seconds, and the average glow time should not exceed 10 seconds. These receptacles should also be able to contain possible fires. There have been a number of incidents resulting from uncontrollable cabin fires starting in lavatory receptacles; for example, a Varig Boeing 707 was forced to crash-land on the approach to Paris in 1973 when both cockpit and cabin were filled with smoke. All but 11 of the 134 on board were killed.

SMOKE AND TOXICITY Smoke from burning cabin materials has caused a number of fatalities after survivable crashes, and airworthiness requirements call for the use of materials which do not emit excessive smoke. There is technical debate about accceptable levels of optical density; many materials used for cabin-furnishing produce asphyxiating and in some cases toxic gases. No airworthiness requirements have been specified and agreed in detail, but designers are expected to avoid materials which smoke and toxic smoke in particular. Airworthiness requirements classify cabin furnishings as "self-extinguishing" (Grade SE); "flame-resistant" (FLR); and "fire-resistant" (FR).

Smoke from electric-wire insulation can quickly fill a passenger cabin or flight deck. Wire and cable insulations which emit less smoke are commercially available.

Airworthiness rules governing smoke are continually under development and review, but typically the limiting optical density (Ds) for textiles, air ducting and thermal insulation might be 100 within four minutes after starting the test: and for electrical wire and cable insulation 15 within 20 minutes after starting the test. Such rules would apply to new production aircraft; the "retrofitting" of existing aircraft with smoke-resistant materials might be required on major overhaul within, say, five years, although electrical re-wiring would be too costly for the operator of older aircraft.

LIFERAFTS Airliners flying for substantial periods and distances over water are required to carry liferafts, equipment and provisions sufficient for all the occupants. Typical of the regulations are those of the British Government, whose Air Navigation Order specifies that an aircraft which flies more than 400 n.m. or more than 90 minutes flying time from the nearest land and airport shall carry:

A lifejacket for each person on board, equipped with whistle and waterproof torch;

Liferafts sufficient for all occupants, equipped with a sea anchor; lifelines; paddles; means of protecting the occupants from the elements (awnings); weatherproof torches; distress signals; half a litre of fresh water for each four persons the liferaft is designed to carry, together with 100 grammes of glucose toffee tablets; and means of making sea water drinkable unless the full quantity of fresh water specified is carried. There must also be a comprehensive pack of first aid equipment in each liferaft, and survival-beacon radio equipment.

ARCTIC SURVIVAL Airliners flying over substantially uninhabited land where, in the event of an emergency landing, polar conditions are likely to be met, should carry the following equipment in addition to the above: gas stove suitable for use with aircraft fuel, one for every 75 people on board; a utensil for melting snow; two snow-shovels; two ice-saws; single or multiple sleeping bags sufficient for one third of all persons on board; and an arctic suit for each crew member.

We do our aircraft utilisation planning algorithmically on an iterative basis.
— Speak English, said Alice. I don't understand all those long words, and I don't think you do either.

---

9 The Uncommon Cause

The majority of airliner accidents are the direct result of human error. There remain the remoter risks — lightning, bird strikes, structural failure caused by the elements, collisions, pilot incapacitation. These risks can be made even more remote by airmanship, engineering, and medical policy.

Just before midnight on August 6, 1966, near Falls City, Nebraska, a One-Eleven of Braniff Airways was seen by witnesses on the ground flying at about 5,000ft, its lights blinking normally, into or behind a cloud illuminated by moonlight. Shortly afterwards it was heard to explode, and burning wreckage was seen to fall. All 42 occupants lost their lives. Witnesses said that the cloud was not cumulo-nimbus storm cloud. They reported no lightning or thunder in the vicinity, but lightning well to the north.

All ops manuals have storm-avoidance procedures. These vary but, in general, pilots are warned to make weather-radar detours of at least 10km at all altitudes depending on temperature. Wide detours are necessary because of the widespread turbulence associated with most storms. But there is no guarantee that steering clear of radar returns will keep the aircraft out of rough air.

The "flank tornado" is not always detectable by radar, or even by eye. It occurs on the outermost edges of the big thunderstorms, sometimes inside clouds of innocent appearance and faint radar echo. The cloud entered by the Braniff aircraft appeared to have been one of a line extending northwards towards the thunderstorm area. The possibility of a tornado was supported by the evidence of a witness who spoke of "a loud swishing noise overhead". This could have been the typical roar of a tornado.

The "flank hazard" is often associated with a squall line connected to a severe thunderstorm. It is now appreciated that these formations may be encountered far from the thunderstorm around which the radar detour is being made, and in clouds of innocent appearance. A 30km deviation of all thunderstorms is recommended at all altitudes.

In the statistics the accident would be listed under a broke-up-in-turbulence heading. But mid-air disintegrations caused by the forces of nature are rare, a tribute to aircraft structural engineers and the airworthiness authorities. In ten years nine airliners are destroyed by the elements — more than one of them, perhaps, while skirting the eye of a storm.

Weather radar fitted in the aircraft nose is a storm-avoidance instrument, and is mandatory equipment on every airliner. It paints a TV picture in the cockpit of storm cells up to 100 miles ahead.

STRUCTURAL FAILURES IN TURBULENCE

Date	Aircraft	Carrier	Location	Type of Flight	Crew	Fatalities Passengers
Aug 20, 1965	Viscount 804 (SP-LVA)	LOT	Jeule	Positioning	4	—
May 3, 1966	B707 (G-APFE)	BOAC	Mt Fuji	SP	11	113
Aug 6, 1966	BAC One-Eleven (N1553)	Braniff	Falls City, Neb	SP	4	38
Jan 15, 1968	DC-3 (SU-AJG)	UAA	Zifta, UAR	NSF	4	—
Mar 8, 1968	F.27 (PI-C-871)	Air Manila	Philippines	SP	4	14
Apr 8, 1968	DC-3 (CC-CBM)	Ladeco	Coyhaigue	SP	3	33
May 3, 1968	Electra (N9707C)	Braniff	Dawson, Tex	SP	5	80
Dec 2, 1968	F-27B (N4905)	Wien Consolidated	Alaska	SP	3	36
Dec 31, 1968	Viscount 720C (VH.RMQ)	Mac. Robertson	Western Australia	SP	5	21

CLEAR-AIR TURBULENCE Less easily detected by the crew is clear-air turbulence (CAT) which does not give a radar "paint". Occurring well away from storm clouds, CAT is not easily detectable by radar or by eye. It occurs at any altitude in clear air. Sometimes a sharp fall in temperature may be encountered first, giving the pilot time to reduce speed and to switch on the "Fasten Seat Belts" sign.

About a third of all serious turbulence incidents and accidents occur in clear air. In the six years 1964-69 in the USA, where there is about half the world's air-transport activity, and records are kept, there were 97 turbulence incidents out of 441 airliner accidents and incidents of all kinds. Of these at least 34 were caused by clear-air turbulence (CAT). It is probable that in the world as a whole about 20 per cent of accidents are caused by turbulence, of which perhaps 6 or 7 per cent are caused by the CAT variety.

CAT is not an exclusively upper-air phenomenon, although usage has tended to define it thus. A DC-10 on final approach to Boston crashed and was written off, fortunately without loss of life, when it encountered a sudden change in the direction and force of the wind. "Low-level wind shear" was cited as the cause of this accident. A more serious "wind-shear" accident befell a Boeing 727 on the approach to New York Kennedy, killing 112 occupants.

What happened in both cases was that a sudden change in the direction or force of the wind occurred at a critical moment during the approach. In the case of the DC-10 a strong tailwind changed to a light headwind between 500ft and 200ft. The pilot was descending normally on instruments and autopilot/autothrottle when, just before the runway threshold, the nose went down and thrust reduced. Before the pilot could take recovery action the wheels hit the approach lights and the aircraft crashed on the runway.

This accident seems far removed from the clear-air turbulence which aircraft encounter at cruising height. Yet it was caused by invisible turbulence which has undone and continues to undo experienced pilots. Because it occurs at 400ft and not at 40,000ft it should not be excluded from the definition of CAT. Wind-shear is discussed more fully in Chapter 20.

WAKE TURBULENCE Aircraft, like ships, leave a wash behind them. Aircraft wakes are caused primarily by vortices or horizontal tornadoes rolling off each wing-tip. Swirl velocities can be as high as 150 m.p.h., 230 kph. Except at high altitudes, where they commonly condense into contrails, they are invisible. Counter-rotating upwards and inwards, they can capsize or upset aircraft following too close, for example in the approach to landing. A DC-9 on a training flight landing behind a Boeing 747 rolled over on its back and crashed, killing the crew of three.

There continue to be incidents and accidents. Unless precautions are taken, these will rise with the number of jumbo jets and light aircraft using airports. Light-aircraft pilots in particular are at risk.

The strength of wake turbulence is a function of speed, weight and drag, the force and direction of the wind, and the distance of the following aircraft. Air traffic control has required spacing between jumbo jets and following aircraft of five or six n.m., compared with the normal three n.m.

There is a difference between wake turbulence and jet or propeller blast. Wake turbulence cannot exist unless the aircraft is flying, because vortices are the offspring of lift. The diameter of a wing-tip vortex increases with distance; it can be 50m in diameter up to five km behind the aircraft, where rotation speed (tangential velocity) can still be well over 25kph. This represents a 120deg/sec roll rate, which is beyond the control power of many light aircraft and disturbing to many airliners. Wash off wings moves downwards; and therefore aircraft on the approach, being above the wake of the aircraft in front, are out of harm's way down to a certain height.

The vortices sink at a rate of 100 to 200m/min but tend to level off at about 300m below the flight path. Below this height, therefore, vortices sink close to the ground where they tend to lie, counter-rotating across the ground away from each other at a lateral speed of about 3 k.p.h. In a steady crosswind of the same speed, while one of the "horizontal tornadoes" will be carried away at 6 k.p.h. downwind, the other may continue rotating in the same spot until it decays, seriously disturbing the air up to 100m above the approach to the runway. In such conditions hazardous moments can be experienced by a following aircraft on final approach. Pilots landing within two minutes or so of a heavy aircraft on a calm day in a gentle crosswind should check with air-traffic control whether wake turbulence conditions exist, and be prepared for them. Similarly, on take-off the prudent pilot — performance permitting — will aim to get airborne before the point at which the big aircraft in front became airborne and started to generate vortices. Or he will consider whether atmospheric conditions call for a few minutes' holding while they decay.

Test pilots of the US National Air and Space Administration, Nasa, flew a small Cessna T-37 trainer behind Boeing 747s. They found that the distance at which they encountered significant turbulence was reduced from eight miles to about two when the 747 was flying level with landing-gear up and modest flap setting. With all flaps and undercarriage down the turbulence was experienced at about five miles. Films of test aircraft following a Lockheed C-5A military jumbo transport have shown a DC-9 rolling through 90°, and a Lear Jet rolling completely through 360°.

The US National Transportation Safety Board has recommended the following action against wake turbulence:

1. Amendment of airline operating manuals to describe more specifically the best wake-turbulence avoidance procedures — for example, a following aircraft should maintain an approach path above the Vasi (Visual Approach Slope Indicator lights) or ILS (Instrument Landing System) glide slope;
2. Definition and publication of the weather conditions which cause trailing vortices to persist in the vicinity of the runway;
3. Warnings by the air-traffic control of separation according to the vortex-generating properties of different aircraft; and in the meantime an increase in separations to at least three minutes in hazardous conditions.

Another effect of vortex wakes is to damage buildings near airports. About 40 cases of vortex-damaged buildings near Heathrow were recorded up to the mid-1970s. In one case tiles weighing nearly 150kg were lifted from the roof of a house. The average number of incidents per year, according to Lee of British Airways, appears to be increasing. Core suctions of up to 55lb/ft^2 can be expected, increasing with the size of aircraft.

Lee proposes the use of vortex generators (VGs) to alleviate the effect of the main vortices. The vortex generators would be small triangular plates — similar to those used commonly on wings, for example upstream of control surfaces, to control the boundary layer — to delay airflow separation. It has been demonstrated that VGs can attenuate the main wing-tip vortices, though not so effectively with flaps down as with flaps up.

Another promising possibility, according to Lee, is a wing-tip spoiler. This might be a retractable plate, placed spanwise normal to the chord. Tests by Nasa, the US National Aeronautics and Space Administration, have suggested that at 1.5 n.m. behind a 747, the rolling moment induced on a following Lear Jet would be about 20 per cent of the normal value. This means that a Lear Jet could fly as close behind as 1.5 n.m. without risking aileron-control loss — very much less than the normal safe 6 n.m. separation.

Flight-tests have been carried out by Nasa to measure the effect of flap-setting on the wake turbulence caused by a Boeing 747. Big improvements were obtained by reducing the deflection of the outer flaps. The rolling moment induced on a Lear Jet half a mile behind was about one third that with normal (30°) landing flap. This is thought to be because the vortex from the tip of the outer flap coalesces with the vortex from the wing-tip with flaps fully deflected, resulting in a stronger single vortex.

The effect of gear down is noticeably worse than with gear up for reasons not really understood. The pilots engaged in the tests judged that with full 30° flaps and gear down on the 747, the separation requirement was about 9 n.m., and between seven and eight with gear up. The separation requirement was very much the same with 30° inner flap and 20° outer flap; with no outer flap, but full inner flap, separation with gear up appeared to be about six miles, and as close as three miles with gear up.

Vortices have been found to linger along the approach path of a runway when there is a headwind of about 5kt, crosswinds of up to 10kt, and rear-quarter winds of up to 15kt. They can be predicted by a suitably placed array of windmill-driven anemometers near the middle marker of the ILS approach, between 3,500 and 4,000ft from the threshold. The Doppler-shift effect of laser-beam pulses can be also used to measure pressure patterns and wind velocities. America's Nasa is testing two scanning laser Doppler systems located about 100m apart each side of and one km from the end of the runway.

A reliable wake-turbulence detector system is still to be perfected. Meanwhile airmanship and good forecasting are the best safeguards.

PILOT HEART ATTACKS See Chapter 19.

BIRD STRIKES Three fatal airliner accidents have been caused by bird strikes. Damage by a single bird is rarely hazardous: windscreens and airframe and engine leading-edge structures are designed and tested to meet the strictest bird-impact airworthiness standards. There was the case of a Viscount which in November 1962 collided with a swan at 6,000ft near Ellicott City, Maryland. The aircraft was destroyed with the loss of all 17 occupants. The accident investigators found the remains of the bird embedded in the tailplane, which had broken off. There have been sightings of geese and other species at over 15,000ft, but collisions are extremely rare. In July 1962 the commander of an Indian DC-3 on a domestic flight was fatally injured by a vulture which came through the windscreen. The copilot landed the aircraft safely.

Complete power failure following the ingestion of flocks of birds into the engine air intakes can be disastrous, as in the case of the Electra which flew into a flock of starlings soon after take-off from Boston in October 1960, with the loss of 62 lives. A similar incident occurred to a Qantas 747 taking off from Sydney in April 1973, without loss of life. In December 1969, also at Sydney, a Pan American 707 was severely damaged when the take-off was abandoned following bird ingestion, although none of the 136 people on board was injured.

Particularly vulnerable to bird strikes are military aircraft which spend much of their lives flying at high speeds and low levels where the bird population is highest. Bird strikes are regarded by most air forces, especially those operating single-engined jets, as one of the routine major safety hazards. The Royal Netherlands Air Force has found that up to a third of its accidents are caused by bird strikes. The United States Air Force reports as many as 700 a year.

About 90 per cent of bird strikes take place below 1,500ft, where nearly 90 per cent of birds fly. Except during migration, more than half the bird population flies below 500ft. More than a fifth flies between that level and 1,000ft. Only 14 per cent is found between 1,000ft and 1,500ft. From there up to 5,000ft is found 9 per cent, and above that level the remaining 4 per cent. All these figures change during migration, when the highest density in many areas is between 1,500ft and 2,500ft.

The force with which a bird strikes an aircraft is proportional to its weight and to the speed of the aircraft. Doubling the weight of the bird increases the impact force by only half; doubling the speed of the aircraft increases the impact force by more than four times. The speed of the aircraft is more critical than the size of the bird.

Airworthiness-certification standards of bird-proofing design and impact-testing are such that strikes are nowadays more of a nuisance than a danger, except in the rare case of power failure caused by a multiple strike. Typical of the windscreen requirements, which vary with aircraft type, is the ability of the A300 to withstand the impact of a 4lb bird at 470 m.p.h.

The airlines expect the airport authorities to control the bird population. They expect also that the air-traffic control authorities, in co-operation with the airport management, will give regular warnings of bird-strike hazards.

Temporary advantages have been gained by broadcasting amplified recordings of distress calls. For a time this is found to disperse the birds; but familiarity gradually makes it less effective. The sudden unsettling of a flock can in any case be dangerous. Recorded distress calls are almost ineffective at big civil airports where the runways are too busy and continually noisy. The British Airports Authority has tried the technique at Stansted but without conclusive results, other than an indication of the cost of the operation.

Some military airfields have employed hawks and other birds of prey to keep down bird life. Falcons operated at RAF Lossiemouth reduced bird strikes by nearly half.

This mediaeval contribution to jet safety requires trained falconers and birds, and is expensive. It has not yet been found possible to colonise airfields naturally with hawks.

The siting near airports of bird-feeding grounds, such as the major sewage lagoons at Heathrow under the western (prevailing) take-off path, is not good safety practice. Ten aircraft in one day were damaged by seagull strikes, according to the Civil Aviation Authority *Civil Aviation Information Circular* of January 28, 1974, at an airport which is assumed to be Heathrow. There have also been numerous warnings about waste food left lying about outside airport restaurants. The dangers should not be exaggerated. Bird strikes have not been a serious danger at Heathrow. This is Europe's busiest airport and it has been bordered by reservoirs and sewage farms for many years. But everything possible must be done to avoid siting bird-attracting amenities near airports, and certainly airports should not be built on sites heavily populated with birds.

The bigger the aircraft the more vulnerable it is to bird strikes. It appears that the number of such incidents is proportional to the size of the air intake. The number of bird strikes for the Boeing 747 is just over

10 per 10,000hr compared with 1.5 for the Boeing 707.

Investigation of an accident in which a DC-10 was totally destroyed, fortunately without loss of life, at New York Kennedy in 1975 revealed that at least two heavy birds and possibly as many as seven in the 2kg class (duck, geese) had struck the No 3 engine fan, causing the fan casing to disintegrate.

FATAL BIRD STRIKES

Date	Aircraft	Carrier	Location	Type of Flight	Crew	Pass-engers	Remarks
					Fatalities		
Oct 4, 1960	Electra (N5533)	Eastern	Boston	SP	3	59	Multiple strike on take-off
July 15, 1962	DC-3 (VT-AVS)	Indian Airlines	Lahore	NSF	1	—	Captain killed by vulture through screen
Nov 23, 1962	Viscount (N7430)	United	Ellicott City, Md	SP	4	13	Hit swan at 6,000 ft. Left tailplane detached

Subsequent debate between the US National Transportation Safety Board and the Federal Aviation Administration disclosed some areas of doubt about bird-strike airworthiness requirements.

An FAA Circular had prescribed that a test engine should ingest flocks of starling-sized birds in volleys of up to 16; gulls, pigeons or small duck in groups of up to 10; and large birds such as duck, geese and buzzards weighing around 2kg fired singly at the test engine fan.

Doubts exist about the effectiveness of firing volleys of birds at different fan radii compared with single shots fired at critical areas such as the blade tips. The "worst case" — hitting a flock of Canada Geese weighing about 3kg each — is being considered by the airworthiness authorities.

COLLISIONS involving airliner deaths average one a year. They are the ultimate failure of the air-traffic control system. The majority of collisions occur in the United States, where about half the world's air transport movements take place, and where there is an extremely high volume of general aviation. Yet of more than five million US airliner movements each year, an annual average over the years of between only two and three has ended in a mid-air collision. In most cases the collision is with a general-aviation aircraft, and in the vicinity of an airport.

Of 71 mid-air airliner collisions between 1946 and 1973, according to Stratton, 41 occurred in the USA, three in Canada, 11 in South America, eight in Europe (of which two were in the UK), seven in India and the Far East, and one in Africa. Of these 71 mid-air collisions, 14 were with airliners; four with military transports; 13 with fighters or other military aircraft; and 40 with light aircraft. According to Stratton, the risk of all occupants of two airliners being killed in a mid-air collision is 55 per cent — a surprisingly good chance of survival. The chances of all occupants of an airliner being killed in a collision with a military aircraft are 92 per cent, but only 23 per cent in a collision with a light aircraft.

In the United States the number of mid-air collisions involving all types of aircraft averages 34 a year, of which just under two a year involve transport aircraft. The majority of these are in collision with light aircraft. The majority of collisions with light aircraft occur during the arrival and departure stages of flight. Half the collisions with other transport aircraft and military aircraft occur en route. Most mid-air collisions and fatalities take place when one or other aircraft is not under air-traffic control.

Collision avoidance systems (CAS) A number of collision-avoidance systems have been developed, but none has been adopted. Their cost and complexity, and the need for all aircraft to be fitted for complete effectiveness, are among the reasons why CAS is not as common as weather radar.

A typical CAS system is the device recommended by the Air Transport Association of America (ATA). This is a "co-operative" system: it operates only when both aircraft are fitted with similar equipment. To be fully effective, therefore, this type of CAS would have to be fitted to military and general-aviation aircraft as well as to airliners.

CAS measures range and rate-of-change of range, and exchanges altitude information with the other aircraft. There is no doubt that it is technically feasible, though it would not work if it "cried wolf". The biggest technical challenge would be to eliminate the possibility of false warnings. The main objection is cost and the difficulty of ensuring that every aircraft flying is co-operatively fitted. CAS could cost as much as £15,000 to fit to one aircraft. There is also the "safety-policy" point that yet another cockpit warning system might lull pilots and air-traffic controllers into a false sense of security.

Although anti-collision devices were first proposed in the mid-1950s, there is a case to be made for the proposition that anti-collision devices blur responsibility for separation, and that avoiding action between one conflicting pair of "co-operatively" equipped aircraft may lead to a greater risk of collision with an unequipped — and thus undetected — aircraft. Until every airspace user, including the jet fighter and the Sunday pilot, has anti-collision devices, responsibility for airliner collision-avoidance rests squarely with air-traffic control. This means not only radar, computers, transponders and qualified controllers, but also rules which private and military pilots can understand and obey.

The US Federal Aviation Administration has carried out a survey of collisions reported in the USA involving civil aircraft (not only airliners) over the eight-year period 1964-1971. There were 271 collisions causing 556 fatalities. Of the 271 collisions only 17 involved airliners. The results, simplified and listed according to phase of flight, may be summed up as follows:

	Collisions		Fatalities	
Near and on airports				
With air-traffic control	31		54	
On runway		0		0
Mid-air		31		54
Without air-traffic control	147		95	
On runway		47		2
Mid-air		100		93
	178		149	
En route and terminal areas				
Visual flight (VFR)	77		150	
Intentionally close flying		25		30
Random collisions		52		120
Instruments (IFR)	2		86	
Terminal area		1		82
En route		1		4
Mixed VFR/IFR	14		171	
Terminal area		10		114
En route		4		57
	83		407	
Totals	271		556	

The fatalities column is important but it is a matter of chance whether the colliding aircraft are carrying a few or many passengers. A light private aircraft in effect takes up as much air space as does a jumbo jet, and thus represents just as great an air-traffic control problem — greater, indeed, because light aircraft are slower.

The main conclusion is that two-thirds of all collisions, 178 out of 271, take place near an airport.

AIR MISSES The number of air-misses is a fair measure of air-traffic control efficiency and safety. Statistics kept and studied by the British National Air Traffic Services, a department of the Civil Aviation Authority, suggests that the number of air-misses increases approximately as the square of the traffic. The basis of these air-miss statistics is the confidential pilot report. Even the air-miss working groups do not know the names of the reporting pilots. The more serious air-misses — about one a year in the United Kingdom — are investigated by the Accidents Investigation Branch.

Some countries require the filing of a full air-miss report so that it can be investigated. Not all are reported — perhaps because the pilot, who may have been at the wrong holding height over a beacon, or not where air-traffic control had ordered him to be, did not want to get involved in the subsequent inquiry. But enough air-miss reports are filed to allow the authorities to compile statistics and analyse trends which are invaluable in the planning of air-traffic control. The United Kingdom air-miss record, published by the Civil Aviation Authority, is as follows:

Total reported "dangerous" near-collisions involving public-transport aircraft in the UK

1963	2	(495,000)	1968	6	(612,000)
1964	7	(522,000)	1969	4	(639,000)
1965	3	(554,000)	1970	11	(706,000)
1966	9	(605,000)	1971	5	(730,000)
1967	5	(617,000)	1972	10	(772,000)

Figures in brackets denote total public-transport movements.

COLLISIONS WITH HIGH GROUND The number of aircraft which have flown into high ground has remained remarkably constant over the years at just under 20 a year on average. The number of such accidents per million flights is highest in South America, at 2.65, and lowest in North America, at 0.39. The European and Asia/Far East rates are each just over one. Nearly half such accidents occur during the descent or approach and just over one-third en route. The remaining 15 per cent take place after take-off during the climb.

LIGHTNING One of the greatest fears of the early aviators was that lightning would be fatal. It was one of those hazards of nature which would seriously limit the development of flying. In fact it has not proved to be a major danger. Good electrical design, bonding and static-dischargers have combined to rank the hazard very low in the list of accident causes.

Only one jet airliner is known to have been lost as a result of lightning. In December 1963, in the USA, lightning struck the fuel-tank vent of a Pan American Boeing 707 and ignited the vapour. The aircraft caught fire and crashed with the loss of all 81 occupants. The fact that the aircraft had been fuelled with higher-volatility JP4 Avgas (wide-cut gasoline) rather than the JP1 (kerosene) is thought to have been a contributory cause. The accident played a part in convincing the aviation industry and safety authorities of JP1's superior safety — though this is more apparent in the crash-spillage case (see previous chapter).

Lightning can pit, dent and sometimes pierce the aluminium skin at the "attachment" points where it enters and leaves the aircraft. This uninvited electricity can damage equipment — especially electrical circuits and electronics — in its way.

Aircraft can trigger off a flash between clouds of different potential and become part of the discharge path. The effect may frighten passengers but the fuselage shell effectively screens them from danger. In the case of ribbon or "blue" lightning the current in any case rarely exceeds a few amps, and the result may only be two pinholes. Fork or "red" lightning of higher current, sometimes thousands of amps, will cause bigger holes; but good bonding — what the mediaeval steeple builders knew as lightning conductors — will protect aircraft against all but the freak lightning strike. The majority of lightning strikes take place below 20,000ft.

FATAL LIGHTNING STRIKES

Date	Aircraft	Carrier	Location	Type of Flight	Fatalities Crew	Fatalities Pass-engers	Total Occupants Crew	Total Occupants Pass-engers
Jan 27, 1951	S-M95B (I-DALO)	Alitalia	Civitavecchia	SP	4	10	5	12
June 26, 1959	L-1649A (N7313C)	TWA	Milan	SP	9	59	9	59
Aug 12, 1963	Viscount (F-BGNV)	Air Inter	Lyons	SP	4	16	4	16
Dec 8, 1963	707 (N709PA)	Pan Am	Elkton	SP	8	73	8	73
Dec 24, 1971	L-188 (OB-R-941)	Lansa	Puerto Inca	SP	6	85	6	86

How would you like to be up there in that airliner?
— I wouldn't like to be up there not in that airliner.

10   Accident Investigation

When an airliner crashes many interests are involved. There is the country on whose territory the aircraft falls (defined by the International Civil Aviation Organisation, Icao, as the "State of Occurrence"); the country in which the aircraft is registered (the "State of Registry"); the countries in which the airframe, engines and systems are designed, manufactured, tested and certificated (the "States of Manufacture"); the countries of nationality of the passengers, which might be termed the State of Bereavement; the State whose air traffic control authority was in charge; and other operators of the aircraft type involved.

According to Article 26* of the Chicago Convention on International Civil Aviation the State of Occurrence shall be responsible for investigating the accident, though other interested States may be allowed to appoint Accredited Representatives. Annex 13 to the Chicago Convention spells out the rights of participation in an inquiry as follows:

5.20—The State of Registry shall be permitted to appoint an Accredited Representative to participate in the investigation.

5.23—The State of Manufacture shall be entitled to appoint an

---

*"In the event of an accident to an aircraft of a contracting State occurring in the territory of another contracting State, and involving death or serious injury, or indicating serious technical defect in the aircraft or air navigation facilities, the State in which the accident occurs will institute an inquiry into the circumstances of the accident, in accordance, so far as its laws permit, with the procedure which may be recommended by the International Civil Aviation Organisation. The State in which the aircraft is registered shall be given the opportunity to appoint observers to be present at the inquiry and the State holding the inquiry shall communicate the report and finding in the matter to that State."

Accredited Representative to participate in the investigation of an accident whenever it is believed that its participation in the investigation could be useful or result in increased safety.

5.26—Any State which, on request, provides information to the State conducting the investigation shall be entitled to appoint an Accredited Representative to participate in the investigation.

5.27—A State entitled to appoint an Accredited Representative shall be entitled to appoint advisers to assist him in the investigation.

5.28—RECOMMENDATION. Participation in the investigation should confer entitlement to:

    (a) visit the scene of the accident

    (b) examine the wreckage

    (c) question witnesses

    (d) have full access to all relevant evidence

    (e) receive copies of all personal documents

    (f) make submissions in respect of the various elements of the investigation.

5.29—RECOMMENDATION. A State which has a special interest in an accident, wherever it occurred, by virtue of fatalities to its citizens, should, upon making a request to do so, be permitted by the State conducting the investigation to appoint an expert to participate in the investigation to facilitate the availability of factual information to the former State. The entitlement to participation of this expert should be limited to:

    (a) visiting the scene of the accident

    (b) having access to the relevant factual information

    (c) providing assistance and information concerning the identification of the victims; and

    (d) receiving a copy of the final report.

The State requesting such participation should justify to the State conducting the investigation the basis for its request.

The world "should" rather than "shall" shows that these are only recommendations. If a State decides, as some have done, that the accident is nobody's business but its own, nothing can be done.

Accredited Representatives should be completely objective members of the inquiry. The purpose of all members of the inquiry should be to discover the cause of the accident, however unpalatable, rather than to promote the interests of the State they represent, or to apportion blame. An English judge and air lawyer, Mr Justice Kerr, has told the Royal Aeronautical Society: "In some cases one finds a conscious or unconscious chauvinistic desire to conduct the investigation in such a way as to absolve from any possible blame the authorities or nationals of the country in which the inquiry is held."

The purpose of Icao's Annex 13, which defines the rights of Accredited Representatives, is stated in its foreword as "the prevention of further accidents." This should be the purpose of all members of an inquiry.

The State of Manufacture as well as the State of Registry should also be allowed to send observers. Manufacturers and airworthiness authorities, backed by their massive technical facilities, are often the most likely to find the cause of the accident.

International procedure When an airliner accident happens the State of Occurrence notifies the State of Registry and the State of Manufacture. Standard reporting forms are provided by Icao. Unless the initial notification specifically states that the State of Manufacture should not send a representative, this State can notify its intention to appoint one to the inquiry. In other words, the primary assumption is that the manufacturer is welcome. This has not always been so. Recognition of the manufacturer's role took some fighting for, mainly by the Americans, British and French. But the State of Occurrence may still not accept a manufacturer's representatives.

The International Civil Aviation Organisation, Icao, has a standard form for reporting accidents. The Preliminary Report, which should be produced within 30 days of the occurrence of the accident, should be in coded format, while the Final Report is required to be sent to Icao in the form of a computer-compatible Aircraft Accident Data Report.

To quote Annex 13: "If the State instituting the investigation considers that the international dissemination of information in the Accident Report would be of exceptional value to the promotion of aviation safety, because of the successful employment of new investigative techniques or the disclosure of the need for significant preventive action, that State should send to Icao copies of the summary of the report, prepared in one of the working languages of Icao, in the format indicated in Annex 13 using the terminology contained in the Icao Lexicon."

It is clearly unfair that the State upon whose territory an aircraft chances to crash should pay the invariably high cost of the investigation. Even if the State could afford to do so it might not have the required experts and facilities. For example, specialist instruments to detect chemical traces of an explosion, or a specialist pathologist to obtain medical evidence from the dead, may be available in only one or two countries. The black-box crash recorder, to give another example, can usually be interpreted only by the maker's engineers in their laboratories. States now take it for granted that wreckage and components like flight recorders may be sent for analysis to the State of Manufacture. This was a procedure that had to be fought for. The exchange of vital components is provided for by Icao in Annex 9, Facilitation.

An accident happened in State A to an American-built jet transport registered in State B. There was reason to suspect that the accident was related to others which had very recently been the subject of US Federal Aviation Administration (FAA) airworthiness-alerts. Several hundred aircraft of this type were in public transport service in many countries. But every inquiry and offer of help by the US authorities, and by the State of Registry, was declined.

Incidents like this are leading to amendments of the Chicago Convention, the international civil-aviation law, in a number of ways. For example, the State of Occurrence should, it is proposed, accept representatives not only from the States of Registry and of Manufacture (as provided for) but States should be given the opportunity to comment on the report before publication. None of this can be denied by a State if it agrees with the Chicago Convention that the object is to determine the cause of an accident.

A most useful Icao air-safety document is the *Manual of Aircraft Accident Investigation* written by experts from six of the leading western civil-aviation States: Australia, France, West Germany, Italy, United Kingdom and the United States.

EVIDENCE Icao recommends that all observers shall be entitled to all the evidence. In practice the world of accident investigation is very small, and usually everyone knows each other well enough to get straight down to the job. The investigators have often co-operated before, and they exchange technical evidence freely and frankly, working as a team. At the technical level co-operation is invariably good; it is when politicians get involved that confidence may dwindle or disappear.

The British legal approach to accident investigation is typical of the best, rooted deep in the law of a country which rates the rights and liberties of individuals highly, and sets the law above government.

The key official of the Accidents Investigation Branch (AIB) is the chief inspector of accidents. He answers direct to the civil-aviation minister. The regulations give the inspector, not the minister, the right to decide whether an investigation shall take place. This helps to ensure that accidents cannot be glossed over for political reasons. The chief inspector advises the minister whether or not an inquiry should be public, but the minister makes the final decision on this. Public accident inquiries are the exception rather than the rule. All reports of all accident investigations are published, though not all the evidence.

The law requires that anyone whose reputation may be adversely affected by a report — say a pilot — shall be given the opportunity to make representations to the inspector. This is known as "11(1)" action, from the section in the Act of Parliament. Those who make representations and are dissatisfied can appeal to a Review Board. This can seriously delay publication because the law requires that a Review Board shall be held if an aggrieved party asks for one. The result is that accident inspectors find themselves taking particular care to respect the rights of individuals, knowing that their reports have to be fair and scrupulous enough to satisfy a judicial court. All this can delay publication, and alter the findings; but the report is ultimately published — sometimes as much as three or four years after the accident. The average time taken is about two years for major airliner accidents.

Somebody has to decide where the greater value lies: in the protection of an individual's liberty, even if he is being vexatious, or in the prevention of other fatal accidents. In practice the dissemination of urgent safety information is not held up by consultation procedures. The chief inspector is prepared to defend the view that lives are more important than protecting the interests of people who cannot make up their minds. The procedure does not prevent "fire brigade" action when, for example, an aircraft crashes because of fatigue in a flap-operating lever. As soon as it is discovered in the wreckage an alert is telegraphed immediately to all other operators of the aircraft.

The Accidents Investigation Branch is independent of everyone except its minister. It can be critical of the body which makes the safety regulations, the Civil Aviation Authority, and it sometimes is — though not as robustly as the US National Transportation Safety Board is of the Federal Aviation Administration.

The British AIB also investigates serious incidents, for example near-collisions with the ground or with other aircraft.

The investigation of accidents which occur in foreign territory can raise problems, because under international law (Icao Annex 13) responsibility for accident investigation is with the State of Occurrence. But most States will co-operate with the State of Registry in helping to establish the facts about, for example, what the local air-traffic control authority said. Sometimes discreet wording needs to be adopted in the report; for example, if the air-traffic control authority of the State of Occurrence is reported to "claim" that it gave a certain clearance, this can usually be taken to mean that the fact is disputed. If the report states that "clearance was given", this may be interpreted to mean that, in the opinion of the accident investigator, it was in fact given.

98

When a British airliner failed to get airborne on take-off at Munich in 1958 the German inquiry blamed the commander, Capt James Thain, for not checking that there was ice on the wings. The pilot's responsibility is to have the wings checked and cleared of ice before getting into the aircraft. Capt Thain did in fact fail to do this, for which he was disciplined and suspended. But he insisted that slush on the runway — the responsibility of the German authorities — had retarded the take-off and had been the cause of the fatal crash.

He fought to get the inquiry findings changed. Eventually the British authorities conducted slush tests, and found that quite shallow amounts of slush can significantly retard a take-off run. The British issued a report supplementing the German report. After an eleven-year fight the pilot, Capt. Thain, who died in retirement in 1975, cleared his name. At the same time air safety had been advanced.

When an accident happens the investigators are very dependent on the honesty of the airline's officials. It is much better for the accident investigators to be told straight away that the airline has a conscience about something. The inquiry will discover this anyway eventually, but confidence will then be lost, and so will the common objective — which is to prevent similar accidents.

Medical evidence Some accidents have been solved solely by pathology. The pathologist's job can be peculiarly difficult if the accident happens in an undeveloped country. Limited laboratory and refrigeration facilities, the emotional atmosphere and local legal and religious observances sometimes make unhurried, clinical analysis impossible. While wreckage can be examined in scientific conditions over a period of months or even years, autopsies have to be performed in days or even hours. Clear and prompt orders should be given by States to their local authorities to recognise the special needs of the pathologist.

In one accident that happened on holy ground the local authorities would allow no doctors near. As a result medical evidence that could have helped to save lives in the future was almost certainly lost. In another accident the magistrate ordered that nothing should be touched while he was away on holiday. In another the authorities allowed reporters and television camera men into the mortuary while the pathologists were trying to do their work.

The importance of pathology examinations for heart disease, alcohol, drugs or other irregularities is obvious. The Chicago Convention entitles pathologists to be part of an accident-investigation team, and to make sure that there is understanding and liaison between them and the judicial authorities.

Conclusive evidence of sabotage has been obtained from X-ray photographs which revealed hundreds of metal particles in some bodies. From their size and positions it was possible to deduce that they had been projected with high velocity, as in an explosion. It proved possible actually to locate the origin of the explosion. The fragments were of mild steel, which is used very little in aircraft manufacture, and the fracture and heating characteristics of the particles were typical of those produced by a bomb detonation. If the local police or judiciary had ordered that the bodies should not be touched, or if entry of the explosives experts had been denied or delayed by minor officials, or if the State had refused to allow the particles to be sent for analysis in a London forensic laboratory, the cause of the accident would have remained a mystery.

LOCAL DIFFICULTIES Most States co-operate wholeheartedly with the investigators, and obstruction is inusual. But ignorance can frustrate investigators, especially in countries unused to foreigners. Foreign experts are not always welcome, sometimes for political reasons, sometimes because the State is so administratively primitive that it is unaware of its obligations under Annex 13 to the Chicago Convention on civil aviation. Government officials of the highest authority may give orders to expedite the entry of foreign air-safety experts; but the work of these experts may still be obstructed by local police, officials, and judiciary. The investigators may arrive at the remote scene of an accident — perhaps days after it happened — to find the wreckage looted, the dead buried. Vital scratches, chemical traces, fire or debris patterns may have been lost by ignorant handling of the wreckage. A British expert, Dr Clancey, has decribed how a Convair which crashed in a war zone had all its seat cushions looted. This could have been serious, because expanded plastic foam is a most effective trapper of bomb fragments, and it was suspected that this crash had been caused by sabotage. This was later proved by other means.

The usefulness of seat cushions in bomb-detection, Dr Clancey has said, "was proved in the now classic case of the loss of a Comet 4 B in the Mediterranean where practically the whole proof of the presence of a bomb, its position in the aircraft and its type was deduced from the scientific examination of a single seat cushion."

The accredited representatives defined in Article 26 and Annex 13 do not include insurance surveyors. It has been argued that insurance experts should be given access to the wreckage, as of right, and that the prompt settlement of claims would be assisted if surveyors were allowed to form on-the-spot judgments. More important, the insurers argue, is the help which their experienced surveyors can contribute to finding the cause of the accident.

One international air lawyer has argued that there is a strong case for passengers to be represented, because their entitlement to damages under the Warsaw Convention can be unlimited if there is wilful misconduct or contributory negligence by the carrier. Some legal authorities urge that accident reports should be comprehensive and objective enough to provide a sound basis for settling or dismissing claims in later damages suits.

In an ideal world all airliner accidents would be investigated by the International Civil Aviation Organisation. Mr Justice Kerr has said:

"There would seem to be a great deal to be said for the creation, under the auspices of Icao, of a number of specialist aircraft accident investigation teams or units. All that would be necessary would be panels of experts in different fields composed of nationals of different countries who are willing to make their services available internationally.

"It would of course be unrealistic at the present time to expect States to accept any obligation to call upon the members of such panels as advisers, or perhaps even to admit them as observers. But the existence of such panels, coupled with the ability of States to select from them persons and nationals of their choice, might well lead to an improvement of the present position. There would then be known to be available an internationally sponsored and recognised means of supplementing the local resources of expert knowledge and experience.

"If the local resources or procedures might otherwise appear to be inadequate to achieve the objects of a full investigation under Annex 13, then the very existence of such panels might well lead States to make use of them in order to convince the general public about the comprehensiveness and objectivity of the investigation.

"As a corollary for permitting their names to appear on such panels there should then no doubt be made available to such experts through Icao copies of the various Annex 13 Investigation Reports as and when they appear, so that their knowledge is kept up to date. This would involve an amendment to Annex 13, requiring the State holding an enquiry to communicate the report and findings to Icao as well as to the State of Registration. This in itself would be an advance, because it would result in a greater pooling of knowledge and experience.

"One would then also hope that Annex 13 might be widened to include not only accidents in the sense of disasters involving death or serious injury, or indicating serious technical defects, but also 'incidents' which have all the ingredients relevant to an inquiry."

PUBLIC INFORMATION The law of almost every State requires an investigation of every "notifiable" accident. The definition of a notifiable accident varies, but in general it means a crash in which lives are lost or gravely hazarded, or the aircraft is badly damaged. The government may decide on a public inquiry.

Almost everything the American National Transportation Safety Board (NTSB) does has to be done publicly. Policy is to relate factual information about an accident to anybody at any time. "If the elevator is here and the engine is there and the rest of the aircraft is somewhere else, that is factual," says the NTSB. There is often argument, especially after an accident, as to what is factual and what is analysis. The gain by being open is the confidence of the public that the authority is doing an objective job; factual information given as soon as possible allows professionals in the industry to look at their own operation. This is accident prevention.

The NTSB accepts the risk of being misquoted. "You lose a little there, and later you have to explain yourself out of it, but on balance we do not believe in the don't-tell-anybody-until-it's-wrapped-up philosophy. Information is an accident-prevention device in itself."

Accidents are best investigated by a body which does not make the air-safety rules. Defective rules are more likely to be changed if the rule-maker is not the judge of their effectiveness. Most of the more mature air-transport countries make a point of separating accident investigation from lawmaking.

BLAME The purpose of accident investigation is to establish the cause, not to attribute blame. This may seem obvious; but the International Civil Aviation Organisation Annex 13, Accident Investigation, did not make this clear until the 1970s. The international and national laws of liability, and the involvement of lawyers seeking compensation for their clients, has often tended to frustrate and even pervert the real purpose of accident investigation. The amended Annex 13 states: "The fundamental objective ... shall be the prevention of accidents and incidents. It is not the purpose of this activity to apportion blame or liability."

The main weakness of the public inquiry system is that lawyers get into the "blame mode". This adversary system, as the Americans call it, does get to the bottom of many discrepancies which official technical investigators may not regard as important, or are too involved to pursue. Accident reports which have been left to the official investigators often leave many questions unanswered, and apparently sometimes even unasked. Only lawyers and journalists believe themselves to be truly independent, but the accident investigators do not always think that they help air safety. Lawyers are, they say, too interested in blame, and journalists trivialise and sensationalise everything. But very often it is impossible to separate blame from the cause. The "blame mode" adopted by lawyers and journalists at accident enquiries can be healthy, provided that it does not inhibit professional frankness, especially about incidents and human errors.

Human fallibility is accounting for a higher proportion of accident causes as technical failures become fewer. There is therefore a strong case for protected incident reporting, to take the blame out and to put safety in.

PILOT ERROR is cited as the cause of a third to a half of all accidents. But pilot error may be an oversimplification. It is often the conclusion of inquiries whose terms of reference are to find "the" cause of an accident. Almost every accident is a combination of several events, none of which would alone be the cause but each of which is an essential ingredient in the final disaster. Pilot error may be present; but so may the errors of aircraft or equipment designers, maintenance engineers, air traffic controllers, and so on.

"PRIME CAUSE" CONCEPT Experts in the field of accident investigation emphasise the need to get away from the legal concept of the "prime cause", or "probable cause". In general the courts do not understand the "multiple-cause accident". The quest for a single cause can mean the overlooking of much useful safety.

CRASH RECORDERS The first evidence for which investigators search at the accident site is the flight-data recorder, otherwise known as the crash recorder or "black box" (which in fact is painted yellow or flame orange). Icao Annex 6 requires all turbine aircraft over 5,700 kg to be equipped with a flight recorder.

Mounted in the more survivable sections of the aircraft, usually in the tail cone, the crash recorder is painted highly conspicuously with the words in black letters: FLIGHT RECORDER — DO NOT OPEN. ENREGISTREUR DE VOL — NE PAS OUVRIR. Mounted on a 20g attachment, the crash recorder is required to survive the most destructive accident. Typically it must be tested to show that it can play back a readable record after, for example, a peak acceleration of 1,000g; an impact force equivalent to a 25 kg steel bar dropped endwise from 2m; a crush force of 2½ tonnes for five minutes; a fire of 1,100°C for five minutes followed by 800°C for 30 minutes and 600°C for 60 minutes; immersion for 24hr in kerosene, oil, hydraulic fluid and extinguishants; and immersion for 30 days in sea water.

The recorder should ideally be fitted with a reliable underwater separation device, so that it floats to the surface if the aircraft crashes in the sea. Some countries require this, and also the fitting of a sonar "pinger", or sound-producing device, to assist detection (see below).

The crash recorder comprises a tape, wire or foil which records, from take-off to touchdown, at least five basic parameters: Time, Speed, Heading, Altitude, Acceleration. Such data are often indispensable to air-crash investigators in their efforts to reconstruct the last moments of a flight.

Crash recorders can be expensive and heavy, and they have to be maintained. A typical reliability requirement is a 100 per cent playback at least 85 per cent of the time. The best safety authorities require regular checks. Some crash-recorder manufacturers offer units with more than five channels, capable of measuring 50 or more parameters such as engine performance, structural stresses, control-surface positions, or whatever the airline wants to measure. Used in this way the crash recorder is a flight data recorder (FDR) — a sort of flight inspector providing reliability data for the engineering and flight operations departments (see Chapters 15 and 19). Only the biggest airlines have such elaborate flight recorders. They require much engineering, particularly wiring, and require expensive computer-aided analysis.

Value of Flight Data Recorders Flight Data Recorders have been fitted to all US airliners of more than 5,700kg, 12,500lb, take-off weight since July 1958. The regulations require records to be kept for 60 days.

Since 1974, following four crashes from which the Flight Data Recorders were not recovered because the wreckage was in deep water, the US Federal Aviation Administration has required recorders to be equipped with devices to assist location under water. Typically, an underwater locater beacon — a small battery-powered acoustic transmitter activated by water — emits an intermittent acoustic signal of specific frequency. Salvage experts searching for the wreckage of an American Boeing 707 which crashed into the Mediterranean detected the beacon's acoustic signal at a depth of over 10,000ft 27 days after the accident.

From 1959 to the end of 1973 the US National Transportation Safety Board received 509 flight data recorders for read-out (not all from fatal crashes). Of these only 41, or 9 per cent, failed to yield readings because they were damaged or (in the case of four) could not be recovered from deep water.

COCKPIT VOICE RECORDERS (CVRs) are compulsory in nearly all major air-transport countries. "If only we knew what they were saying in the cockpit during the last ten minutes" is a wish often expressed by accident investigators. Every word spoken on the flight deck — radio messages, checks, commands or even the joke with the stewardess — is recorded by the CVR. Like the crash recorder, with which it is sometimes integrated, the CVR is resistant to fire and impact. In deference to the pilots' wishes the tape is recycled after a given play, typically 30 minutes. Icao requires all radio communications to be

Today, as when airlines began just after the First World War, safety ultimately depends on the aircraft designer, the engineer, the management and the man in the sharp end – the pilot.

Above: The standards of engineering integrity required for blind landings are such that the electronics have to meet a theoretical failure rate of not more than one per ten million landings. This Trident of British Airways landing in Category 3 conditions has a triplicated autolanding system.

Left: Air crashes are so rare, and so dynamically and physically complex, that attempts have been made to simulate crashes in order to analyse them under controlled conditions. In this dramatic sequence an old, specially instrumented DC-7 is observed and filmed by the US Federal Aviation Administration taking off under its own power (in a remote desert area near Phoenix, Arizona). After reaching about 100 m.p.h. and catching fire the aircraft crashes to its destruction.

Top: Inflatable chutes down which passengers can slide to the ground or water are designed into the floor near each door. They double up as life rafts, with capacity sufficient for all occupants of the aircraft. They eject and inflate automatically in the event of a ditching or crash-landing.

Bottom: An A300 demonstrates its ability to land crosswind safely on a wet runway, coming to rest without overheating the brakes or overworking the thrust reversers, and well within the scheduled runway length. Note the "lift dumpers," which get the weight of the aircraft off the wings on to the wheels and brakes immediately after touchdown.

Top: Paradoxically, some of the most difficult approaches have the best safety records. Here an Air-India Boeing 707 approaches Kai Tak, Hong Kong.
Bottom: Ditchings by airliners are extremely rare, and in this case it was the result of a premature descent during an approach in difficult visibility. There is only one known case of a fatal jet ditching resulting from fuel shortage. Here a DC-8 which prematurely descended into San Francisco Bay is lifted out of shallow water and loaded onto a barge for shipment to a repair base.

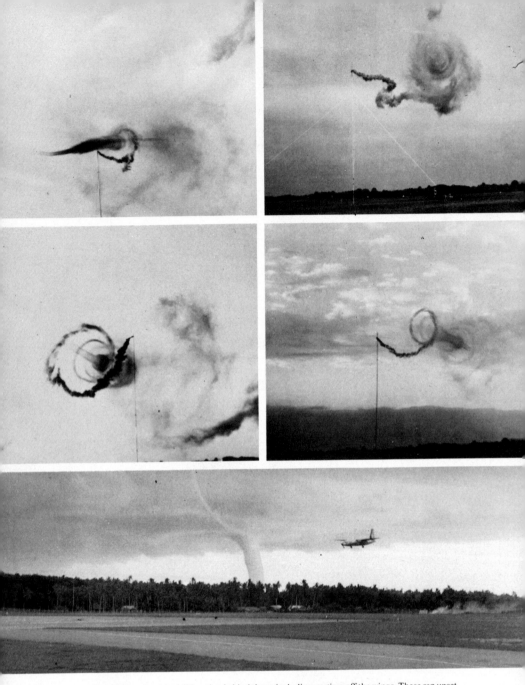

Top: Airliners leave invisible wakes behind them, including vortices off the wings. These can upset following aircraft, especially near the ground at airports. The heavier the aircraft the stronger the wake vortex. Here the US Federal Aviation Administration flies test aircraft (not visible) past a smoke tower, vividly rendering the wake vortices visible.

Above: "Wind-shear is most often associated with thunderstorms. Although the squall line may be . . . . ahead of a thunderstorm, a clue to the pilot that shear may be lying in wait is the presence of the thunderstorm itself" – an Indian Airlines Fokker F.27 beats a "twister" on short finals to Bombay.

Right: "Landing accidents and incidents, veering off and over-running the runway, account for about three per cent of airliner accidents and serious incidents of all types. In two out of three airport accidents and incidents airport conditions are cited as a cause or contributory cause." Though damaging to the aircraft, as in this case involving a Boeing 707, few such accidents result in death or injury.

Emergency exits and flame-resistant cabin furnishings are nowadays mandatory, as in the Boeing 747 cabin. The wicker chairs and ripping panels of the 1920 Handley page W10 would make today's airworthiness engineers shudder.

similarly recorded by air-traffic control.

A cockpit voice-recorder playback after an accident almost always makes a key contribution to the investigation. If it does not pinpoint the cause it may well eliminate many possible ones. The following is an example of a CVR playback from a Convair 600 of Texas International Airlines which crashed in Arkansas in September 1973 with the loss of all the occupants — eight passengers, a stewardess and two pilots, whose voices during the last half hour of the flight are transcribed. The aircraft crashed into a mountain, at a height of 2,025ft, and the wreckage was not found for three days.

The CVR helped the accident investigators to determine the probable cause, which was that the captain was attempting to fly by visual flight rules (VFR) at night in instrument weather, and that he descended below safety height for the terrain while "there was no evidence that [he] was concerned about his position or track over the ground." Two minutes and 40 seconds before impact, after the captain's ordered descent to 2,000ft, the first officer said: "Man, I wish I knew where we were so we'd have some idea of the general terrain around this... place."

LEGEND

CAM	Cockpit area microphone
-1	Voice identified as Captain
-2	Voice identified as First Officer
*	Unintelligible
#	Nonpertinent word
( )	Questionable text
...	Pause
Time	Minutes and seconds from the start of the CVR

20:14.5
CAM-2 How'd I get all this # speed?
CAM-1 You're all right
CAM-2 (Pile it on) we'll keep this speed here?
CAM-1 A little while
CAM-2 There ain't no lights on the ground over there
CAM-1 Yeah, I see 'em behind us
CAM-1 See stars above us
20:40.5
CAM-2 I got some lights on the ground
CAM-1 There's just not many out here
CAM-2 Maybe... could be somethin' else, coach
CAM-1 Aha, we're gettin' rid of the clouds
CAM-1 We'is in the clouds, Fred
CAM-2 Are we?
CAM-1 Yeah
CAM-1 No, we're not

105

21:16.5
CAM-1 I can see above us
CAM-2 We got (ground) up ahead?
CAM-1 I can see the ground here
CAM-2 Yeah, I can see the ground down here, too
CAM-1 Yeah***
CAM-1 North is a fair heading, north
CAM-2 Now, what have we got here?
CAM-1 Naw, you're all right, I can see some lights over here
CAM-2 I'll tell ya what, coach...
22:02.5
CAM-2 That's probably Hot Springs
CAM-1 Yep, could be
CAM-1 Yeah, that might be either it or Arkadelphia
CAM-2 Well, I'm getting out of the clouds here Mac, but I'm getting right straight into it
CAM-1 Oh, looks like you're all right
CAM-2 Do you see any stars above us?
CAM-2 We're going in and outta some scud
CAM-1 Yeah, we've got a little bit here
CAM-2 I sure wish I knew where the # we were
22:49.0
CAM-1 Well, I tell you what, we're, ah, on the two fifty... two sixty radial from, ah, Hot Springs
CAM [Heavy static]
CAM-2 Figure I can kick her on up here, maybe I can outrun it
CAM-1 I don't, I don't think you can get up
CAM-2 Well, I, I got the # thing pointed almost straight up to see what we got out here
23:27.5
CAM-2 Paintin' ridges and everything else boss and I'm not familiar with the terrain
CAM-2 We're staying in the clouds
CAM-1 Yeah, I'd stay down. You're right in the (some) right in the base of the clouds
CAM-1 I tell you what, we're gonna be able to turn here in a minute
CAM-2 You wanna go through there?
CAM-1 Yeah
24:04.5
CAM-2 All right
CAM-2 Good, looking good, Mac. Looking good
CAM-1 That's all right, wait a minute
CAM-2 Well, I can't even get, ah, Texarkana any more
CAM-1 I'll tell you what, Fred
CAM-2 'kay, boss
CAM-1 Well, ah, we'll just try that, we'll try it. We're gonna be in the rain pretty soon. It's only about two miles wide
CAM-2 You tell me where you want me to go
CAM-1 Okay, give me a heading of, ah, three forty
CAM-2 Three forty?
25:25.5
CAM-1 Three forty

106

CAM-1 Steady on
CAM-1 We got ten miles to go 'n' we're gonna turn...
CAM-1 To the left about ah, 'bout fifty degrees
CAM-2 Want me to turn, did ya say fifty?
CAM-1 Yeah, fifty left
CAM-1 Oh about, uh, two ninety
CAM-2 Two ninety
25:59.5
CAM-1 Ya got six miles to turn
CAM-1 Three miles south of turn
CAM-2 We're in it
CAM1 Huh?
CAM-2 We're in solid, now
CAM-1 Are we?
CAM-2 Hold it
27:01.0
CAM-1 Start your turn... standard rate
CAM-1 Level out and let me see it... when you hit two ninety
CAM-2 Aw, okay
27:20.0
CAM-2 There's your two ninety
CAM-1 Steady on
CAM-1 Should hit in about a half a mile. Should be out of it in 'bout two
       miles
CAM-1 You're in it
CAM-1 Are you through it?
28:05.0
CAM-1 Turn thirty left
CAM-2 I can see the ground, now
28:20.5
CAM-2 There's thirty left
CAM-2 Naw, that's thirty-five #
CAM-1 Keep on truckin', just keep on a-truckin'
CAM-2 Well, we must be somewhere in Oklahoma
CAM-1 Doin' all the good in the world
CAM-2 Do you have any idea of what the frequency of the Paris VOR is?
CAM   Nope, don't really give a #
29:15.0
CAM-1 Put, uh, about two sixty-five, heading two sixty-five
29:19.0
CAM-2 Heading, two sixty-five
CAM-2 I would say we # up
CAM-1 Think so?
CAM-? [Laughter]
CAM-1 Didn't we?
30:23.0
CAM-1 Fred, descend to two thousand
30:25.0
CAM-2 Two thousand, coming down
30:42.0
CAM-2 Here we are, we're not out of it
CAM-1 Let's truck on

31:01.5
CAM-1 'bout five to the right
CAM-1 Shift over a little bit if you can
CAM-2 Sure can
CAM-1 That's all right
CAM-2 Right #
CAM-1 That's all right, you're doin' all the good in the world
CAM-1 I thought we'd get, I thought it was moving that way on me only, we just kinda turned a little bit while you was looking at the map
CAM-2 Look
CAM-1 First time I've ever made a mistake in my life
CAM-2 I'll be #. Man, I wish I knew where we were so we'd have some idea of the general # terrain around this # place
CAM-1 I know what it is
CAM-2 What?
32:01.5
CAM-1 That the highest point out here is about twelve hundred feet
CAM-2 (That right)?
CAM-1 The whole general area, and then we're not even where that is, I don't believe
CAM-2 I'll tell you what, as long as we travel northwest instead of west, and I still can't get Paris
CAM-? [Whistling]
CAM-1 Go ahead and look at it
CAM-? [Whistling]
CAM-? #
CAM-? [Whistling]
33:18.5
CAM-2 Two hundred and fifty, we're about to pass over Page VOR
CAM-2 You know where that is?
CAM-1 Yeah
CAM-2 All right
33:34.0
CAM-1 About a hundred and eighty degrees to Texarkana
33:37.5
CAM-2 About a hundred and fifty two
33:40.0
CAM-2 Minimum en route altitude here is forty-four hund...
33:42.0 Sound of impact

SEARCH AND RESCUE All contracting States of the International Civil Aviation Organisation are expected to arrange for search and rescue facilities within their territories, available on a 24-hour basis. In areas of undetermined sovereignty, notably the high seas, responsibility for search and rescue is determined by regional air-navigation agreements.

Having defined the SAR region for which it is responsible, each State establishes a Rescue Co-ordination Centre (RCC). If necessary, sub-centres are established also. In addition each State designates public or private services as alerting posts — police stations, coastguards, lifeboat and lighthouse stations, military bases, and so on. Each Rescue Co-ordination Centre must have the means of immediate communication with local air-traffic control, rescue centres, and appropriate radio stations capable of alerting vessels and aircraft and of position-fixing. Each RCC must be able to communicate rapidly and reliably with all rescue units in the region, all adjacent RCCs, and all met offices and alerting posts.

Rescue units are designated for the SAR task by all States. These can be military, government or private services — helicopter operators, fire and ambulance services, hospitals, police, salvage services, and all air force, army and naval units.

All SAR aircraft communicate on the distress frequency of 121.5MHz (and 243MHz). They should be equipped with homing devices to locate the survival-radio equipment or emergency locating beacons (Elbas) which public-transport aircraft are required to carry. On board each SAR aircraft must be a copy of the "International Code of Signals" (see below) in case of communications difficulties.

States should provide, at appropriate airfields, survival packs for dropping from any type of aircraft. These packs should have their contents indicated by the standard international colour code and, where appropriate, by explanatory signals. A red pack indicates medical supplies; blue indicates food and water; yellow indicates clothing and blankets; and black indicates miscellaneous equipment such as stoves, axes, compasses, and so on. The contents should include instructions printed in at least three of the Icao working languages (English, French, Spanish, or Russian). All States are required by Icao to permit immediate access of another State's SAR units to its territory, preferably by prior agreements setting out the conditions of entry with the fewest possible formalities. Diplomatic authority should be delegated to the Rescue Co-ordination Centre for the duration of the emergency. In practice, where human lives are at stake, only a most uncivilised country would make difficulties for the rescuers of other nations. Difficulties can still arise, especially over who gives the orders to whom; but these too can be smoothed by prior agreements and by the common sense of the people on the spot. The rescue services of one State are not going to take over from those of another in the middle of an operation, even though the crash may be on its own territory. Indeed, it would expect its rescue services to take orders from the foreign units concerned.

All States are enjoined by Icao Annex 12, *Search and Rescue*, to carry out joint training exercises to promote communications and efficiency. In addition, every RCC should make available all its radio frequencies, call-signs, hours of watch, the positions of known wreckage which might be mistaken for the missing aircraft, and the places where emergency droppable packs are stored.

Emergency phase When an emergency is declared, following the "uncertainty phase" and the "alert phase", the RCC declares the "distress phase" and immediately:
(a) Initiates action by its SAR units
(b) Ascertains as closely as possible the position of the missing aircraft, and indicates the extent of the area to be searched
(c) Notifies the operator of the aircraft
(d) Notifies adjacent RCCs
(e) Alerts the air traffic control services, unless they already know
(f) Seeks the assistance of all aircraft, vessels and coastal stations to maintain a listening watch on 121.5 MHz and 243 MHz
(g) Plans the whole conduct of the search and rescue operation, communicates it to the authorities responsible for the actual rescue, and keeps the plan amended.

Finally the RCC should notify the State of Registry of the aircraft, and also the appropriate accident investigation authority — a representative of which should, if possible, accompany the first rescue units to arrive at the scene of the accident.

If ever there is any doubt as to which RCC is responsible, it will be the centre in whose region the last reported message was received; or, if this was on the border, the region to which the aircraft was heading; or, if no message was received, the region to which the aircraft was thought to be destined.

Search and Rescue signals If an aircraft wants to direct a surface craft towards the site of an accident it should circle the craft at least once and then cross its projected course close ahead at low altitude, rocking its wings (or, less preferred, opening and closing throttle) and then heading in the direction desired.

The international code for use by survivors and by rescuers is clear and simple. Examples:

Require doctor	I
Medical supplies	II
Food and water	F
Probably safe to land	**Triangle**
Require fuel and oil	L
All well	LL
No	N
Yes	Y
Not understood	L with another L "in mirror"

Require engineer	**W**
Indicate direction to proceed	**K**
Require firearms	Two **Vs** in chevron
We are proceeding in this direction	**Arrow**
Operation completed	**LLL**
All safe	**LL**
We have found some personnel	**╫**
We cannot continue and are returning to base	**XX**
Wreckage is in this direction	**Arrows** (one above the other)
We can find nothing but are continuing to look	**NN**

I have survived six accidents so I must be doing something right.

11 Accident Liability

Almost every chapter of the air-law textbook was on board the Turkish Airlines (THY) DC-10 which crashed at Ermenonville near Paris on March 3, 1974, killing all 346 occupants.

The liability of an airline was first governed by the Warsaw Convention of 1929. Accidents in the tender years of the air-transport industry forced the nations to agree upon standard procedures, not only to regulate claims but also to protect the infant airlines. The principle of Warsaw has stood the test of time. Without Warsaw a claimant would have to prove negligence before he could recover damages. With Warsaw the dependants of international airline passengers do not have to prove negligence. In exchange for this privilege they accept that the airline's liability is limited.

Warsaw thus uniquely unified the law internationally by taking the burden of proof off the injured party in exchange for limited compensation. Warsaw only exempts an airline from liability if it can prove "unavoidable accident," which is usually difficult. A claimant can break the damages limit only by proving "wilful misconduct" or a ticket defect, but this too is difficult.

Air transport is now a grown-up industry with a responsibility to society far greater than it was in 1929. And the value of money has not stood the test of time. The Warsaw compensation limit was set at 125,000 Poincare gold francs, worth $10,000 at 1976 rates. This figure increases as the price of gold rises but is worth less and less in relation to passenger incomes. The Warsaw limit was doubled by The Hague Protocol of 1955. But even $20,000 is not regarded as adequate by some countries. The United States Government threatened to denounce Warsaw unless the limit was substantially increased. The result, in 1966, was the "Montreal Agreement" among airlines operating to, via or from the USA to increase the limits to $75,000 by special contract with passengers.

The Montreal Agreement was not, like Warsaw or The Hague, an agreement of States. It was an inter-airline bargain, struck under pressure from the US Government to give passengers — especially Americans — a better deal. More than 100 "Warsaw" airlines are parties to the Montreal Agreement.

A Protocol drawn up at Guatemala in 1971 attempted to take all states to $100,000, unbreakable by "wilful misconduct" or any means whatsoever. But Guatemala has never been ratified by the USA or by the UK and is nowhere in force.

For the passenger there is, of course, always personal insurance. For less than the cost of an in-flight movie an insurance slot machine at the airport can cover him for $100,000 or more. And most prudent families will ensure that they are covered at all times, not only for air travel.

THE DC-10 ACCIDENT The DC-10 was on a flight from Paris to London, between two States — the United Kingdom and France — which are parties to Warsaw and The Hague. The carrier, Turkish Airlines, THY, is registered in a State which is not a party to Warsaw (nor, therefore, to The Hague). But many of the contracts of carriage, being between two Warsaw States, were governed by the Warsaw Convention.

The compensation which dependants can recover depends among other things on the point of departure and from which airline the tickets were bought. Sitting next to one another in the same row of seats in the DC-10 could have been passengers with "entitlements" varying from possibly very little to "the sky's the limit" with, in between, $75,000 for Montreal Agreement passengers, £8,723 for Warsaw/Hague-carriage tickets, or just £4,362 for plain Warsaw carriage. To quote the secretary and solicitor of British Airways Overseas Division: "If... you should feel that the present situation is both complicated to the point of incomprehensibility, and capable of leading to great unfairness between one passenger and another, you would be quite right."

There was a further complication for the dependants of the passengers who had been ticketed by British Airways, and who switched flights at the last moment because of a strike by that airline's baggage loaders. BEA made special "Montreal" contracts with passengers travelling on its services. This raised the question of what happens when the actual carrier, in this case THY, is not the contracting carrier, in this case British Airways (or strictly speaking, at the material time, BEA). The air lawyers had thought of this one in the convention drawn up at

Guadalajara in 1961. This makes the actual carrier equally liable with the contracting carrier. But Guadalajara was signed before the Montreal Agreement; and it does not provide for the transfer of the "Montreal $75,000" liability to an airline which is not a party to it. British Airways claims that it offers $75,000 only on its own "services," and that the THY flight was not such a service (though it might have been had it been a BEA charter).*

It was alleged that a Paris airport employee had failed to latch the door according to the correct procedure used in hundreds of thousands of previous DC-10 departures by a score of different airlines. The below-deck aft cargo door had blown off at about 12,000ft, causing the deck to buckle and jam the flying controls. It was alleged also that the Turkish airline might have added unauthorised shims to the lock-limit warning switch (to correct a flickering warning light) and misrigged a lock-pin in the mechanism from +0.25in to the -0.175in found in the wreckage.

These allegations were made by McDonnell Douglas to mitigate its own liability (or, it further alleged, that of its design and manufacturing subcontractor responsible for the component concerned, General Dynamics) for an indisputedly poor original door-lock design; and for delivering the aircraft (DC-10 ship 29) to Turkish Airlines without certain safety modifications recommended by McDonnell Douglas itself in its *Service Bulletin* SB 52 37.

That SB followed a "carbon-copy" incident, fortunately not fatal, more than a year before the Paris disaster (involving American Airlines DC-10 ship No 1 over Windsor, Ontario). That incident also had followed a departure with an incorrectly latched cargo door.

Also involved in liability allegations was the US Federal Aviation Administration, the airworthiness authority. The FAA had not made the "Windsor incident" modifications mandatory by means of an Airworthiness Directive, and had further failed to order floor-venting modifications as recommended by the US National Transportation Safety Board after the Windsor incident.

The widow of a British passenger killed in the subsequent Paris disaster sued McDonnell Douglas in an American court (actually in California, the State of Manufacture). Heavy damages have been awarded by US courts in manufacturer-liability cases. The highest damages that could have been won in this case by sueing the Turkish

---

*There has been dispute about the liability of an airline for passengers who are killed in the course of embarkation or disembarkation. According to the Warsaw Convention they are the responsibility of the airline; and a US court has found that TWA was liable for passengers killed by terrorists in a transit lounge at Athens Airport in August 1973. The passengers had been checked in by the airline for New York and had passed through passport and currency control and security before boarding. The terrorists apparently mistook them for passengers of another flight to Tel Aviv.

airline in a European court would be the "Warsaw" limit with all the complications listed above; and there was little doubt about the potential liability of the manufacturer. The result, reached in the US District Court of Los Angeles, was an agreement by the defendants and their insurers to offer compensation in return for being relieved of legal liability. The plaintiffs were not involved in the time and expense of proving and allocating liability among Turkish Airlines, the FAA, McDonnell Douglas and its subcontractor General Dynamics.

MANUFACTURERS' GENERAL LIABILITY About 50,000 aerospace-manufacturing companies in the world supply airliners, engines, autopilots and everything down to wiper blades. Nearly every component can contribute to an accident.

The airlines have the Warsaw/Hague/Montreal system to limit their liability. Yet in some United States courts a manufacturer — of any nationality — is vulnerable to "strict-liability" claims that his product was defective, and to the penalty of huge damages awarded by juries.

The American jury system tends to favour the widows and orphans rather than heavily insured giant corporations. "Blame" lawyers working on commission — sometimes up to 30 per cent of the damages — have combined with the strict liability of manufacturers in some US courts to produce big awards. Further, some US courts award punitive or exemplary damages. These are intended not only to compensate the victims but to punish manufacturers of defective products. In 1971, for example, $17.25 million was awarded against Beechcraft. Although this award was later reversed on appeal, because the jury was held to be wrong on a point of fact, a design error in an aircraft system could put an inadequately insured manufacturer out of business.

In some US jurisdictions the claimant has succeeded merely by showing that he was indirectly injured by a defect. And US case law has established that a manufacturer is liable for his product even though it is many years old, has had more than one owner, and has been substantially modified since manufacture.

There are few signs that US judgments are favouring the manufacturer, although in many US courts proof of contributory negligence by the claimant can be a successful defence.

A manufacturer may be liable for his product, however humble. As an English air lawyer, Mr Peter Martin, has written: "If the forger of a metal used in the manufacture of a turbine blade uses less than reasonable care in his preparation of the metal and if the turbine blade fails as a result of that negligence and if, as a result of that failure, the aircraft suffers an accident in which personal injury or death is caused to the passengers, then ultimately, if the negligence of the forger can be proved, he may be responsible for every penny of damages which may be ultimately payable."

Aircraft manufacturers do not always accept total contractual responsibility to purchasers and third parties. There may be exculpatory clauses in purchase agreements with suppliers of components, who may thus become involved in product-liability cases. Manufacturers who find themselves in US courts are expected to produce the most detailed evidence of design, manufacture and testing. To quote an actual subpoena: "You are commanded to bring all design data, documents, inter-office correspondence and drawings and all other papers and records pertaining to the design, production and manufacture of the aircraft..." As a Lloyd's underwriter has advised: "Keep this in mind next time you put pen to paper. Consider how it will sound when read in a courtroom four or five years from now — possibly out of context."

Suppliers are well advised by insurers and lawyers to consider the exculpatory provisions of their agreements with prime contractors. How liable is the supplier of a seal or valve, or even a complete engine? Mr David Higham of the Lloyd's brokers Willis, Faber & Dumas says: "A person injured by a defective product no longer needs to prove that the defect resulted from any negligence. In certain jurisdictions he need only show the defect, the connection between that defect and his injury and damages. Furthermore, in most US jurisdictions the injured party need only prove that the defective product contributed to his injury; it need not be the sole cause."

It is no good complaining, an underwriter has said — "If you wish to have the economic advantages of trading in their markets then you have to accept their legal system." He might also have added that the dependant of an American citizen killed outside the USA in an aircraft made by a non-American manufacturer can sue that manufacturer, if he is doing business in the USA, in a US court. This long arm of the US law could catch almost every major non-American aircraft manufacturer.

Clearly, the liability of the aerospace industry is very different from that of the airline industry. An airline's liability is limited even though it may have been negligent; an aircraft manufacturer's liability may be unlimited even though it took every possible care, and even though its product was only indirectly to blame. The aerospace industry does not enjoy the protection of a Warsaw Convention. The proposition that their liability should be limited is now a matter for respectable discussion by manufacturers — though they have yet to accept automatic liability as the price of limited liability. This is why they have got nowhere in their pleas for a limit.

There are cases where Governments themselves may be directly involved — perhaps by negligent air-traffic control, or defective safety

116

procedures. The US Federal Aviation Administration could theoretically be sued for allegedly not having made certain DC-10 cargo-door modifications mandatory.

The insurance premiums for product-liability cover paid by the world's aerospace manufacturers — suppliers as well as prime contractors — are probably now about $60 million a year (much directly or indirectly on the London market). The total world aviation insurance premiums paid by the airline industry are probably nearly $1,000 million annually.

An American-made aircraft operated by a Turkish airline carrying a majority of British passengers crashed in France following a defect in the cargo-door latching mechanism, killing all 346 occupants of many nationalities. If ever there was an accident which demanded international action to reform and standardise the liability laws, this is it. To quote a distinguished American lawyer, Lee S. Kreindler: "Intelligent laymen can only have contempt for what lawyers, governments and airlines have created."

The chairman of MEA, Sheikh Najib Alamuddin, has said that those bereaved by an air disaster should be speedily and fully compensated without the law's delay. International Air Transport Association members should, he says, get together to finance a common insurance policy. Manufacturers and government agencies, whose liability is so often intermeshed with that of the airlines, might well feel the need to co-operate in such a policy, and form a liability partnership with airlines. Their insurers are largely common to both.

The Warsaw formula, in which an airline in effect accepts automatic liability in return for limited compensation, could apply to manufacturers and public services just as well in principle as it does to operators. And The Hague, Montreal, Guadalajara and Guatemala modifications of Warsaw could be integrated in a common international convention devised to cover suppliers and regulators as well as the operators of air transport. Claimants should not have to "shop around" the courts, going for the airline and then the manufacturers and possibly eventually for a public authority.

One solution could be for presumed liability always to be attributed by claimants direct to the operator, who would decide later whether to have recourse to his supplier or regulator. This system of operator-liability applies in the European nuclear power station field under the 1960 Paris Convention — though the analogy is slender because in this field the operator is the designer, and the state accepts ultimate responsibility.

There is not much doubt that there must be a limitation of liability: the Warsaw principles have stood the test of time and should be cherished. But the limit should be higher — at least as high as the $100,000 of Guatemala. The real argument is over the question of whether the limit should be breakable or unbreakable.

On balance, the best compromise would seem to be unbreakable but much higher limits of liability.

Everyone knows the difficulty of getting international agreement. But the wide and enduring international support for the Warsaw Convention and, to a lesser extent, for its amending protocols gives grounds for optimism.

Accidents like that to the DC-10 should jolt every government, every airline, every aircraft manufacturer and supplier, and every lawyer, into realising how urgent is the need for reform.

Aircraft salesman: We must blow our own trumpet a bit more about the excellent structural characteristics of our new aircraft.
Chief engineer: Not too loud or it might fall apart.

---

12 Hazardous Cargo

In the small hours of November 3, 1973, an American all-cargo Boeing 707 en route from New York to Scotland crashed trying to make an emergency landing at Boston. The aircraft was on final approach to runway 33L when it pitched up and crashed into the ground on to its nose and left wing, killing the crew of three.

The cause of the accident was found to be improperly loaded nitric acid which had ignited its packing material. Smoke disabled the crew, and control was lost. Also included in the seven-ton shipment of chemicals were sulphuric acid, hydrofluoric acid, inflammable liquids such as isopropanol, xylene, acetone and methanol, containers of acetic acid and hydrogen peroxide, and a poisonous solution identified as "stripping solution A-20". There is no evidence that the captain was even aware that hazardous cargo was on board.

In the United States, on December 31, 1971, two passenger flights — a Boeing 727 and a Douglas DC-9 — were loaded with improperly packed shipments of 32-Curie Iridium 192. Radiation of up to 12 rems — double the safe annual limit allowed for radiation workers — was experienced by the 171 passengers and crew and the 31 ground handlers.

About 750,000 radioactive packages a year are carried by air, many of them in the company of passengers. Air cargo is big business. In the mid-1970s the world's airlines were carrying about 15,000 million ton-miles compared with 5,000 million 10 years before. Boeing estimates that by 1985 the ton-mileage will be more than 30,000 million.

Now the United States Federal Aviation Administration (FAA) has published new rules about hazardous cargo. Only radioactive materials intended for research or medical treatment are allowed on passenger flights. All radioactive packages have to be scanned with radiation counters. The permissible radiation level at the surface of any package loaded into a passenger aircraft shall not be more than 0.5 millirems an hour.

Rules about the packing and labelling of dangerous cargo are issued by the FAA. But the American Airline Pilots' Association (Alpa) is still not satisfied, and is implementing its own rules about the carriage of "hot" cargo. If a captain feels that any of these rules are being infringed he asks to see the cargo manifest; and if in his opinion any item does not meet the Alpa requirements he asks for the shipment to be off-loaded.

The American pilots will allow the carriage on passenger flights of radioactive pharmaceuticals, dry ice and magnetic materials, but nothing else. Up to 30 flights a day have been delayed by pilots dissatisfied with cargo manifests.

The United States is not satisfied with the International Air Transport Association's *Restricted Articles Regulations*. These are specified in the dangerous-materials laws of other countries, including the United Kingdom, and are indeed thorough. Certain articles are prohibited altogether by these regulations — explosives, poison gas, inflammable liquids and gases, and certain volatile chemicals. Restricted articles have to be packed, labelled, handled and loaded in accordance with the Iata regulations. "Danger" labels are recommended by Iata and are recognized and observed throughout the industry. A "cargo aircraft only" label is used for packages which are not to be loaded in passenger aircraft.

The FAA has revised the Federal Aviation Regulations, Part 103, governing radioactive materials shipped by air. The United States Department of Transportation is considering further changes to the law, and the American Hazardous Materials Regulations Board considers what changes are required to improve safety to the travelling public and flight crews.

The carriage of animals by air also can be hazardous and has to conform with Iata's live animals regulations. Aircraft can be easily damaged or unbalanced by loose or distressed animals, and there are strict rules about their containment. The floor of one freighter aircraft had to be replaced after corrosion by gallons of elephant urine during a CL-44 flight from Delhi to Frankfurt. The electrical system of another freighter was short-circuited by saline solution seeping through the floor from tanned hides.

In both cases the aircraft were landed safely, but the hazards of carrying animals cannot be underestimated. They have to be treated as "wet cargo" and cages or compartments must make provision for all the animal's environmental needs including ventilation. Cages must be accessible in flight and at transit stops; animals which are natural enemies should not be adjacent; and human remains should not be loaded near to animals.

Hold doors must be opened and closed with the greatest care, and only by qualified staff. The cargo world was a rough-and-tumble one long before the advent of the aircraft, and the meticulous safety disciplines of the air are unfamiliar to some cargo practitioners. Strict laws and training are essential.

WEIGHT AND BALANCE Every aircraft has weight restrictions defined in its Flight Manual and Certificate of Airworthiness. These must be observed when loading. The main limitations are taxi weight; take-off weight; landing weight; and "zero-fuel" weight.

The most critical wing-bending case is with zero fuel in the wing tanks and maximum payload in the fuselage. Aerodynamic lift and fuselage weight combine to bend the wings up. This bending is alleviated by the weight of fuel in the wing tanks. Any increase in payload above zero-fuel weight could cause the wings to bend upwards towards their structural limit.

Basic Operating Weight This is the "hangar" weight of the aircraft ready to load for service. Adding crew, catering and spares gives:

Dry Operating Weight Adding fuel to this gives:

Operating Weight Adding payload (passengers, cargo and mail) to this gives:

Take-off Weight This may be exceeded only by adding fuel to give taxi weight. Subtracting take-off fuel and trip fuel gives, respectively:

Zero Fuel Weight and

Landing Weight.

All aircraft have a safe centre-of-gravity (c.g.) range, and the load is distributed between the front and aft holds accordingly. For example, 3000kg in the front hold might take the c.g. forward of the safe limit; the addition of 4000kg in the aft hold might — depending on the aircraft — bring the c.g. back into the safe range. But mistakenly transposing these loads might result in a nose-down unbalance and possibly disastrous consequences for the flight.

Safe range is specified by the manufacturer and is usually expressed in terms of Mean Aerodynamic Chord (MAC). The aerodynamic chord of a wing may be visualized in cross-section as the internal "stream line" joining the leading edge to the trailing edge. The chord may vary according to span, because in plan view the leading edge and the trailing edge of a wing usually taper towards the tip. The average or mean aerodynamic chord (MAC) is selected as the reference line for defining centre-of-gravity range. The safe range is expressed (for example) as 10-40 per cent MAC. In other words, if the c.g. is aft of the limits, that is to say more than 40 per cent, the aircraft has been improperly loaded and may be unstable.

The strength of the aircraft structure, and of the floor in particular, also limits the loading of cargo. The manufacturer's Aircraft Weight and Balance Manual specifies the maximum permitted load on each section of the fuselage, above and below the floor. The sections near the wing will bear the heaviest loads, because here the structure is very strong and loads are least likely to affect balance. Separate account has to be taken of local loadings in holds and especially on the floor of the passenger cabin, which is stressed primarily to carry passengers and their seats. The permitted maximum local loadings — for example, $150kg/m^2$ — are given in the Aircraft Weight and Balance Manual. A small but heavy load could buckle the floor, so spreader boards are used.

Cargo must be lashed to prevent in-flight movement endways, sideways and upwards. Each airline provides guidance on methods of lashing and the various types of tie-down equipment, including nets, webbing, straps, cables, tensioners and ordinary ropes. The floors and, sometimes, walls of the aircraft are fitted with lashing points and rings.

Cargo which is loose (i.e. not packed in containers or pallet-mounted igloos or webbed onto pallets) is called "bulk" cargo. Pallets, igloos and containers are used in all the larger cargo aircraft. Packed in the warehouse, perhaps far from the aircraft, by shippers or agents, they require special care — especially when dangerous chemicals and substances are included. Loading into the aircraft, on to floors fitted with suitable roller tracks, is quick and simple. Loaders merely follow the balance and floor-strength regulations and tie the unit to the hold fittings.

Containers are strong enough to withstand the movement of cargo inside caused by flight loads, and may be loaded into holds which are not strong enough to withstand the battering of bulk cargo or cargo packed into so-called Uncertified Containers. Cargo loaded on to the main passenger deck, whether in containers or not, should be forward of the passengers and against a stressed bulkhead to protect the crew in the event of a crash landing. In some aircraft, because of the cargo door's location, the cargo has to be loaded behind the passengers on the main deck. Especially strong restraints must be applied to safeguard the passengers in the event of a crash landing. This method of loading, like the use of passenger seats for the carriage of light boxes and parcels, is not recommended.

"Bulk" cargo, such as baggage or other loose pieces, is becoming rarer as container and pallets are used to carry more and more cargo. The same safety rules about loading and restraint apply. Modern aircraft have a bulk-cargo hold, suitably fitted with nets and webbing.

Aircraft are also vulnerable to damage by carelessly operated ground vehicles. The blades of a fork-lift truck can ground a £10 million jumbo jet by puncturing the fuselage skin. Even the slightest scratch or dent in the skin must be reported immediately, because pressurised hulls can be endangered by even minor deformations or cracks. The best ground vehicles have automatic cutouts which stop the hydraulic extension as soon as the rubber buffer touches the aircraft.

Ground staff should wear proper clothing — gloves, fluorescent jackets, hard hats, and ear defenders. This is not necessarily or even primarily for personnel safety reasons but because "uniform dress" fosters the team spirit and hence professionalism which is the surest guarantee of safety.

Yuckspeak Library: Having a high structural integrity and a demanding fatigue spectrum = Strong.

13   Air Navigation

The early pilot navigated by looking at the ground and comparing it with the map. Railway lines, lakes, coastlines and rivers were the best navigation aids, just as they are to the amateur pilot today. The RAF DH.9A pilots who pioneered the air-mail and Imperial Airways routes from Cairo to Baghdad in 1921 are said to have followed plough lines across long sectors of the desert.

As ranges increased the pilot used a magnetic compass to steer a course. This he computed with the triangle of velocities — knowing his own airspeed, desired track and the strength and direction of the wind. He checked this Dead Reckoning (DR) by comparing the ground with his map. He remembered to adjust his heading for variation of the Earth's magnetic field and for deviation caused by ferrous metal in his aeroplane. At night he was lost unless — like Alcock and Brown, Lindbergh, Chichester, Henshaw and other long-distance pioneer pilots — he could read the stars. And in bad weather he was soon lost too. His only navigation aid then was a handkerchief to wipe his goggles.

Today the relaxed pilot is still the one with a map on which he can see his position. Gyros and electronics now do the DR, presenting the pilot not only with his position but also with his heading, groundspeed, and time to the next point. Electronics even do the steering for him through the autopilot.

Radio was first used experimentally to communicate with aircraft before 1914. During the Great War it was used for directing artillery fire and reporting on enemy movements, often from balloons. The Direction-finding (DF) properties of radio stations soon became evident. As any transistor-radio owner knows, a radio may be rotated until the signal from the tuned station is strongest.

In the 1920s the loop antenna was developed so that pilots could tune in to radio transmitters and fly from one to another. The DF loop, rotated by hand, received the signal most strongly when the loop was end-on to the station. The voltages induced in the loop by the signal cancelled each other and the signal was "null". The pilot would read the bearing of the station from a scale on the loop, or on a Radio Compass on his instrument panel. Tuning in to another station then gave him a "fix" — actually a running fix — on his map. Or he could home on to the beacon by keeping the Radio Compass needle on zero, making due allowance for drift. By superimposing the Radio Compass on the magnetic-compass card the bearing of the station could be read off directly instead of having to be computed.

Such a radio compass was known as a Radio Magnetic Indicator (RMI). The loop would be automatically rotated by an electric motor, the power of which was a function of signal strength, so that the loop maintained the null position. This was Automatic Direction-Finding (ADF). Modern ADFs do not have loops, which stick out into the airflow and cause drag. They now have antennae faired into the skin of the aircraft.

Non-Directional Beacons (NDBs) operate in the medium-frequency (MF) band. Non-directional means that the beacon is not limited to fixed beams, but emits radio waves equally to all points of the compass. A morse identification is superimposed on the waves.

NDBs have limitations. Their medium-wave transmissions are distorted by mountains, coastlines, thunderstorms and "night effect". At night the Kennelly-Heaviside and Appleton layers (the E and F ionised layers) of the Earth's atmosphere weaken, allowing sky-wave propagation and hence false reception of MF radio signals. After sunset these approach the antenna from above.

The Radio Range appeared in America in 1927, before the radio compass. It became widely established in the USA, Europe and

---

The frequency bands used by navigation systems are:

VLF	Very Low Frequency* 3 to 30 kHz*	(10,000n.m. range)
LF	Low Frequency 30 to 300 kHz	(long-range)
MF	Medium Frequency 300 to 3,000 kHz	(liable to distortion)
HF	High Frequency 3 to 30 MHz	(long-range, reflected from ion osphere)
VHF	Very High Frequency 30 to 300MHz	(short-range, line-of-sight)
UHF	Ultra High Frequency 300 to 3,000MHz	(radar, TV)

*1 Hz = 1 cycle/sec

---

elsewhere by 1939. Radio stations suitably located under the main air routes transmitted dots in the medium-frequency (MF) band from one antenna and, in the intervals, dashes from another. When flying "on the beam" (one of many aviation terms to pass into the English language) the dots and dashes merged so that the pilot heard a steady note (equi-signal) in his headset. Any deviation produced dots or dashes, and the pilot steered accordingly to get the continuous note. The airways system was founded on radio ranges. But they were prone to the same distortions as were the DF loop and radio compass, and they could lay down only a small number of tracks, typically four. They were also a headache — literally — for pilots.

In good weather simple flashing lights on the ground, each Morse-coded "A", "B" and so on, marked the way for the new mariners. One was in service in California until 1972, and is now in the Smithsonian Air and Space museum in Washington.

From the Radio Range the Germans developed Lorenz, a radio beam to guide aircraft towards airfields for approach and landing. Dots and dashes in the pilot's headset told him whether he was to the right or to the left of the runway. This was operational in Europe before the Second World War.

From Lorenz was developed SBA, or Standard Beam Approach. This included marker beacons to help the pilot to work out whether he was on the correct glideslope as well as "on the beam" directionally or in azimuth. An outer marker beacon two or three miles from the runway threshold warned the pilot to check that he was at a certain height for a glideslope of, say, 3°. At 150m from the threshold the inner marker told him that he should be down to 30m, 100ft. This system was to be replaced by GCA, Ground-Controlled Approach and later by ILS, Instrument Landing System (Chapter 20).

During the Second World War Lorenz developed a long-range navigation system based on dots and dashes. Known as Sonne, it was used with great effect by U-boats and Focke-Wulf Condor maritime-reconnaissance aircraft in the German anti-shipping and U-boat offensive. Though easily jammed, it was unmolested by the Allied air and naval forces, who used it themselves. Sonne was the first long-range navigation system devised to require no more than an ordinary MF receiver in the aircraft.

After the 1939-1945 war Sonne was further developed by the British Marconi company, who named it Consol. This was a long-range navigation aid. It was still used more than a quarter of a century after the Second World War. Three antennae transmitted MF signals phased and rotated in such a way that the pilot or navigator heard dots, dashes and an equi-signal. He interpreted these to get his bearing. By referring a number to a chart overprinted with a Consol pattern he obtained a position line. Several sectors of the Consol chart had an identical radiation pattern and experience was needed to overcome ambiguities. The system suffered also from the ionospheric limitations of MF radio transmissions, though in good day-time conditions range was up to about 2,000 miles, 3,000km.

During the first part of the Second World War the British invented Gee, a radio-navigation aid working on the hyperbolic pulse system. It was more difficult for the enemy to jam than were the point-source dots and dashes. Loran (short for long-range navigation) also is a hyperbolic system, and was still being used in Loran-C and -D forms in the 1970s, though requiring the services of a human navigator.

Loran has two or more transmitters up to 1,000km apart, each pair forming a chain. One transmitter, the master, emits a number of uniformly spaced pulses per second. The slave transmitter emits a corresponding series of pulses at a different phase. The phases of the master and slave transmissions are precisely timed. A computer in the aircraft (or ship) measures the difference between the times taken for the master and slave transmissions to reach the receiver. It is then possible to plot on a chart a number of hyperbolae for known difference-values. Loran charts are overprinted with the hyperbolic pattern, and the pilot or navigator refers the difference-value to his Loran grid to get a position line. At the end of the 1939-1945 war Loran chains covered a quarter of the Earth's surface. Loran was a step towards "area" navigation as opposed to beacon navigation.

Area Navigation permits aircraft to fly off airways. Decca, like Consol and Loran, is a hyperbolic aid which works on the principle of phase-locked master and slave transmitters. The radio waves from these transmitters lay down an imaginary hyperbolic lattice. A Decca chain typically consists of a master station with three slaves around it at intervals of about 120°. The distance (or baseline) between the master and each slave is 80km to 160km, say 50 to 100 miles. The lattice of hyperbolic position lines so created may be overprinted on a map. A phase-comparison meter displays the position of the aircraft on a roller map in the cockpit.

Decca is extremely reliable and accurate. It is used by ships as well as by aircraft. It is standard on most British Airways European Division airliners and is extensively used by helicopters in North Sea gas and oil exploration. A chain is installed also in the New York area, where it is used by helicopters and ships.

Whether aircraft are flying by area navigation or by beacon navigation, they still have to be separated and sequenced for the approach to the airport. Some will argue that it is better to bring the traffic in along "rails" than to have it coming into the station from all over the countryside, as with area navigation. Although area navigation may not replace the airways system, it facilitates the construction of new airways, more intense use of existing ones, and the more flexible separation of inbound, outbound and overflying traffic.

Area navigation could have been adopted in the 1950s as the international standard. But VOR beacon navigation was being developed, especially in the US (see below). The preponderance of American civil and military aircraft and the alleged cost of Decca area-navigation ground stations decided the adoption of VOR/DME as the standard international navigation aid. This was to last for more than 25 years.

The limitations of medium-frequency (MF) beacons led to the introduction of very-high-frequency VHF Omni-Range (VOR) beacons. These have been an International Civil Aviation Organisation standard for navigation since the late 1950s.

VOR operates in the very-high-frequency VHF band, radiating two transmissions. Both are of constant frequency but one remains stationary as the other rotates. The receiver in the aircraft compares the difference in phase, this being proportional to the magnetic bearing of the VOR beacon. The receiver in the aircraft is a phase-comparison meter. In its simplest form it drives a left-right needle on the VOR instrument which tells the pilot which way to steer to maintain the radial he has selected. In due course, provided the pilot follows the needle, the aircraft arrives over the beacon. There is a "to" indicator on the VOR instrument. This changes to "from" over the beacon. As with the NDB (see above) a morse identification is superimposed on the VOR transmission so that the pilot can make sure he is tuned to the right beacon.

The VOR beacon, unlike the NDB, transmits individual radials. This makes it useful to off-airways pilots. It is a "line-of-sight" aid, being VHF, and signals can be masked by high ground, but it does not suffer from the ionospheric effects of MF. Range depends on the power of the beacon and the height of the aircraft, and is typically about 200 miles, 300km, at 25,000ft.

VOR is the basis of airways systems all over the world. It is simple and reliable and can be coupled to the airliner's automatic pilot to steer the aircraft along the required path. Combined with DME (Distance Measuring Equipment) VOR provides an almost complete navigation aid. VOR/DME is similar to Vortac (from VOR and Tacan, or Tactical Air Navigation, an early American form of DME).

In DME coded UHF pulses transmitted by the aircraft interrogate a receiver at the VOR site on the ground. The DME responder transmits a similar coded pulse back on a different frequency. The time difference is converted into a distance.

By the mid-1970s experience was being gained with an improved beacon called Doppler VOR. In this the modulations are reversed (the reference signal becomes amplitude-modulated) and electronic switching avoids the need for a rotating aerial. The wider-aperture aerial reduces ground interference. The net result is a more accurate, more reliable VOR and easier to site (see Chapter 14, The Airport). But it is more expensive, costing about $¼ million to install and $5,000 a year to maintain.

A forerunner of VOR/DME was the British-invented Rebecca/Eureka system of World War Two. Eureka was the responder beacon part of an airborne VHF (200 MHz) Rebecca interrogator. The system gave RAF aircraft a bearing and distance to a beacon. An inconvenience was that the heading of the aircraft had to be altered to get an equi-signal — there were two aerials, typically one on each side of the nose — but in the absence of Gee (see above) excellent fixes could be obtained. The system was developed to produce a very accurate Blind Approach Beacon System (Babs).

The development of the airborne computer made possible area navigation using existing VOR/DME or Vortacs instead of master-and-slave chains. The Decca chains installed in Europe and elsewhere, notably New York, are used by suitably equipped aircraft — including off-airways light aircraft and helicopters — and by ships. But the computer's adaptation of VOR point-source aids to area navigation — R Nav — was to prove almost as important to the airman as the self-contained aids like inertial platforms and Doppler. The computer's ability to offset a waypoint — to "ghost" a VOR station — was an important advance in air navigation. So was its ability to estimate climb and descent paths to assist air-traffic control. Point-source beacons no longer constrained traffic to the airways "tramlines" between them. As Sir George Cayley said in the nineteenth century, "the air is an ocean that comes to every man's doorstep." Aircraft are the only form of transport able to move in all three dimensions. Air navigation has still to take full advantage of this.

Inertial-navigation systems (INS) are totally contained in the aircraft. They are the first pilot-navigation aids since the human eye to make aircraft independent of the outside world. INS is a "non-co-operative" aid. It needs no outside radio like VOR, though such aids may be consulted to check the accuracy of — to "update" — INS. The inertial platform was initially developed, as was so much advanced electronics, for guided weapons. It is expensive: a full triplicated installation costs £100,000.

INS consists of a platform, three gyros spinning at 20,000 r.p.m. or more, two or three accelerometers, and a digital electronic computer. The platform is mounted on three gimbals whose axes are in pitch, roll and azimuth. Like a coin held between the fingers, it can be rocked from side to side, fore and aft, and rotated. The gyros keep the platform stable or completely horizontal, whatever the movements of the aircraft.

The accelerometers mounted on this stable platform measure the movements — which mean accelerations — of the aircraft, however slight. An accelerometer works on the principle of a weight whose displacement is proportional to the force applied to it. Each accelerometer in an INS is precisely positioned in a known system of co-ordinates and remains thus throughout the flight, even in turbulence.

A digital computer keeps track of all changes of time, speed and direction as sensed by the accelerometer. The computer has been given longitudes and latitudes and the required flight path or navigation "program". Before take-off the pilot simply dials the co-ordinates of the required waypoints.

The computer memory compares the required flight-path with the actual flight-path as sensed by the accelerometers. The pilot is presented — on a moving map if desired, or on his instrument panel — with a continuous display of position, heading, groundspeed, distance to the next waypoint, and so on. The computer issues commands to the autopilot so that the aircraft is automatically steered along the desired flight-path. Before each waypoint a light blinks; over the waypoint the aircraft is turned automatically on to its new heading. New waypoints can be inserted in flight, when a diversion is necessary to another airfield for example, or to avoid a storm.

Although INS is independent of radio beacons on the ground, and is duplicated or even triplicated, VOR/DME and other outside aids may be used to update it. The gyros and accelerometers of inertial platforms are highly sensitive, but no bearing is perfect and friction leads to long-term inaccuracies. Left to themselves, inaccuracies build up and the aircraft drifts off track. A drift of more than 1km/hr is unusual.

Though INS technology will get better and better it may always benefit from an outside check, especially if it is expected to steer the aircraft from cruise to descent and cloudbreak for a precision capture of the airport instrument landing system. Clearly, at the end of a ten-hour flight, or even a one-hour flight, INS would not alone be accurate enough for a precision approach and landing — although Microwave Instrument Landing Systems, MLS, should be good enough to cater for fairly big INS errors. MLS (see below) has a beam which outstretches 120°.

Some airlines regard INS as the ultimate navigation system. It permits world operations independent of ground-navigation facilities. It is a true area-navigation system. With it an aircraft can fly "across-country" instead of from one beacon to another.

Doppler is another "non-co-operative" aid, that is to say one which makes an aircraft independent of ground aids.

The Doppler effect is best illustrated by the sound of a train whistle. As the train passes the listener the decrease in pitch, the same thing as a decrease in frequency, is proportional to the speed of the train. Thus a radar wave transmitted by an aircraft at a certain frequency will be reflected from the ground and received back at the aircraft at a different frequency according to its speed. This difference — the Doppler shift — is proportional to the velocity of the aircraft. A Doppler aerial which transmits beams in four directions provides an integrated Doppler shift. This is displayed to the pilot as groundspeed and drift. Doppler is limited over calm seas, which do not reflect well. This is one reason why it has not been developed into a primary navigation system, as has INS.

Omega is another area-coverage aid. Eight Very Low Frequency (VLF) radio transmitters are maintained by the US Defence Department at various points on the Earth* so that aircraft and shipping, with simple radio receivers and Omega charts, can find their position wherever they are. VLF provides extremely long-range (up to 10,000 n.m.) signals. Omega was introduced primarily as a military aid but it is used also by civil airliners. It is hyperbolic and is a sort of very-long-range Loran.

Each Omega station is pulsed or time-locked with respect to the others by atomic clocks. The receiving computer compares the time taken to receive 12kHz signals from different transmitters, and converts these into a position.

Omega suffers from various errors due to signal distortion and night effect, but these errors can be diminished or overcome by so-called Differential Omega. An Omega receiver is installed, say, at an airport. The difference between the theoretical signal for that spot and the actual signal received is continuously passed as a correction to all aircraft in the area. Omega may be used to update inertial navigation systems. It may well be replaced by VLF navigation or navigational satellites.

One of the problems with Omega is that the transmitters are not very powerful (10kW) and their pulsed operation is complex. Civil airlines are making use of another global system of VLF radio transmitters.

*Argentina, Australia, Hawaii, Japan, Liberia, N. Dakota, Reunion Is., Trinidad.

Known as VLF Navigation, this system employs ten transmitters around the globe* which are used by the US Navy and Nato for communicating with submarines. The beacons are very powerful (50kW-1,000kW) and being of low frequency (16kHz-24kHz) they are very long-range.

The aircraft needs a computer, receiver, atomic clock and display, but usually no special aerial. The computer compares the vectors to different beacons by resolving the time and frequency differences, and produces a track. It also compensates for the diurnal movement of the ionosphere, off which VLF waves are reflected. The Ontrac navigation system is one of a number which use VLF.

Navigational Satellites The northern star is still, as Shakespeare said, "as constant as any fellow in the firmament." Astro-navigation has been used since *homo sapiens* first gazed at the stars. Navigators by sea and air are still taught how to use the sextant. Now Man has learnt to make artificial stars, fixed relative to a spot on Earth, in so-called geostationary orbit.

Artificial satellites have a major advantage over stars: they are active rather than passive. They can transmit data and do not need to be interrogated. The efficiency of air traffic control is diminished by the line-of-sight limitations of VHF and the atmospheric limitations of HF radio communications. Satellites may prove most valuable for communications, giving air traffic controllers the data they need — speed, heading, height and position — to separate and sequence traffic.

For as far ahead as can be seen, aeronautical satellites will complement ground aids. Many airline companies with heavy investments in INS have been reluctant to subscribe to satellites when they are already paying for ground aids. But as satellites become more and more established in the world of communications the airlines will recognise their communications and navigation potential.

Air Traffic Control (ATC) The purpose of air traffic control is to speed the movement of aircraft and to prevent collisions. The three-dimensional nature of air traffic and its varying speeds, headings and altitudes (and rates of change of altitudes) presents ATC with a particularly complex computing problem. ATC capacity is ultimately determined by runway capacity — by the amount of concrete available for landing and taking off. The critical factor is the rate at which aircraft can be got off the ground.

An aircraft occupies a runway for an average of between 50 and 60

*Australia, England, Hawaii, Japan, Maine, Maryland, Norway, Panama, Puerto Rico and Washington State.

seconds. Thus in theory a runway should be able to handle up to 60 movements an hour. In practice the peak rate is about 40. This is the most that can be sustained by ATC in instrument weather. The Sustained Capacity Rate, sometimes known as the Standard Busy Rate, is about 30. This is the most that can be sustained indefinitely by highly skilled human controllers. In practice, the average hourly rate for 24 hours a day 365 days of the year is not as much as 20. This is a mere third of the theoretical runway capacity of, say, half a million movements a year. A single runway should easily average 150,000 movements a year.

Delays occur when the ATC system fails to keep pace with the growth of air traffic. This causes lost aircraft utilisation, higher fuel consumption and passenger frustration. In the USA typical peak-hour delays at the major airports have averaged between 40 and 75 minutes. This comes close to the generally accepted "severe congestion" peak-hour delay of between 45 and 90 minutes.

Controlled airspace is defined by the Recommended Standards and Practices of the International Civil Aviation Organisation. The centre of a Control Zone, or CTR, may be a major airport. This CTR extends to perhaps 20 miles from the airport, and up from the ground to 10,000ft or higher. No aircraft may enter without permission. Around the Control Zone is a Terminal Area, or TMA. This usually starts at 3,000ft and extends up to 25,000ft. Joining all these TMAs are the airways. These are corridors typically 10 miles wide and extending from 3,000ft to 25,000ft. Each airway is marked out with radio-navigation beacons and Mandatory Reporting Points. The area above 25,000ft is Upper Airspace.

Separation standards are laid down by the International Civil Aviation Organisation. They are 1,000ft vertical separation; 10min flying time horizontal separation; climb or descent through an occupied level typically to take no more than five minutes.

Over the North Atlantic at any moment there are on average nearly 100 subsonic aircraft, fewer in winter and more in summer. They fly between 20 or more major city-pairs in Europe and the United States and Canada.

Flight Information Regions, or FIRS, extend from ground level up. Pilots flying within them but outside controlled airspace will be supplied, on request, with flight information such as weather and airfield serviceability.

Flight Level (FL) is the altitude related to the standard atmospheric-pressure barometer reading of 1013.2 millibars or 29.92in of mercury (Hg). Flight level is always quoted in hundreds of feet. For example, FL30 is 3,000ft and FL280 is 28,000ft.

Before 1920 air traffic control consisted, as it does today at non-radio light-aircraft airfields, of visual signalling. Men with red and green flags or lights, or boards laid out on the ground, directed the pilot. Human eyes were extended by light beacons (1925) and later by radio (1930). With radio, pilots and control towers could at last talk to each other, and, as recorded, the directional properties of radio were used to tell pilots where they were.

In 1940 the Battle of Britain proved the power of radar. Originally it was called radio-location by its British inventors, but the American acronym for Radio Direction and Ranging, RADAR, became universally adopted.

The combination of radar and voice-radio (radio telephone, or RT) revolutionised the control of combat aircraft from the ground, and by 1950 radar had revolutionised civil air traffic control (though the military origin of radar is still apparent in its terminology — for example, the use of the word "target"). Radar plays two major roles — primary and secondary — in air traffic control.

Primary (or Surveillance) Radar finds and tracks aircraft up to 300km away, depending on radar power, position, weather and target size. It is "passive" — that is to say the target does not know it is being surveyed. Secondary Radar is "active," interrogating a transponder in the aircraft and reading its identity and height.

A Transponder is a radar receiver-transmitter which selectively responds to interrogation on a specified frequency (Squawk). A limitation of radar is that the ground-controller's display shows merely a target of unknown altitude and identity. Transponders tell the controller the identity of the blips or targets on the radar displays. This is the principle of military IFF, Identification Friend or Foe, which tells ground forces or other aircraft whether an approaching target is friendly or not.

The radar controller can identify a non-transponding target by asking the pilot to make an identification turn, but this is not practicable in rush hours. As air-traffic movements increase the controllers have less time to interrogate, separate and sequence traffic for landing. Traffic eventually gets beyond the capacity of the human controller. Delays and collision-risks increase. Before this happens equipment has to be improved. Thanks to Mode C transponders, blips on the controller's radar display can be annotated with their altitude. A "leader line" indicates the direction in which the target is moving. These Alphanumerics put on the controller's radar screen the information he needs about each target in his zone. A transponder can have more than 4,000 channels. There are transponder codes for radio failure, emergency and hijacking which flash on the controller's radar screen and gain immediate attention.

The computer helps to reduce the controller's workload. By key-punching each pilot's Flight Plan (see below) into the computer before departure, a controller can obtain a pre-printed Flight Progress Slip. The computer detects conflicts with other flight plans, and if necessary recommends alternative altitudes or routeings.

A development of this is a computer program which predicts conflicts among the actual — as opposed to the planned — traffic. The human controller, looking at a radar display with perhaps 50 targets moving in five dimensions of space, speed and time, cannot be expected to predict conflicts. There may be unknown traffic — military or private without transponders — and complications may be caused by aircraft with transponder or radio failures, and by emergencies. Very advanced software* is required to process so much dynamic data, to predict conflicts, and to recommend avoiding action. None is yet in service. Some air-traffic control systems do not have the equipment to cope even with transponding aircraft.

Traffic flowing into a terminal area starts to be streamed while en route. The controller arranges the aircraft into sequence for the approach and landing. Each may have a different performance, cruising speeds varying from 150kt at 10,000ft and 500kt at 30,000ft to 1,200kt at 60,000ft. The computer helps the controller to manage the speed and height of each target, ordering speed and altitude changes.

When the volume of traffic becomes too great the controller may order en-route aircraft to a holding pattern, or stack, though this wastes time and fuel and is going out of fashion. The computer is making it possible for the controller to "stack horizontally" by speed-sequencing the inbound stream, aircraft being given a height and time over a beacon.

Vertical stacks are still used where ATC equipment is still inadequate. Aircraft descend from cruising height to a radio beacon located perhaps 30km from the airport. Separated in layers of 1,000ft, each aircraft starts a turn as it passes over the beacon, and after flying the outbound side of the racetrack for a prescribed time, a turn is made "inbound to the beacon". When the aircraft at the lowest level, say Flight Level 60, is told to leave the stack to approach, all the others above it are told to descend 1,000ft.

The lowest aircraft in the stack is given clearance to begin its approach by Approach Control, which gives the pilot his altitudes and altimeter settings. The altimeter setting QNH gives him his altitude above sea level, QFE his height above the ground. Allowance has to be made for the fact that most airports are above sea level. Obviously, when the

---

*Software is the paperwork required to program a computer. Program in this context is the correct spelling, not programme.

altimeter is set to QNH, it does not read zero when the aircraft is on the ground unless the airport is at sea level like Schiphol. When the altimeter setting is QFE the pilot reads height above the airport.

The aircraft may finally be handed over to an approach director, who will vector it by heading and altitude instructions to the beams of the Instrument Landing System.

Consider the flight of a scheduled passenger airliner departing from London Heathrow. At least an hour before take-off the captain or, with bigger airlines, the flight dispatcher or operations staff file a Flight Plan. This gives the air traffic controller a full statement of the pilot's intentions: destination and alternates, route and desired altitude, number of passengers, times of departure, aircraft type, and call-sign. The airport tower and air traffic control have the required information 20 minutes before the flight departs. When the doors are closed the pilot asks for permission to start his engines; clearance to taxi to the runway; and airways clearance to, say, Amsterdam.

The tower is given the clearance by the Air Traffic Control Centre, which is responsible for providing the required separations while taking the aircraft out of the Terminal Area (TMA) and specifying the airway and levels at which to fly. This is typically done by naming the airway, the VOR navigation beacons, and the levels at which to fly over them.

The Air Traffic Control Centre computes progress based on the flight-plan information already filed. This is done for each aircraft so that the controllers can calculate the required separations. At the appropriate point the pilot is handed over to the Amsterdam Control Centre. The controller switches his target to the controller of the next sector by pressing a button which transfers it to the appropriate computer and radarscope, which blinks until the new controller acknowledges it. This is known as a Radar Hand-off.

At busy times aircraft are cleared out of the London terminal area at a rate of one every one-and-a-half or two minutes. More than 2,000 aircraft a day pass through the area. Of these, 40 per cent are over-flying aircraft, the rest arriving or departing. Computers do much of the controller's thinking, leaving him more time to work out the moves in this game of high-speed, three-dimensional chess. The computer senses conflicts and can give instructions to change heading or height to avoid a collision. Such computers have to solve data-processing problems and require programs more complicated than any operation yet attempted by man, including spaceflight.

THE FUTURE OF AIR NAVIGATION There are two schools of thought about the future of air navigation. One says that ground radar is the answer, that the controller on the ground must "see" every aircraft regardless of the equipment it carries. This school requires the computer to monitor and process all radar information, and predict conflicts.

The "data-link" school argues that because so many parts of the world lack radar, and even radio beacons, the onus is on the aircraft to tell the controller its position. The data link could be voice radio or telemetry. Instead of radar seeing the aircraft and painting a blip on the controller's radar, the navigation equipment on board the aircraft transmits its position, height, speed, heading and other data to the controller. The "data-link" school holds that the best information about position, height, heading and so forth is already available to the pilots. The air traffic control system, it argues, largely duplicates data which the airliner itself knows best and can transmit to the controller.

The two philosophies, radar and data-link, will probably co-exist. Radar will dominate air traffic control systems well endowed with ground aids, and data-link will be required where ground aids are lacking, as they are in so many of the poorer countries.

Whatever the system, the object of air navigation and air traffic control remains the same. Equipment in the aircraft and in the Air Traffic Control Centre must tell pilots and controllers where every airliner is, what its intentions are, and warn pilots of impending conflicts, though final command decisions will always remain with the captain.

There is an argument that air traffic control should be able to deny a captain permission to land or take-off, perhaps in certain weather conditions. While it is likely that the captain's decision will always be final, advice from air traffic control is usually taken.

The early aviator flew from A to B looking at the ground, checking what his eyes saw against his map and his magnetic compass, computing in his brain the correct headings according to the wind, and commanding his hands to steer the controls accordingly. This "contact flying" is still how amateur private pilots navigate.

Today's aviator can fly from A to B without seeing the ground. He dials his present position co-ordinates and those of his destination into the inertial navigator. Computers then command the automatic pilot to steer the aircraft accordingly. Technology can even provide a map with the aircraft position constantly marked on it, supersonic at 50,000ft above the clouds over desert at night, or subsonic at 1,000ft on a sunny day over Windsor. Technology, and above all the inertial platform and the electronic computer, have in effect reproduced the simple map-flying navigation of the primitive air navigator.

14 The Airport

Landing accidents and incidents, veering off and overrunning the runway, account for about 3 per cent of airliner accidents and serious incidents of all types. In two out of three airport accidents and incidents airport conditions are cited as the cause or contributory cause. Of 34 such accidents studied by the US National Transportation Safety Board over a period of 12 years, 15 are attributed to wet runways, seven to ice or slush, three to snow, and the rest to running into the soft shoulders of the runway.

The safe airport is a compromise between the airline's need for the best equipment and the airport owner's need to make a profit. The equipment is costly, demand is difficult to forecast, and capital often cannot be spread over a long enough period to be covered by revenue. But still the airliners come. Airports are capital hungry, needing almost double the investment per employee compared with airlines. Revenue from landing fees, concessions and other sources is less than half the capital employed; many airlines turn their capital over every year. This is why airports try to achieve a greater margin of revenue over expenditure to get a return on capital.

Nobody knows how much is spent on airport equipment, but it must be approaching $600 million a year. American airlines alone are spending nearly $200 million a year on ramp and servicing equipment around the terminal. The airport — or in some countries the civil aviation authority — provides approach aids and approach lighting, runways, runway lighting, runway cleaning, taxiways, taxiway lighting, aprons, jetways and terminal buildings.

LANDING AIDS The airliner approaches to land at the well equipped airport by ILS (Instrument Landing System). The International Civil Aviation Organisation, Icao, and the International Air Transport Association, Iata, recommend that all airports with scheduled jet services should have ILS. The best airports put it in for regularity and reliability as much as for bad weather (see Chapter 13 and Chapter 20). Most of the ILS systems on the market, thanks in part to the automatic-landing programmes, have attained high standards of accuracy and reliability. The cost of installing a Category 3* ILS can be more than $½ million.

There is a trend towards MLS (Microwave Instrument Landing System). MLS permits a choice of approach paths and two-gradient (3° and 6° perhaps) glide slopes. It is claimed that MLS will increase the capacity of airports. MLS could have a big future if it were compatible with existing airborne ILS receivers, and if air traffic control and pilots were to accept multiple approaches and glide slopes (see Chapter 20). Distance information can also be derived from MLS, which does not require marker beacons four miles from the threshold, as ILS does. It can be contained within the airport.

Small airports handling only a few scheduled jet movements can get by with VOR (VHF Omni Range). As an approach aid it is cruder than ILS, giving guidance in azimuth only; but with DME (Distance Measuring Equipment) it can play the dual role if sited and maintained properly. From DME information the pilot can derive, with height from the altimeter, his glidepath. A radar should be available at the airport to allow the air traffic controller to monitor the approach.

VOR can be prodigal of land, and is getting expensive to site. Doppler VOR, with phase-comparison using Doppler shift, is more expensive than standard VOR but is easier to site, being less sensitive to certain obstructions. It is suitable for airports with land problems, with neither the traffic nor the weather to justify full ILS, Vasi and lighting approach aids (see Chapter 13).

Precision approach radar or PAR, which provides ground-controlled approach (GCA), is going out in favour of radar-monitored letdowns and ILS. Even military users are moving away from PAR and GCA. Many airports find radar a valuable partner for ILS. Surveillance radar is normally used for terminal-area navigation, but radar letdowns on the ILS tend to produce greater air-traffic control capacity than ILS by itself, with the lengthier procedures required to establish aircraft in the ILS groove. Surveillance radar expedites aircraft from airways on to the extended centre line of the ILS localiser.

Visual as well as instrument landing aids are the mark of a good airport. The visual approach slope indicator, or Vasi, is not of course a substitute for ILS, being an "airfield-in-sight" aid. Bars of lights at the side of the runway are set to show the pilot when he is below the

---

*"Category 3" defines the lowest landing visiblity — see Chapter 20.

139

glidepath (undershooting), when he is correctly established, and when he is too high (overshooting). The majority of pilots, and hence airport owners, consider that Vasi is a necessary aid (see Chapter 20).

LIGHTING Airport lighting standards are laid down by Icao. The Calvert centreline and crossbar approach lighting system consists of a centreline and normally five crossbars. The system provides the pilot with information in the three principal axes. For runways served by ILS the high-intensity five-bar approach lighting is augmented by supplementary lighting over the inner 1,000ft of the approach consisting of white centreline barrettes and red sideline barrettes.

Because approach lighting is so closely related to the ILS, integrity must be up to the standard of air and ground electronics. Airports with poor weather and heavy traffic like Heathrow have five levels of brilliance control, solid-state reliability, automatic-start standby power, and one-second switching-in of a secondary power supply. Pilots can be badly placed if the approach lighting suddenly fails at a critical moment. A Turkish F.28 crashed in 1975 when this happened at a Turkish airport, with the loss of all on board.

Approach lighting can be very expensive. Will airlines pay the cost of the airport aids required for round-the-clock operation in the worst weathers? There appear to be second thoughts about the economics of Cat 3 operations, though the quest for this ideal has lifted the standard of all aids — ILS, Vasi and approach lighting — in average instrument weather. The number of hours in the year when landings have to be made in Cat 3 conditions can be very few indeed. Peak brilliance of Heathrow's approach lighting is 30,000 candelas, though there is not a requirement to see approach lighting for a Cat 3 landing.

Touchdown zone lighting is recommended by Icao, and is nowadays considered to be best airport practice. ILS, approach lighting and Vasi — whether Cat 1, 2 or 3 — have to be matched by threshold, runway and taxiway lighting standards.

White runway centreline lighting is standard at the best airports. There is a trend towards reducing the spacing of this lighting from 100ft to 50ft as all-weather standards move towards Cat 3. This could mean expensive digging and recabling, and additional controls and switching, unless the airport has provided for expansion at an early stage of design. Digging up runways and delaying traffic can be expensive. Centreline lighting provides take-off guidance as well as steering reference during the landing roll. Centreline runway lighting at Heathrow peaks at 10,000 candelas depending on the weather.

Runway edge lighting is also essential. The more guidance that can be given to the pilot, during take-off and after touchdown, the better. The random maze of blue taxiway lighting has become confusing at the bigger airports. The move is away from blue edge-lighting to green taxiway centreline lighting. Some airports consider that the best practice is green taxiway centreline lighting with edge reflectors. The pilot likes to know that by taxying over the green centreline he will get where he wants to go. Green lights of 25 candelas represent good practice.

A real problem for the future is to decide how much provision to make for Cat 3 visibility operations. Even high-intensity taxiway lighting can be inadequate when visibility falls to about 100 metres. This raises the need for enormously costly automatic taxying guidance. The aircraft so expensively landed in the worst visibility cannot sit on the taxiway until the weather has cleared.

First-class taxying control systems are needed, especially in poor visibility, to prevent ground collisions. Complex taxiway networks can be provided with selective switching to provide the pilot with his guiding green lights. Red stop bars at taxiway intersections are mandatory at the busiest airports. Obviously such standards are way beyond the needs of most; but the prudent airport manager will make provision for these developments, if he can, during planning and construction. He will also ask industry for the highest standards of reliability, fault-monitoring and cleaning when buying lighting.

A growing problem as airports get busier is the maintenance of runway and taxiway lighting. Jet exhaust deposits reduce the brilliance of the lights, which can distort measurements of runway visibility (see below). Regular light-cleaning is essential, and lamps must be designed for quick change without disrupting traffic. Icao is beginning to specify automatic fault-monitoring.

Runway visual range (RVR) instruments are nowadays expected at all airports with scheduled jet services. While the human eye is still the best way of measuring visibility, the trend is towards the instrumented RVR which, at the busier airports with bad-weather records, may be cheaper than a man sitting for hours at the end of the runway counting the runway lights, converting them on a table to allow for the approaching pilot's slant visibility, and relaying RVR to the tower for transmission to pilots. The British Civil Aviation Authority has installed RVR systems at Heathrow, Gatwick and Manchester (see also Chapter 20).

FOG DISPERSAL Jet engines can be used for fog dispersal. Mounted in underground chambers near the threshold of the main runway, their hot jets are ducted to particular areas, dispersing the fog. The principle is similar to that of the Fido torch system of the 1940s, without the spectacular and potentially dangerous flames. The jet-exhaust method of fog dispersal can be expensive, though it is in use at some airports, for example Paris Orly.

SLIPPERY RUNWAYS The coefficient of friction of a dry runway is between 0.75 and 0.9. This falls to 0.1 or less for glazed ice, the worst case. As speeds and aircraft size increase, wet runways and cross-winds require better measurement of braking conditions. "Mu-meter" trailers towed along the runway produce the required friction (μ) and skid-resistance data on which the pilot can base his decion to land. Development of Mu-meters has increased knowledge of runway friction coefficients and has led to improvements in surface design by grooving and friction courses.

Runway grooving is helpful and grooves can be machined on to concrete; but ¼in cuts spaced 1½in apart soon gather dirt and water does not flow away. A wire brush on an un-grooved concrete runway is very effective, but if sand is used to help increase the friction of, say, glazed ice, big industrial vacuum cleaners have to be used after the thaw to prevent grooves and friction courses from getting clogged. Grooving increases the runway coefficient of friction. Another effective method is to lay a friction course on top of the runway. This provides a honeycomb drain through which the water percolates and falls away.

Wet runways can cause aircraft to aquaplane, or skim a film of incompressible water. The brakes are less effective even than in a skid, because there is no adhesion at all between the wheels and the surface.

Of nearly 2,000 runways used by airlines in the USA, less than 40 airports have one or more grooved runways. A study by Stephens of McDonnell Douglas lists 18 cases of jet-airliner veer-offs, or ground-loop/swerves, and 21 cases of overruns in the period 1962-1973. Half the accidents are attributed to pilot error as the primary cause, and a third to airport conditions. Stephens feels that weather and visibility should share responsibility.

Only about 20 US airports during the period studied had porous friction-course overlays on their runways. Stephens points out that a stabilised approach, correct speeds, a firm touch-down and delayed brake application until wheel spin-up can reduce the number of veer-off and overrun accidents.

Also helpful, US air-safety expert Jerome Lederer points out, would be the installation of more visual approach slope indicators (Vasis) (see Chapter 20). Of 2,000 runways used by US airlines in the mid-1970s, nearly 1,700 were without Vasis, which reduce the chances of undershooting or landing too fast and too long.

SNOW AND ICE In snow-clearance systems the trend is towards trains incorporating ploughblade, brush and blower followed by snow-cutter. The level of investment depends upon snow statistics and runway area, and is particularly difficult to judge in countries such as those of northern Europe, where snow may come as light powder one year and 6ft deep and wet the next. Snow vehicles have to work fast and efficiently when needed.

First comes a large blade plough on the front of a vehicle which tows a large rotary power brush assisted by a high-pressure jet of air. Each of these trains can clear a swathe approximately 9ft wide. Several trains operating in echelon create a snowbank which is then dispersed by a snow-cutter and blower. Snow removal is a heavy task. A runway of 12,000ft x 200ft, its 16,000ft or so of taxiways and vast parking aprons are covered with 900 tons of snow after a half-inch fall.

Snow can also be cleared by heating the surface of the runway with electric grids. The electric load is very heavy, and can be equal to the total electric-power capacity of the airport. Heating a 12,000ft runway 200ft wide at 15 watts/sq ft — the rate for heating road surfaces — would produce a demand of 30 megawatts.

Ice can be removed or prevented by spraying the runway with a liquid chemical such as a glycol-based fluid.

Future developments in snow-clearance envisage thermal blowing by gas-turbine engines. This was tried early in the life of the jet engine, but proved to be expensive and not too effective. Recent developments are showing promise and units are beginning to appear on the market. A consideration here is that light fittings pose clearance problems with mechanical systems.

FIRE AND CRASH SERVICES Without doubt the airport's least utilised capital assets are its fire, crash and rescue vehicles.

The use of larger aircraft has required big increases in the quantities of fire-extinguishing media. The trend is towards a "knock-out punch" — a large quantity applied in 1 minute to control the fire so that people can be got out. A knock-out blow depends on the size of the fire; but 5,000 Imp gal of foam a minute — the capacity of some of the big water and foam fire tenders on the market — can certainly be considered in this category. A typical type of fire engine would carry up to 2,000 gal of water and 300 gal of compound.

The trend is also towards faster emergency vehicles. As runways increase in length and distance from the terminal the ability of the fire and rescue services to get there in time has to be maintained. At the biggest airports substations are becoming necessary to reduce emergency reaction time.

The UK Civil Aviation Authority requires that fire crews should reach the scene of an accident within two and at the most three minutes. This is difficult for heavy fire trucks, so the best airports — for example those of the British Airports Authority — use rapid intervention vehicles (RIVs) which can move at 100km/hr, reaching the accident scene in perhaps half the time taken by the heavy trucks.

A vehicle weighs seven tonnes, carries water and compound for 2,000 gal of foam, has a crew of two or three, can accelerate from 0 to 80km/hr in about 20 seconds, and has a broad wheelbase and low c.g. for fast cornering.

Rescue vehicles carrying cutting and breathing equipment, ladders, axes and all the other rescue tools and paraphernalia specified by the authorities are often the first on the scene of an accident. The trend is towards what the Americans call Quick Dash Trucks with the priority objective of getting to the scene of the accident as quickly as possible. Also known as rapid-response vehicles, they may carry fire-fighting equipment as well — typically 200 gal of water and 15 gal of foam.

Icao categorises airport emergency rescue requirements very precisely. There are eight categories of airport. National authorities may have their own requirements, and these may be more stringent. The best airport will have a minimum of two fire engines and a spare, together with at least one rapid-response vehicle. For airports near water rapid response obviously requires amphibian or marine fire and rescue vehicles. This at least doubles the investment in emergency equipment.

Airports are not expected to provide full hospital facilities, and local authorities usually provide the ambulance fleet. But the well equipped airport will provide comprehensive first-aid. One authority, for example, keeps inflatable casualty reception tents readily available. The airport emergency orders provide for the quick notification of local authorities' supporting services such as police, fire, ambulance and hospitals.

Measures must be taken to protect aircraft and their occupants in the unlikely event of over-running the runway after an abandoned take-off, braking failure, or a misjudged landing. Arrester wires and nets, as used on aircraft carriers at sea, have been tried, but are not suitable. A successful if expensive method is to lay beds of plastic foam, typically Marcus Langley mixed cement and urea formaldehyde, in the overrun areas. A typical bed would be 36ft wide and 300ft long. All runway embankments and lighting ducts and other obstructions must be ramped so that they are surmountable by aircraft which may have veered off the runway. All equipment such as lighting must be breakable ("frangible").

When the landing has been safely completed both tower and pilot need to know the position of the aircraft on the airport in relation to terminal and runway. The best practice here, though a luxury for all but the biggest and busiest airports, is the airfield surface movement indicator, or ASMI. Ground surveillance radars at high points around the airport display what they see on an indicator in the control tower. The controller knows where every aircraft is and prevents taxying collisions. The electronics industry is developing a secondary type of radar so that transponder-equipped taxying aircraft may be identified with a callsign or flight number.

Runway cleanliness is considered next to godliness by most airline maintenance engineers and pilots. The general phrase "runway contamination" covers jet oil, tyre-rubber, glazed ice, compacted snow, standing water and general debris. Maintenance repair costs for damage caused by foreign objects on runways are high enough to require a considerable airport investment in runway vacuum cleaners and sweepers. Cleanliness means safety too, as at least one accident after a tyre burst at speed has underlined. Tremendous sweeps of concrete are involved, and airports may have large industrial vacuum cleaners going for hours a day.

One of the biggest sources of engine damage is material blown on to the runway by wind or jet blast, and ingested by aircraft. Rollers are employed at many airports to keep the grass edges compacted. Table-top cleanliness of runways is the rule at even the smallest airports, especially those served by jets.

BIRDS There appears to have been an increase in the birdlife around airports. This could be the result of the growing practice of switching on landing-lights during the day as well as at night. This is done to make aircraft as visible as possible, especially to smaller aircraft that may have strayed into the control zone, or to aircraft lining up for take-off. But these lights, like lighthouses, may well attract birds. Another suspicion is that birds are becoming wise to the fact that vibration from jet engines brings worms to the surface. Jet noise may mean food.

At one airport with a bird problem, Copenhagen Saltholm, ornithologists go to the nests with hypodermic formalyn needles, leaving one egg in the nest untouched (if the eggs are merely taken the bird will lay again).

Airport authorities are seeking vegetation which is able to thrive in ground which can withstand the weight of aircraft, but not attract birds. The general rule is to eliminate rubbish dumps, especially those containing food, and to avoid cereal farming.

The bird-strike hazard is discussed in Chapter 9.

SUMMARY The well equipped airport must be paid for. The economic facts of life are that whoever buys the equipment will seek to cover his costs either direct from the passenger or through landing fees. The passenger ultimately pays through the price of his ticket.

Facilities which at first sight seem desirable may be less so when the economics are seen in perspective. Zero-zero blind landing ability may be desirable, but is one landing worth £1 million? This is an exaggeration; but the well equipped airport is always a compromise between meeting the airline requirement for safe and punctual operation in all conditions of traffic and weather, and landing fees that do not price airline or airport out of the market.

Finally, any investment decision in airport equipment has to allow for growth in traffic, airline size and technical developments, particularly in ever-improving electronic aids. Forecasting mistakes in the airport business can be very costly indeed.

Lady Controller: Roger, may I turn you on at five miles?
Captain: You may certainly try, madam.

---

15 Maintenance and overhaul

Stacked one on top of another the servicing, maintenance and overhaul manuals for a modern airliner can rise to the height of a small house. The three terms are loosely used but might be defined as follows:

Servicing Between-flights attention on the ramp
Maintenance Medium attention in the hangar
Overhaul Heavy attention in the hangar

The object is to reduce technical delays without reducing safety level. The technical delay rate of the Boeing 707 when it entered service was 11 per 100 take-offs (a delay of 15 minutes or more). This was down to four 15 years later but beginning to show an increase as major airframe maintenance was required.

The technical delay rate of the Boeing 727 and 737 started off at about three per 100 take-offs, and levelled off at between one and two. The Boeing 747 levelled off at about four after starting at 15.

The advantage of buying a modern aircraft is evident from its maintenance and overhaul times. As the following Atlas-group table shows, a Boeing 747 needed less maintenance than did the Boeing 707 after many years of service.

Maintenance and overhaul

Check	A	B	C	CS	D
Frequency	8-16 days	4-6 weeks	4-5 months	2 years	4 years
Duration	—	12hr	1 day	1 week	2-5 weeks
707	100hr	320hr	1,200hr	7,000hr	14,000hr
727	100hr	320hr	1,500hr	6,000hr	12,000hr
737	85hr	320hr	1,200hr	5,000hr	10,000hr
747	170hr	600hr	2,400hr	8,000hr	16,000hr
DC-10	170hr	*	2,400hr	8,000hr	16,000hr
A300	135hr	350hr	1,200hr	5,000hr	10,000hr

*Covered in Checks A and C

In addition are checks carried out before and between flights — the turnround checks or preflight check or pre-departure inspection (PDI). This involves the standard "walk-round" by the station engineer or flight engineer. He looks for fuel leaks and damage, especially to cargo doors, engines and undercarriage. The turnround check requires the opening of a few access hatches to systems and servicing points; the cabin and galleys are refreshed and any Technical Log "no-go" snags are cleared.

The Check A involves changes of a few "hard-time" components, that is to say components with fixed lives as agreed by the airworthiness authority.

The Check B or Service Check involves more hard-time component changes; the Check C or Intermediate Check involves further changes and refurbishing of the cabin including the seats. The Checks CS and D or Major Checks involve, in addition, structural inspections and repairs and engine changes.

DESIGN FOR MAINTENANCE Airliner components must be designed so that they are accessible, easy to remove, interchangeable, and above all easy to inspect without removing or breaking them down. They must also be designed with "Murphy's Law" in mind. If a hydraulic valve can be assembled so that a control movement is reversed or the flow one way is prevented, someone will one day so assemble it, perhaps with fatal results. A designer must make it impossible for components to be incorrectly assembled, in case the man doing the job is distracted for some reason in the middle of his work.

The rate at which components are removed prematurely, usually as a result of failure, increases with the complexity of the aircraft. A small twin-propeller airliner might have a premature (or unscheduled) removal rate of 80 components per 1,000hr. This might be 160 for a twin-jet and more than 200 for a four-jet airliner. The premature removal rate for a jumbo jet might be over 300 components per 1,000hr.

Each type of aircraft has an alert level for the number of Tech Log entries per 1,000hr. This might be set at, say, 5 per 1,000hr. Below this level failures are a matter for the engineering department, and no manufacturer design action is required; above it the matter is referred to the manufacturer and to the airworthiness authority.

In the first or second year the number of Technical Log* "alert" entries can be as high as ten, falling to five per 1,000hr; after about the fifth year of service the entry rate is usually down to below one. It will rise again as the effects of aircraft age or wear are felt.

---

*The Technical Logbook is the legally required serviceability record of an aircraft. Defects are entered by the crew after each flight. See Chapter 2.

The trend is towards On-condition Servicing aided by Flight Data Recorders (FDRs) and towards design for inspection "in situ" by borescope and other techniques. This leave-well-alone maintenance came about for economic reasons. It is obviously wasteful to remove equipment just because it has reached a certain "hard-time" life and is in perfectly good condition. The development of design techniques to permit regular and intimate inspection of components is of benefit obviously to safety as well as to economy.

A borescope is an optical instrument which can be "plugged in" to specially designed inspection ports located in high-wear areas such as engine compressor and turbine blades. The subject is illuminated by a fibre light-guide cable. It can be inspected through an eyepiece or, as this can be tiring for the inspector, by projecting the image on to a closed-circuit television.

CONSORTIUM MAINTENANCE Typical of the trend towards common maintenance is the Atlas consortium comprising Air France, UTA, Lufthansa, Alitalia and Sabena. Their agreement shares overhaul and maintenance work among members (see preceding table). The airframe of the 747 is overhauled by Air France, that of the A300 by Lufthansa, DC-10 by Alitalia, and Concorde by Sabena. Lufthansa is the overhaul agency for 747's Pratt & Whitney JT9D turbofan, while Air France does the General Electric CF6 engines of the DC-10 and A300 as well as of the GE-powered 747s.

Atlas began by being limited to sharing overhaul work only, but the tendency since has been to include maintenance and flight operations. The DC-10 operated by Lufthansa could well be operated by a flight crew from Alitalia.

The effect of Atlas-type consortia is to increase also the tendency towards the common purchasing of standard-specification aircraft with common systems, avionics and cockpit layouts.

BRITISH AIRWAYS MAINTENANCE and overhaul are typical of the best airline-industry standards. The airline's separate divisions specialise in the different techniques required for long-haul and short-haul operations; and the airline is based in a major aircraft-manufacturing country. As a pioneer of new aircraft and techniques (turboprops, subsonic and supersonic jet transports, blind landing) British Airways has had to develop the most advanced maintenance and overhaul systems.

The differences between the engineering divisions of the two old Airways Corporations, now joined together as British Airways, arise directly out of their different missions. The European Division is the

149

short-haul, high-frequency operator with something like 350 movements a day through the main London Heathrow base in the peak period and an average flight time of 1 hour. The Overseas Division is the long-haul, lower-frequency operator with aircraft away from base for three or four days, a maximum of 45 movements a day at Heathrow and an average flight time of 4½ hours. Yet there is a surprising amount in common between the two great engineering factories which lie within a few minutes' walk of each other at Heathrow, employing a total of nearly 10,000 people. As "flight-test departments" of the British aircraft industry and pioneers of its products for more than a quarter of a century, both have highly developed reaction procedures — more so perhaps than any other airline.

The European Division system is called React, the adventitious acronym of Reliability Evaluation and Control Technique. The Overseas Division system rejoices whimsically in the name of Sordid, which stands for Summary Of Reported Defects, Incidents and Delays. The two divisional systems differ considerably in detail, but their intentions are the same: to achieve the fastest possible reaction to defects in the interests of safety and economy.

The heart of the European Division defect-management system is the monthly document React. Inputs begin with the aircraft Technical Log which, with the associated documentation such as flight snag and check sheets, records by law all aircraft defects. Pretty well everything from these sources goes into React, which plots the behaviour of each aircraft type, system by system. There is an alert level for each — for example, "target" delay tolerated for the Trident 2 fuel system is 5 minutes per 100 departures, with an alert level of 7.5 minutes.

React shows monthly levels of zero, 2.9, 4.7, zero, 6, and then, suddenly, 20.2. Obviously the cause will be established long before React appears; but further reaction will be necessary if the level continues to be above "alert".

Special groups, focusing on component improvement and systems, analyse React each month. If a problem fails to respond to treatment by these groups it is passed for consideration to a Problem Control Group under the chairmanship of the chief maintenance engineer. He meets his key engineers for situation reports each morning. The Problem Control Group's members, in addition to the airline engineers, include representatives of the aircraft manufacturer and also the vendor if a particular component or system is intractable.

The time taken from reporting a defect to clearance has been monitored closely. European Division claims that while 80 per cent of defects took eight days to clear in 1967, the 1975 rate was about two days. On the Trident only 30 per cent were being cleared in one day in

1967 compared with 75 per cent ten years later.

These are levels which, according to the chief maintenance engineer, sustain the confidence of the pilot. The technical judgement is that of the engineer and the pilot, who will consider the limitations of the allowable deficiency list (known as the minimum equipment list in the USA and the acceptable deferred deficiency list by the Overseas Division).

BEA's work on automatic landing led to a Civil Aviation Authority (CAA) requirement that the airline should demonstrate a certain level of system integrity in routine line service. This level should be at least as high as that demonstrated in manufacturers' testing, and over many more landings. The requirement resulted in the expansion of the flight data recorder (FDR) carried in each aircraft. About 40 measurements, direct or derived, were agreed to be relevant. Some 64 measurements are sampled each second, from 1 to 8 times for different parameters.

The European Division has demonstrated more than 5,000 automatic landings in good visibility, with the captain in a position to take over. On this experience the CAA has approved the automatic landing system for Category 3 weather, in which cloud base and visibility are too low for manual landings and the aircraft is under automatic control to touchdown.

All recordings analysed in European Division for auto-landings are also simultaneously subjected to a flight operational analysis, which searches for non-standard events. Events without direct safety implications do not go to the flight manager, who is responsible for discipline as well as for safety, but to a specialist air-safety pilot, a retired captain whose professional discretion is trusted by pilots and by the management. Aberrations are dealt with quietly and informally. Nobody knows who the erring pilot is, but every pilot knows that the fleet performance is being monitored by the FDR.

The objective is safety, not discipline. Handled this way the flight data recorder — especially one recording so many parameters — may be regarded by the pilot as friend rather than snooper. (See also Chapters 2 and 19).

Cost of the European Division's flight data analysis programme is about 40p per aircraft flying hour — about £70,000 a year. Some of this money is recovered under a contract with the British Government to supply data for CAADRP (Civil Aircraft Airworthiness Data Requirements Programme) to check and update the British Civil Airworthiness Regulations (BCARs) and other operational standards.

Would the European Division have fitted such comprehensive flight-data recording if the CAA had not required it? The chief engineer says that it would, for management as well as for safety reasons. In any case the CAA requires all airlines to increase the number of channels from six to 40-plus — enough to derive much more about the flightpath.

The new CAA crash-recorder philosophy is to find out what the pilot was actually doing, rather than just deriving the flightpath. The CAA requirement for cockpit voice recorders (CVRs) was defined in the mid-1970s and British Airways was already installing CVRs in all its fleet.

The European Division is putting particular emphasis on engine health monitoring (EHM), using readings from the flight-data recorder to do various analyses, one of which is plotting vibration against spool speeds and comparing each flight vibration level with "signature" levels. European Division claims that this method detects a single broken turbine blade and that this, with other analyses which warn of impending engine trouble, can save one in five serious engine failures.

A small staff of engineers in the division's Early Failure Detection Centre know by the shape, size, quantity, colour and texture of metallic particles on magnetic plugs and oil filters where mechanical failure is incipient. The Rolls-Royce Speys of the Trident and Super One-Eleven fleets feature two well designed and located magnetic plugs in each engine oil system, and these are removed for inspection every 50hr. The main oil pressure filters are also examined at intervals of 600hr and 750hr respectively on these fleets. A complementary oil-inspection technique is spectroscopy, whereby a drop of oil is electrically vapourised and sub-microscopic particles of bearing-metal traced by its characteristic wavelength.

In a typical year of European Division's operations nearly 25 per cent of all engine premature removals are predicted early. This represents 75 per cent of all possible detection, with a monetary saving amounting to approximately £300,000 net that would otherwise be expended on engine repairs.

Engines as expensive as the RB.211 will have to do better than earlier engines. The alert-level shutdown rate per 1,000hr is generally accepted as being about 0.3. This is a great improvement on previous levels, especially the 0.7 of the piston era; but it is probably too high for the big modern and very expensive subsonic and supersonic engines.

The RB.211 of the TriStar has an elaborate Teledyne electronic engine monitoring system. Unlike the older turbine engines it is designed from the start for borescope and easy X-ray inspection. It also has improved design features for magnetic plug and oil filter metallic particle monitoring.

Out of the high frequency of European Division operations has evolved the BeaTech system. All defects are notified inbound to London by the captain about 20 minutes before landing. This gives the Engineering Division time to arrange for the appropriate specialists and spares. Even before the passengers have disembarked a senior engineer is on the flight deck for a discussion with the captain.

Overseas Division has a quarter of the European Division's despatch rate. But its aircraft are often up to 80 hours away from base, while those of the European Division come home to roost every night.

Overseas Division operates a maintenance check cycle, administered by a Maintenance Review Board on which the airworthiness authority is represented. This Board decides, on the basis of defect histories, which components have to be inspected or removed during checks. These are sub-multiples of the "intermediate" check, which varies according to aircraft from 1,200 hours to 1,600 hours. The 747 took one year to reach 1,500 hours, the VC10 eight years, the 707 nearly 15 years. The time has long since passed when aircraft were ritually dismembered every year and found, to nobody's amazement, to be in perfect order.

The old BOAC used to establish its maintenance schedules by eye and ear, but with the 747 a more scientific approach was essential. Aircraft of this size are such an enormous maintenance task that over-engineering could easily break their owners. A Maintenance System Guide was evolved, incorporating the experience of not only the Overseas Division but of Pan Am, TWA, United, American and Air Canada, among others, and the airworthiness authorities. (Similar maintenance guides for Concorde have been evolved by British Airways. Air France, and Iran Air with the British, French and US airworthiness authorities).

On the 747 a third of the maintenance manhours involve components being changed "on condition" — say following borescope inspection — and 16 per cent are accounted for by changes of components whose failure rates have called for a hard-time (HT) life. The rest — 53 per cent of the maintenance manhours on the 747 — is devoted to condition monitoring.

For each system and component condition-monitoring is defined and refined by inputs from various sources — delays, pilot reports, hangar and workshop defects, in-flight engine shutdowns, flight data recorder, manufacturers' Service Bulletins, other airlines' defects, as reported in the FAA's Service Defect Reports, and plug and filter analysis. All defects from all sources are coded on to an IBM card and a computer investigates and prints out trends.

Every problem comes up at the regular morning maintenance meeting at which a flight operations representative is present. If failure histories are worsening for a particular system or component an HT limit is called for.

Overseas Division claim to have more experience than many airlines of condition-monitoring big turbofan engines, in its case the JT9D. Engine-condition monitoring (ECM) compares observed values with "signatures", and plots deviations. Data on nearly 300 installed engines reported in standard form and Telexed to London go into the computer, which prints out trends. These are analysed each morning and problems are communicated to all station engineers. For example, immediate borescope inspections would be required after any turbine failure.

The borescope is proving of great value to operators of the newer types of engine, there being no such method of checking JT3Ds or Conways. The trend in ECM is towards letting the computer analyse and present data to compare an engine with its shipmates rather than with the brochure — in other words, to show what the pilot sees.

Now being evaluated is a technique to print-out only the "exceedences" to cut down paperwork. The ultimate objective is a computer actually in the aircraft displaying engine misbehaviour in real time to the crew.

All 747s are fitted with flight data recorders, or Airborne Integrated Data Systems (AIDS). Blocks of data from each engine regime — take-off, climb and cruise — are reduced to a single "snapshot" of exhaust-gas temperature and other parameters, and converted to standard conditions for comparison with brochure. The ultimate objective of engine condition-monitoring is to change 100 per cent of engines at the home base.

Overseas Division engine shutdown rates are below the "accepted industry average" of 0.3/1,000hr. In 1975 the JT9D-7s of the 747 fleet were running at 0.276; the Conways of the VC10 fleet at 0.138; the Conways of the 707-420 at 0.104; and the JT3Ds of the 707-320s at 0.076.

Yuckspeak Library: Our high-capability facility offers optimum rectification work = We do repairs.

---

16 Power

Nothing influences the safety, reliability, economy, speed and comfort of air transport more than the engine does. The early transport jet engines raised cruising thrust from around 2,000lb in the piston-engined 1940s and 1950s to 5,000lb in the 1960s and above 10,000lb in the 1970s. Aero-engine technology brought down specific fuel consumption (lb burnt per hour per lb of thrust) from above the 1.0 of the first jets in the 1950s to 0.5 in the 1970s. This approached the specific fuel consumption of the piston engines.

Direct operating cost went down from 3 cents per seat-mile in the piston era to 1.75 in the jet mid-1960s and to 1.5 in the wide-body-jet mid-1970s. Speed — the prime commodity of air transport — went up in the same period from 330 m.p.h. to 550 m.p.h.

Time between removal, strip and overhaul never got above 2,000hr for the piston engine. By the mid-1970s turbofan jet engines were staying on the wing for 10,000hr or more, and the airlines had introduced the concept of on-condition or "leave-well-alone" maintenance. The airworthiness authorities, after careful monitoring, permitted the engine and its ancillaries to be overhauled according to condition instead of stripping everything down regardless after so many hours. Modern engines are designed for on-wing inspection, removal and replacement of major assemblies or "modules" such as turbines and compressors.

Overhaul lives were actually decreasing as the piston engine reached the higher stages of its power development just before the turbine age. Technology, stimulated and financed by market demand, achieved with the turbine superior economy as well as safety.

Consumption, weight and overhaul life will continue to improve per lb of thrust. New materials and methods of construction to reduce weight and increase operating temperature will continue to evolve. So will new design and maintenance techniques, especially in-service sampling and monitoring.

The hydrocarbon-fuel turbine engine is unlikely to be replaced by a hydrogen-fuel or other radically new type of engine until well into the twenty-first century. Meanwhile technical effort will be devoted to improving fuel consumption. A 10 per cent reduction in the specific fuel consumption can reduce direct operating cost by more than 12 per cent over North Atlantic ranges, and by more than 6 per cent over short-to-medium ranges.

Reductions in weight are continuous too. Savings here of 10 per cent can reduce direct operating costs over long ranges by up to 2 per cent. Increases in engine purchase price of up to 10 or even 20 per cent have a smaller effect on operating cost.

Aero-engine technology more than any other decides the safety and economy of air transport. In the piston-engine era there were about 60 engine failures or shutdowns for every 100,000 flying hours. By the mid-1960s the failure rate had fallen to about 10, and by the mid-1970s it was less than 5. The very best, the Pratt and Whitney JT8D of the Boeing 727 and 737 and the McDonnell Douglas DC-9, was less than 1.0. Engine failure at V_1 (take-off decision speed) is experienced once in 100,000 flights approximately.

The cost of designing and developing a new engine, and of getting it into public service with demonstrated safety and reliability, is high and is getting higher per lb of thrust. The airlines paid about £6 per lb of thrust in 1960; by 1970 they were paying more than £10, and by 1975 up to £15. In other words an engine delivering 50,000 lb of thrust will cost nearly £1 million — as much as a complete Constellation or DC-6 airliner in the early 1950s. The launching cost of an aero engine in the 1970s might well be 400 times the selling price per unit — say £300 million, or as much as the launching cost of the airliner's airframe.

In the 20 years from the first subsonic jet airliners to the first supersonic airliner the power of the civil commercial jet engine has increased sixfold, from the 25,000 thrust horsepower of the Boeing 707 to the 140,000 thrust horsepower or more of Concorde. This achieved an increase in cruising speed of from Mach 0.8 to Mach 2.0.

In terms of safety and reliability, the quest for higher power with greater efficiency and less noise is along the road of higher bypass ratio and better materials and manufacturing processes such as air-cooled turbine blades.

In the period 1950-1970 bypass ratio, the ratio of the flow through the fan to the flow through the turbine has increased from zero — i.e. all the flow going through the turbine — to 5 or 6. At the same time compression ratio has increased from less than 5:1 to about 30:1; and as compression has increased — thanks to the efficiency of compressor design — so has turbine inlet temperature gone up from about 1,200°K to 1,500°K and above.

156

ENGINE HANDLING Modern turbine aero-engines are remarkably robust, and can take a lot of mishandling. Overspeeding has to be considerable before an engine flies to pieces. The most damaging experience for an engine, including bird strikes and compressor surge, is overheating of the hot turbine section. Turbine temperature limits have to be observed meticulously. An overheat of up to 30°K or even 40°K for five minutes, to get the aircraft out of an emergency, would probably not damage the engine — though it might take some life out of it — but if the overheat went up to 100°K trouble would begin. In a dire emergency there are not many pilots who would not push all the levers "through the fire wall" to get full power.

The pilot's measure of thrust in the cockpit is the engine pressure ratio (EPR). This is the ratio of the pressure in the jet pipe nozzle — the primary measure of engine thrust — to the ambient atmospheric pressure. If the "Flight-Manual" EPR is not reached on a cold-day take-off from a low-altitude airport, the pilot would almost certainly "snag" the engine.

DISC FAILURES A turbine engine contains large wheels, or discs, on which are mounted turbine blades, compressor blades, or fan blades. These discs are made of steel or titanium alloy, and are one of the few areas in which a single failure can have catastrophic results for an aircraft.

Fatal failures of discs are extremely rare. Of 40 disc failures reported to the US National Transportation Safety Board (NTSB) between 1964 and 1975, none caused fatalities. Seven of the 40 resulted in penetration of the cabin by engine fragments, two of these causing injuries. These results appear to be within the airworthiness criteria of not more than one fatal failure in 10 million flights.

Of the 40 disc failures examined, seven involved the front fan; 19 the compressor; and 15 the turbine. But there are six times the number of compressor stages as turbine stages, on average; the compressor failure rate is thus much lower than that of the turbine disc.

The majority of failures, 58 per cent, took place during the climb when the engine was still at full power; 15 per cent took place during the take-off roll, and 10 per cent as the aircraft reached rotation speed to lift off the runway. Only 15 per cent occurred during the cruise, and only 2 per cent during the descent.

Disc failures are very often traced to improper machining or heat treatment of the forged steel or titanium castings. The heat treatment process, which is designed to relieve forging and machining stresses, is a particularly important part of the manufacturing process. Crack-detection tests are carried out during manufacture and overhaul.

Although all turbine engines are designed and armoured to contain blade failures, the containment of disc bursts would require unacceptably heavy structures. Disc failures frequently follow blade failures, because of the resulting vibration, although engines are designed to withstand very large amounts of vibration without failure.

The end of developments in aero-engine materials, aerodynamics, design and production is not in sight. The 50,000lb-thrust subsonic engines of the 1970s will grow into the 100,000lb-thrust engines of the 1980s. The 40,000lb supersonic engine, which presents its own special design problems such as reheat, will grow equally dramatically. Each step up will be accompanied by improvements in noise, economy, reliability, and safety.

The new engine is coming along fine, fine. The only problem at the moment is that the weight is what the thrust should be and the thrust is what the weight should be.

---

17 Noise-abatement

Jet noise is caused by a number of sources, including the intake, but mainly by the air-shearing blast of high-velocity exhaust gas. Special noise-abatement procedures are in force at airports, requiring take-off and landing manoeuvres which have prompted pilots to raise questions of safety. Before considering these questions we need to look at some of the first principles of aircraft noise.

The quietest engines are those which produce most of their thrust with a big fan, like turbofans or propeller-driving turbines (turboprops). Turbofans are sometimes called high-bypass-ratio jets, because of the amount of cold air which they duct past, rather than through, the turbines.

The turbojet or pure jet pushes most of its gas through the turbine. This is the noisiest form of propulsion. The supersonic Concorde has turbojets; high speed means high jet velocity, which is why this aircraft is noisier than the subsonic Boeing 747, DC-10 and TriStar, whose turbofans have bypass ratios of the order of 5:1.

New models of subsonic airliners presented for certification to the American and British authorities in the 1970s were expected to meet noiseworthiness standards. The rules did not ban the jet airliners designed in the 1950s and early 1960s which were still in widespread service, and in some cases still in production, but the noiseworthiness code provided for minimum eventual standards for new production aircraft.

The rules apply to three phases of flight: take-off, sometimes called "flyover"; sideline; and approach. The measure of noise is the Equivalent Perceived Noise Decibel, EPNdB, sometimes termed EPNL (Equivalent Perceived Noise Level).

The plain decibel, or dB, is no more than a measure of sound pressure. It does not distinguish loudness or noisiness. In the late 1950s, when jet noise first began to distress airport communities, the Port of New York Authority's noise consultants Bolt, Beranek and Newman invented the Perceived Noise Decibel, or PNdB. This took account of noisiness and human reaction to it. It was mathematically derived from the dBA (decibel in the A scale) and from the different tones which make up a noise. It got nearer to recording noisiness as it is measured by the human ear. The PNdB was in due course further refined to take into account tones and, for the first time, duration of the noise. It became the EPNdB, or EPNL. It was adopted in 1966 by the United States, the United Kingdom and by Icao, the International Civil Aviation Organisation, as the standard measure of aircraft noise, to be used in aircraft certification.

The mathematical convenience of using a logarithmic base for the decibel scale confuses many people. A reduction of 10 EPNdB from say 115 to 105 means in effect halving the noise. Similarly, an increase of 10 EPNdB means doubling the noise. An aircraft which produces 100 EPNdB is thus four times noisier than an aircraft at the same height emitting 80 EPNdB — the noise level which is in fact about the same as a quiet back street, or a man's voice a metre away.

The noiseworthiness standards adopted by the Americans * and British** and Icao† for new types of subsonic airliner introduced from 1972 differ in detail but are broadly as follows:

	Noise-monitoring point		Limits (E=EPNdB or EPNL)
Take-off ("Flyover")	6.5 km (3.5nm) from start of take-off roll (over this point aircraft may be at varying heights depending on performance)	108E	For aircraft above 280,000kg (600,000lb) max. certificated take-off, e.g. 747
		93-108E	According to take-off weight down to 30,000kg (75,000lb) e.g. DC-10, TriStar, Boeing 707/727/737, DC-8 DC-9, Trident, One-Eleven, and all but the lightest airliners
		93E	DC-3
Approach	1.85km (1nm) from the runway threshold (over which all aircraft are on the standard 3° approach or glideslope at 112m, 370ft)	108E	For aircraft above 280,000kg (600,000lb) e.g. 747
		102-108E	From 34,000kg (75,000lb) e.g. from DC-9, Boeing 737 and One-Eleven
		102E	34,000kg and below, e.g. DC-3
Sideline ("Lateral")	0.65km (0.35nm) at any point parallel to the runway for four engines, 0.45km (0.25nm) for three engines	108E	For aircraft above 280,000kg (600,000lb)
		102-108E	For aircraft from 34,000kg (75,000lb)
		102E	34,000kg and below, e.g. DC-3

*US Federal Aviation Regulations Part 36
**UK Air Navigation Order, 1970
†Icao Annex 16

Airports differ in their limits according to the intensity of public protest. Typical limits are 110 by day and 102 by night, and at many airports a total curfew on night jet movements.

Noise levels are monitored by the authorities, and airline pilots have to schedule their take-off climb angle accordingly. Normal angle is about 15°, anything much higher tending to make passengers apprehensive. Approach height and power settings tend to be fixed by the 3° angle of the ILS (Instrument Landing System) glidepath or glideslope. The suffering airport neighbours, including those who live or work 15 or 20 miles upstream and downstream of the runways, protest that the limits are inadequate and that the monitoring points are in the wrong places.

When the rules were introduced in the 1970s none of the older jet airliners could comply. The DC-10 and TriStar did, though the early 747 was above limits on take-off and approach.

Some of the noisiest airliners were the early Boeing 707 and the DC-8. Concorde was not noisier than these two except in the sideline case (i.e. on each side of the runway during take-off). But it did not appear likely, even with further treatment of the engines, to meet subsonic certification rules.

The aircraft noise problem can be dealt with in a number of ways. Pilots can use special noise-abatement procedures for the approach and landing, making turns where possible to avoid overflying houses, cutting back power, and restricting take-off weight for the steepest climb-out (see below). Airports can be sited away from built-up areas. Curfews can be applied. The public can be given house-soundproofing grants, or may even be rehoused. Technology can tackle the problem at source, by making engines quieter, or allowing climb and descent gradients to be steeper, or by a combination of the two.

In the interests of efficiency and low fuel consumption, engine designers began to use fans to pump greater masses of air at lower velocities. As the development of these turbofans progressed, so the bypass ratio (BPR) increased. This is the ratio of cold air going through the outer part of the fan to the hot gas which it surrounds and mixes with — exhaust from the jet nozzle. The early turbofans like the Pratt & Whitney JT3D and the Rolls-Royce Conway (which was the first bypass jet) had a BPR of less than 2:1. The big turbofans like the Pratt & Whitney JT9D, the Rolls-Royce RB. 211 and the General Electric CF6 have BPRs nearer 5:1 from big fans which produce up to 80 per cent of the thrust. Not only is heat energy converted more efficiently into thrust: the thrust is produced more quietly.

The big fan engines brought dramatic improvements in noise. The DC-10 and TriStar, for example, were more than 10 EPNdB quieter than the untreated Boeing 707-320C and Douglas DC-8-63 in the take-off, approach and sidelines cases — in other words, half as noisy.

A level of 90 EPNdB is frequently suggested as the highest that anyone could reasonably describe as "acceptable". The noise experts' reference is the contour around an airport enclosing an area or noise "shadow" or "footprint" normally subject to 90 EPNdB or more. This shadow, if visible, would look like a long thin blade with the runway in the middle.

The subsonic jets designed in the 1960s produce after take-off a 90 EPNdB contour 2km wide extending 40 or 50km beyond a 3km runway. On the approach their 90 EPNdB shadow extends 20 or 30km back under the 3° ILS (instrument landing system) glidepath. The noise-footprint area in which people outside the airport are subjected to 90 EPNdB every few minutes is therefore anything up to 160sq km.

This contour area is reduced to less than 40sq km each time the TriStar, DC-10 and A300 take off and land, a substantial reduction which has led to intensified public protest against the earlier jets and a campaign for the "muffling" or "hush-kitting" of their JT3, JT8 and Spey engines.

The 747, though quieter than the 707 and DC-8 it replaced, was not at first as quiet as the TriStar, DC-10 and A300, but further developments of the JT9D engine brought the aircraft below the 108 EPNdB limits.

The ultimate solution to the jet noise problem lies inside the engine. Special take-off and approach techniques help, but in principle these are like wearing a raincoat in a house with a leaking roof. Schemes for soundproofing windows, rehousing or even moving airports to remote areas may all help, but they do not tackle the noise problem at source.

The first task is to isolate noise sources. Fan noise varies with tip speed (the slower the quieter) and with compression or pressure ratio, aerofoil section and pitch, and number of blades. It also depends on the distance between the fan and the flow-straightening guide vanes downstream — which can act as a siren — and on the ratio between the number of fan blades and the number of guide vanes. Reducing the velocity of the core jet is also a reducer of EPNdBs. Lengthening intakes and jetpipes and double-skinning them with sound-absorbent honeycomb sandwich material further deadens flow, machinery and combustion noise. Research into the physics of the acoustic material has big dividends still to yield.

Noise research has been a combination of advanced mathematics, particularly into the nature of turbulent flow, and experiment. A modification to reduce noise may impair efficiency, and therefore noise research is always a matter of compromise between — for example — a fan tip-speed of 300m/sec which is quiet and one of 450 which is low-drag but annoying.

The early versions of Concorde will always be noisy, though they will be accounting for less than one per cent of the total movements at the major international airports until well into the 1980s. By then, and certainly by the end of the century, when supersonic airliners will have probably become the normal method of long-range transport, technology will have quietened the supersonic transport too.

NOISE-ABATEMENT PROCEDURES The first part of the take-off, known as the noise-abatement first segment, is flown at full power climbing as steeply as is consistent with safety, bearing in mind the possibility of an engine failure. Thus the aircraft carries its noise as high as it can away from the listener outside the airport boundary and as far as possible from the houses. This is why higher power, even though it may mean more "sideline" noise each side of the runway, can paradoxically mean less noise to airport neighbours. A steeper climb is made possible by higher power.

Just before the noise-monitoring post, at a point usually determined by a given number of seconds from brakes off, the throttles are eased back to a setting which leaves the aircraft in a gentle climb. This is known as the noise-abatement second segment. Full climb power is reapplied after the noise-sensitive area is cleared. The power-cutback procedure may be combined with turns arranged further to avoid polluting populated areas with noise. Power reductions and manoeuvres obviously mean extra work for the crew at a busy time. While noise-abatement procedures can limit loads, they are not allowed to compromise safety. The procedures may be dropped without hesitation if the captain for any reason considers that they will hazard safety. But no professional airline will deliberately ignore noise-abatement procedures in computing loads during flight-planning.

Many airports have automatic noise-monitoring posts. These record samples and with the help of computers alert the airport authority to violations. Airlines which constantly infringe will be required to explain themselves.

THE "TWO-SEGMENT" APPROACH No standard noise-abatement procedures have been generally adopted for the approach, although this is a phase of flight which can be most disturbing for listeners below the standard glideslope, which must be maintained by power. Long low-altitude approaches with engines roaring are obviously avoided by pilots and air traffic controllers, who like traffic established on the standard instrument paths for other reasons.

Why not fly the early approach well above the 3° glidepath, joining it from above, closer to the airport, thus keeping most of the approach noise high above communities? This so-called two-segment approach has been tried experimentally, and actually operated in passenger service in the USA with some noise-reducing benefits. The advocates of the two-segment approach claim that it can provide reductions of between 5 and 15 decibels in noise levels depending on the type of aircraft and approach altitudes. The procedure would provide the most benefit at distances of 5 to 12km from the landing runway along the ILS approach path. The so-called 90 EPNdB shadow — the "acceptable" noise area — would be reduced from about 30sq km to less than 7sq km.

A typical two-segment ILS approach might begin with an upper-segment glide angle of between 5° and 6° depending on the aircraft type. The second segment would be flown at the existing 3° glideslope. The transition between the two segments would be accomplished far enough from touch-down to allow stabilised conditions at 700ft above ground level. The transition would normally begin about 5km from touchdown, and be completed at about 3km.

A stabilised approach usually means that below 1,500ft, and on reaching the outer marker, the aircraft is operated at constant airspeed, glideslope (flight-path) angle and rate of descent, with only small power adjustments. Failure to achieve a stabilised approach has been the cause of many accidents, and is the reason for strict training disciplines to ensure that fewest possible departures from the 3° glideslope.

A stabilised approach is difficult enough at the best of times, and especially when wind-shear and turbulence are experienced. The added difficulty of changing glideslope angle, with all the adjustments of power and trim involved, is not acceptable to the majority of pilots. (They also think that the required sudden power increase will disturb more people under the 3° slope than were spared under the quieter 6° slope.)

There seems little doubt that the two-segment approach, properly executed, will disturb fewer people on the ground; but it is unlikely to be implemented while pilots remain unconvinced of its safety.

LOW-DRAG APPROACH An alternative to the two-segment approach is the "low-drag, low-power" approach. Flaps cause drag, drag requires thrust, and thrust causes noise. One European airline claims a 50 per cent noise reduction during the low-drag approach, at least up to the outer marker of the Instrument Landing System (ILS).

The height at which the aircraft is fully stabilised, with undercarriage and full flaps down, is delayed to about 1,000ft. Descent to within about 240kt to intercept the ILS glidepath at 3,000ft is "clean," using idle power. Below 3,000ft speed is reduced to 160-170kt, with take-off flap and appropriate power for speed. The glidepath is followed to about 500ft above the normal height for crossing the outer marker. The undercarriage is then extended, the flaps are fully lowered and power is increased so that the aircraft is stabilised and ready for landing on passing the outer marker.

Procedures vary and in tests a computer advised the pilot when to lower the flaps and increase power in order to arrive at, say, 500ft two miles from touchdown with landing flap and at the right landing speed.

Lower flap-settings require less power, and hence generate less noise; they also save fuel and engine wear. It has been estimated that the use of 40° flaps on a Boeing 727 causes unacceptable noise over ten square miles during the approach. The use of 30° flaps reduces this area to just under five square miles. It is claimed for the low-drag approach that noise levels upstream of the outer ILS marker (more than 5 miles from the runway threshold) are reduced by between 7 and 12 equivalent perceived noise decibels (EPNdB).

A disadvantage of the low-drag approach is that the aircraft lands faster and requires a longer landing run. The use of 30° rather than 40° flaps on a Boeing 727, for example, increases landing field length from 4,720 ft to 5,060ft, without thrust reversers. The use of full 40° landing flap is therefore necessary in rain, snow, sleet and ice, which all increase the distance needed for landing.

Again, flying with less than full landing flap means higher airspeeds, and this can complicate air-traffic control procedures at busy airports. A Boeing 747 would approach at its maximum permitted landing weight at 220kt without flap, at 160kt with 10° of flap, and at 140kt with full 30° flap. The slower the speed the higher the drag and the more noisy and fuel-consuming the approach.

Low-drag approaches are sometimes called managed-drag approaches, the general procedure sometimes being referred to as Drag Management.

Some airlines are more socially conscientious about noise-abatement procedures than others. An airline which has been particularly commended is Northwest, the US domestic airline. It chose as its climb-out speed $V_2 + 10kt$. For most subsonic jet aircraft this is very near the speed for minimum drag, and hence the speed for the best climb gradient. At $V_2 + 10kt$ pitch attitudes tend to be greater than at higher speeds, varying from 9° at heavy weight to about 23° when light, depending on the type of aircraft. The margin above the stall at $V_2 + 10kt$ — about 30 per cent at heavy weight and about 40 per cent light — is also less than at the higher speeds. There is therefore less margin in the event of a power failure. Northwest crew-training takes care of these differences, and does not regard them as unsafe. For example, in gusty weather, when at V_2+ 10kt a load of about 0.8g can stall the wing, the speed margin is "padded" at the discretion of the pilot.

Northwest crews climb at V_2+ 10kt and at 1,000ft lower the nose and accelerate to allow flap-retraction. The cleaning up of the aircraft increases forward speed and thus lowers the jet velocity relative to the airstream, helping to reduce noise level. The engines are throttled back. At 3,000ft normal climb thrust is applied, and the aircraft accelerated to about 250kt. This procedure reduces noise in two ways. It increases the distance between the aircraft and the people on the ground by climbing at V_2+ 10kt, the highest practicable climb angle. It also reduces noise at its source as much as possible. Northwest call the quiet climb thrust setting "Quiet EPR" — Engine Pressure Ratio, a direct measure of thrust (Chapter 16). Flap retraction, both during the climb and on the approach, is believed also to reduce airframe noise substantially. A 500-ton airliner gliding with all engines shut off would still make a considerable noise (its "noise floor") and one object of current noise research is how to quieten airframes as well as engines.

Noise? Our aircraft don't make a noise. They have an acoustic signature.

18 Economic Strength

A safe airline is not necessarily financially sound, but an unsafe airline cannot be. To be unsafe is not only socially unacceptable: it is also bad for business. Yet there is evidence to suggest that financially unsound airlines are accident-prone. "It is expensive to run an air carrier operation," a former head of the US Federal Aviation Administration has said, "and for the financially embarrassed the temptation to cut corners in maintenance, training and other areas vital to air safety is very strong...

"In one company we found a series of discrepancies such as lack of certification of records, inadequacy of training aids, inadequate flight manuals, and other matters that each on its own would not justify a suspension or revocation. A separate investigation by the Civil Aeronautics Board [the body responsible for the economic regulation of America's airlines] found that the same carrier was in poor financial condition."

One famous engine company plots its airline customers' spares orders; when these slump it chases after their debts. It is noticed too that airline failures are often preceded by dirty aircraft and equipment. In other words, economic strength and the financial disciplines which it demands are safe.

Economic weakness does not mean direct skimping on safety items like engineering or pilot-training. The risk of a fatal crash is not one which any professional airline engineer or pilot would tolerate, however unscrupulous the owners might be. Economic weakness may manifest itself as subtle corporate incapacitation, possibly leading to a creeping management shambles which degrades the discipline and morale so essential to safety. The way in which subtle corporate incapacitation can develop is described at the end of this chapter.

THE FINANCIAL DISCIPLINES A prime product of air transport, at least until cargo overtakes passengers, is the Seat-km — one seat flown one km. This is sometimes expressed as the Available or Capacity Seat-km. Obviously, an airline carrying large passenger payloads over short sectors is producing a different seat-km from an airline carrying smaller payloads over long sectors. As aircraft get bigger and seating layouts more varied — from 260 to 400 in differently operated TriStars — the Seat-km may have to be reconsidered. A "square metre of passenger deck" might become more realistic than the seat.

A standard international unit of operating cost is the US cent per seat-km. This cost, comprising direct and indirect expenses, can be precisely defined and measured. An economic airline is not necessarily the one with the lowest operating cost. The other side of the coin is revenue. Seat-km must be converted into Passenger-km. This is largely achieved by commercial skill and judgement. The measure of an operator's skill — choice of aircraft, pricing, scheduling, and passenger service — is Passenger Load Factor (LF), the percentage of seat-km converted into passenger-km.

An LF of 60 per cent is accepted as a reasonable compromise between overbooking and flying too many seats empty and at a loss. A load factor of 100 per cent may be achieved at peak times, and a very low load factor at thin times. The "target load factor" is used to calculate fares. At the end of the year the Break-even Load Factor must be exceeded.

Load factor is the index of economic success — the result most closely watched as the daily, weekly and monthly figures come in. If this falls below budget — if traffic falls too far short of capacity — urgent measures have to be taken to increase it. The quickest way to do this is to reduce capacity — to cut frequencies, use smaller aircraft, or, in extreme cases, to cut routes. But nothing is more expensive for an airline than idle airliners, equipment and staff. The load factor may be increased, but the saving in operating cost — in fuel, landing fees and maintenance — is little more than half the total. Wages and capital charges still have to be paid.

Load factor may also be improved by cutting fares, but this cannot be done by management decision alone: changes may not be made without the approval of governments, domestically or internationally. Fare-discounting is practised at times of serious excess capacity to boost load factor; but the break-even load factor is now different because the Revenue Rate — the revenue yield per passenger-km — has been reduced.

Hard selling is another way to boost load factor when traffic flags, but this must be done without increasing promotion and sales costs too much.

Achievement of a profit-making passenger load factor is not, however, enough. The seat-km is only part of an airline's product. The total unit of production is the Capacity (or Available) Tonne-km. This takes into account cargo and mail capacity, which tends to become a much more important part of an airline's output as aircraft size increases. It follows that Cost per Capacity Tonne-km is the most complete airline cost index. It is otherwise known as unit cost, unit operating cost, cost level, or unit cost of production. As with the seat-km, the capacity tonne-km comes in different forms: a short-haul airline may produce the same number of tonne-km as a long-hauler, but in many more flights.

An airliner may be able to make a profit on passenger traffic with the cargo holds empty. But the productive capacity is not being used to the full, unless of course the airliner is designed like Concorde mainly to carry passengers. Thus an important airline economic index is Weight Load Factor, sometimes known as Overall Load Factor — the percentage of capacity tonne-km filled with Load Tonne-km. The key Revenue Rate is thus the Revenue per Load Tonne-km.

The major component in most airlines is the passenger revenue rate, but all the productive capacity of the airliner must be fully used. The economics of air transport are related to cost per capacity tonne-km and to revenue per load tonne-km.

There are various methods of defining airline Operating Cost. Airline cost-control systems vary. Some airlines do not even have a system; others, like Northwest and Delta in the USA, have cost-control disciplines which are among the toughest in the business, producing profits — or at least manageable losses — in years when others are in deficit.

All scheduled airlines return to their governments the two standard International Civil Aviation Organisation financial reporting forms, Balance Sheet and Profit and Loss Statement. These are published in the Icao statistical digests. They are the only source of published information in the case of many airlines. Operating costs are sometimes referred to as Direct and Indirect. The dividing line varies from one airline to another. A typical breakdown might look like this:

Total Operating Cost

Direct		Indirect
Fixed	**Variable**	Stations
Interest	Flight operations	Passenger services
Depreciation	Maintenance and	Ticketing, sales, etc
Insurance	overhaul	Administration

Direct Costs are in general the expenses — typically about 60 per cent of the total — which are incurred by the operation of the aircraft: fuel, flight-crew and maintenance, hull insurance, interest on capital, aircraft rental, landing fees, depreciation. Some of these Direct Costs are "fixed" (or "standing") and do not vary with the amount of flying — for example, depreciation, insurance, interest. They account for between 12 and 20 per cent of total operating cost. The rest are variable (flight operations, maintenance and overhaul).

Indirect Costs Typically 40 per cent of the total, these include passenger services; ticketing, sales and promotion; administration; and station costs. "Indirects" include the wages involved in all these activities. These again may be broken down into fixed and variable.

The Direct Cost per hour depends on Aircraft Utilisation. The more hours the aircraft flies — over 4,000hr per aircraft in a year may be achieved by efficient airlines in favourable conditions — the lower the cost per hour.

Cost per Capacity Tonne-km, or unit operating cost, is Cost per Hour divided by aircraft productivity in tonne-km per hour. Productivity is the payload in tonnes multiplied by the block speed in km per hour. Cost per tonne-km varies with range to produce a U-shaped cost curve. The higher the utilisation (in other words the lower the cost per hour) the lower the cost curve.

The bigger and more modern an airliner, the likelier it is to have a lower unit operating cost. This is because the weight of constant-size components becomes a smaller proportion of total weight, and crew costs tend to be a lower proportion of the total Direct Cost despite the salary increases usually demanded for flying bigger aircraft.

Long-range air transport is often supposed to be inherently more economic than short-range. Aircraft Utilisation, which lowers the cost curve, is easier to achieve on long hauls. But the short-haul operator has advantages too, including a geographically more compact market to help ticket-selling.

The distinction between long-haul and short-haul routes diminishes as speed increases. London-Washington, which Concorde flies in three or four hours, is as short a journey as London-Hamburg by DC-3 in 1946, or New York-New Orleans by Boeing 727 in 1966.

Whatever the length of the route, Route Density has a large effect on economics. High traffic volume permits the operator to get down to mass production. He can use bigger aircraft with lower unit costs at the higher frequencies which have a beneficial effect on load factor.

The higher the frequency the higher the load factor that can be achieved without turning traffic away, and the higher the utilisation of expensive stations and staff. Route Density, or tonnes per route-km, is a key economic index. Extensive route networks may look impressive in advertisements, but the load per km may be quite uneconomic. There may be political reasons for showing the flag once a week at some distant airport; but low-density routes are a quick way to deficit and subsidy, and the bigger the aircraft the heavier the deficit. Route Density is important in the management of the airline economy. Few routes are spared seasonal peaks and troughs, and these can be severe in certain areas. The summer holiday migrations in Europe and across the North Atlantic are examples. For every five aircraft in the fleet of a "summer-holiday" airline perhaps only one may be fully needed in January or February. An airline can ameliorate the peak problem by scheduling major maintenance in off-peak times, and by pricing policies designed to promote off-season traffic. All this helps to increase Route Density and Utilisation.

DIRECT COSTS Like depreciation, Interest is a Fixed (or Standing) Charge which the airline has to pay whether the aircraft flies or not. Interest may be regarded as an operating cost like fuel or maintenance — or depreciation. But, as with depreciation, an airline can fly without paying interest, or by paying it well below the general money-market rates charged to other industrial borrowers. Governments may decide to waive or reduce interest on the capital they provide to the airline they own. This is in fact a common form of subsidy, although it is not always made clear in the public accounts. While depreciation conserves capital, profitability decides the airline's ability to raise new capital for buying new aircraft and equipment.

Some airlines find leasing more convenient than buying. Depreciation and interest charges are avoided and replaced by rentals. The decision to buy or to lease depends to some extent on the tax system — for example on depreciation allowances — and on how easy the airline finds the raising of new capital. Lease-purchase arrangements worked out by the banking and leasing institutions and brokers help to offer the airlines the best of both ways of acquiring new airliners.

Depreciation Capital equipment has to be replaced either because it is worn out or because competition has made it obsolete. Depreciation (or amortisation or obsolescence) has to be charged against the operating account. Though not a cash cost, it is an operating cost like fuel, wages or maintenance. It is the cost of staying in business — the means by which an airline provides for the replacement of its equipment and keeps its capital intact. The amount charged for depreciation is a matter for the commercial judgement of the airline. Ideally the fleet should stand valued on the books at or below the value it would fetch on the market. This ideal is rarely possible to achieve; ups and downs constantly affect second-hand values, and taxation allowances on depreciation vary. Some governments do not allow full depreciation as a tax allowance.

A straight-line depreciation of the purchase price over seven years with a residual value of 25 per cent, or depreciation over ten years to a residual value of zero, used to be the classic depreciation policies adopted. By the 1970s depreciation lives were being stretched to 14 and even 16 years as the subsonic jet airliners became well established and developed, with supersonics not yet mature.

Supersonic-airliner depreciation will depend on resale value. This depends on the timing of the competitor, and structural fatigue life.

It is of course possible to adjust depreciation according to trading circumstances. In times of recession depreciation can be reduced or even waived to scrape home with a profit on the operating account. This is a matter for the judgement of the airline and its auditors. It is likely to be a self-deluding expedient, because full costs are not being covered.

In the long run, usually when the time comes for raising new capital, the current capital has to be accounted for. Depreciation of borrowed capital cannot indefinitely be deferred, any more than trade creditors can. A consistently soft depreciation policy may end either in bankruptcy or in a capital write-off by an indulgent government.

Classic aircraft like the DC-3 and the Boeing 707 show that depreciation in the airline business is not always forced by technology. There are hundreds of DC-3s still giving safe and sound public service 30 or 40 years after they were built. There are Boeing 707s with 50,000 flying hours. Eventually the cost of spares, modifications and maintenance will become higher than the cost of buying and operating new aircraft — though the economic life of well maintained airliners is often longer than originally expected. The economically strong airline is the one that applies a well judged depreciation policy.

Insurance Like depreciation and interest, insurance is a fixed or standing charge. Airlines do not have to insure their aircraft hulls against damage or loss, but very few do not. A condition of most loans for the financing of aircraft is that the borrower shall insure the hulls against the normal risks of operation. The premiums usually include third-party cover, and vary widely. For obvious reaons they are never published. A big, long-established scheduled airline with a large fleet of proven aircraft and a good safety history may get cover for 2 or even 1 per cent of the fleet's replacement value. An airline with a small fleet and a mixed or unproven operating record will be rated by the underwriters as a higher risk. The premiums could be as high as 5 per cent. Passenger cover is usually by a separate policy, and the premium is related to passenger-miles flown.

London has long been the world's biggest and most experienced aviation insurance market. More than 50 aviation underwriters are associated with Lloyds, and others of equal quality and expertise are not.

The daily newspaper *Lloyd's List* publishes the reports which it receives from Lloyd's agents and other sources on every accident or incident to civil aircraft likely to lead to claims, from major disasters to minor taxiing accidents. The confidential Lloyd's Blue Book is compiled from this and other sources. It covers every known civil-aviation operator and its accident and incident records enable the underwriters to assess the risks they may be called upon to cover.

Big, well established airlines with first-class safety records pay insurance premiums which average between 1 and 2.5 per cent of the replacement value of their fleets. For example:

	Flight equipment replacement cost	Flight equipment insurance	
	$m	$m	%
Pan American	721	8.6	1.2
Qantas	166	1.6	1.0
SAS	158	3.3	2.1
Air-India	45	1.0	2.2
	1,090	14.5	1.3

By contrast, the higher-risk airlines pay rates which average, from an examination of their accounts, as follows:

	$m	$m	%
Asian	46.0	1.10	2.4
South American	24.0	0.55	2.3
North African	6.2	0.13	2.1
Middle Eastern	2.6	0.10	3.8
Arabian	14.6	0.70	4.8
	93.4	2.58	2.7

Five national scheduled airlines whose names have appeared more often than some others in the accident and incident tables pay insurance at rates of up to 3 per cent.

The difference between insurance rates for scheduled and non-scheduled services is apparent from Icao figures for British Airways and leading British independent airlines. Fleet equipment insurance cost per

Capacity Tonne-km is, respectively, 0.5 and 1.9 US cents.

There is nothing in the safety statistics to suggest that the hull of a charter airliner is nearly four times more likely to be wrecked than that of a scheduled airliner. The trend is for the charter operator to be as safe as the scheduled operator. Therefore the trend in insurance rates is towards parity. One medium British independent pays 1.225 per cent on its jets and 2.4 per cent on its turboprops. There is also the point that premium percentages vary with the value of an aircraft: the higher the value the lower the percentage premium. This is mainly due to the element necessary for the possiblity of repairs to the lower-value aircraft. In general the scheduled airlines have a higher proportion of higher-value aircraft.

Also covered by insurance are the airline's liabilities for damage to third parties — persons and their property on the ground — and for death or injury to their passengers. Most national laws require all airlines operating over their territory to be covered against third-party claims. The passenger liability cover is commonly referred to as "Warsaw cover". The premium for "Warsaw" passenger and third-party cover is usually related to the size of the airline, measured typically in terms of passenger-miles or hours flown.

The worst case for the insurance market would be a mid-air collision between two big airliners over a densely populated city. When the big second-generation subsonic airliners like the 747 were ordered there were fears that the insurance rates would be too high. The airline industry — which had already been setting aside more and more reserves for self-insurance — examined the possibility of starting its own insurance company. This was at first encouraged, but when the size of the subscriptions became known, and when the market rates began to fall before the threat of the airlines' own insurance company, support ebbed away. The airlines drifted back to the normal insurance market. Though rates were high at first, the excellent safety record of the second-generation subsonic jets soon led to a fall in premiums. The pattern will probably be repeated in the supersonic era.

Flight Operations are easily the biggest item of airline expenditure. They comprise crew costs, training and fuel costs together with landing fees and en-route charges, and account for up to 30 per cent of total costs. Flight operations costs include Crew Costs. Although crew work load does not usually increase with aircraft size — and may indeed be reduced by greater comfort and automation — the trade unions argue that pilots are entitled to a share of higher aircraft productivity, and that having more lives in their care entitles them to payment for higher responsibility.

These arguments, though difficult to sustain intellectually, are usually won. An airline paying its pilots an average of £8,000 a year for flying 707s can expect to pay the same pilots at least £12,000 to do a similar, or easier, job on a 747. This is in addition to the cost of his conversion training on the ground and in the air.

Crew costs vary widely from country to country, even for flying the same type of aircraft on the same route. At the beginning of the 1970s the average annual earnings of pilots employed by Pan American was $30,000; British Overseas Airways Corporation, $14,000; Air-India, $9,300; Iberia (Spain) Airlines, $18,200; United Arab, $10,000; East African Airways (mostly expatriate Europeans), $11,200; LAV (Venezuela), $11,000; and KLM, $27,000.

Airline pilots are among the highest-paid professional members of society in most countries. They are highly paid in relation to the senior management and board members of their own airline. Their responsibilities are high; their working life — retirement at the age of 55 in most countries — is relatively short; their hours and domestic lives are usually irregular; and unlike members of most professions their technical competence and medical condition are regularly examined, usually twice a year, failing which they lose their licences.

The industrial bargaining power of airline pilots is very great. They can make idle aircraft costing $20 million or $30 million. (So of course can baggage loaders and maintenance staff.) Yet despite big pay increases, flight-crew cost per seat-km remains remarkably constant.

Some airlines, notably in America, pay an annual salary plus a rate per flying hour. At the beginning of the 1970s crew costs of American 707s and DC-8s were $200 an hour, or less than half total flight operations costs; a smaller trijet 727 crew cost $160 per hour; and the crew of a twinjet One-Eleven $140 per hour.

Traditionally safe airlines may spend up to 2 per cent of their total expenditure each year on crew training — checking, refreshers and type conversions. This cost goes up to as high as 5 per cent when a new airliner type is introduced. Training expenditure is then particularly heavy, and it is common accounting practice to amortise it as a development cost over the introductory period of the new equipment — say three years.

The law varies from country to country, but the International Civil Aviation Organisation recommends that all pilots shall be tested every six months for their ability to handle the aircraft in normal and emergency situations and for their knowledge of procedures. Simulators which reproduce exactly the flight deck of a particular type of airliner, and respond to pilot actions exactly as the aircraft itself does, can cost two or three million dollars. The cost of using big aircraft for crew

175

training, and the revenue-earning hours lost, is uneconomic, and taking airliners to all the limits required for thorough pilot-training can also be hazardous.

Crew-training costs also have to take into account route-checking flights. The law requires these to ensure that a pilot is familiar with the airports to which he is flying and with the diversion alternatives designated for weather or other reasons. Some airlines make much use of films for route training. For best economy an airline will arrange its live route-training so that instructors accompany and observe the performance of flight crews in service. Base training is best carried out at an airport unrestricted by traffic or weather and where favourable bulk-discount landing fees can be negotiated.

The economics of training may be summed up by the air-safety motto that an airline's best investment is a well trained pilot.

More than half the total flight operations bill goes in fuel costs — rather less than half in the case of the shorter-haul airline with twinjet and trijet rather than four-jet aircraft. The four-engined DC-8s and 707s were costing about $250 per hour in fuel at the beginning of the 1970s; trijet 727s, $175; twinjet One-Elevens, $120 — and all these costs were trebled after the oil crisis of 1973-74. Since fuel accounts for up to 30 per cent of total direct expenses, even small fuel economies matter.

A good pilot and flight operations department will flight-plan to achieve the best fuel economy. Some pilots take the trouble — air-traffic control permitting — to get a take-off clearance before starting engines, and go for the most economical power-settings, speeds and altitudes. They can save their airlines the equivalent of their own salaries in fuel costs over the year.

Landing and en route charges are sometimes accounted for under station costs, but they are more logically thought of as a flight-operations cost. They are usually levied by government or airport authorities to pay for runways, lighting and air traffic control services, and all the other airport operating facilities. Some countries provide their national airlines with airport navigation services free of charge — a hidden subsidy which has always made comparisons of international airline costs a risky business. Fees not only vary widely: they change frequently. In the early 1970s New York Kennedy charged a 747 operator just over £100 according to the weight scale (a flat rate per thousand lb); a ramp parking charge during rush hours of more than £80 an hour; porterage (about the same at all hours); £330 for "general terminal and inspection space" charges; and 52p an hour for rubbish burning. Typical total: well over £500.

For the same aircraft at London Heathrow the charge is nearly £700 depending on whether it is an international or a domestic flight. This includes a £120 airport ATC services charge. If the aircraft goes on to land in Switzerland it will be charged just over half the Heathrow fee.

Landing and en-route charges account for about 8 per cent of operating cost for a short-haul airline compared with 5 per cent for a long-haul operator. This entitles the airlines to demand that safety standards are the highest. These costs put the safe airline in a strong position to campaign for good air traffic control, full landing aids, well maintained runways, well trained and equipped rescue services, and proper security checks of passengers before embarkation.

Maintenance and Overhaul About 15 per cent of an airline's budget is spent on Maintenance and Overhaul. The objective is to keep the fleet flying at revenue-earning times at high utilisaton while fulfilling the safety requirements of the Maintenance Schedule. This document, part of the certificate of airworthiness, lays down the checks that must be made, and "lifes" each component according to its reliability in service. In the early days, up to the mid-1950s and in some airlines later, component changes had to be done at stated overhaul intervals: Check 1 every 100 hours, Check 2 every 400 hours, Check 3 every 800 hours, and the big Check 4 — requiring the airliner to be out of service for some days — every 1,600 hours.

As aircraft became more expensive the economic need for higher utilisation became greater. At the same time component reliability increased. The system of progressive maintenance, or "little-and-often" maintenance, kept the fleet flying, while "on-condition" rather than "hard-time" component changes kept costs down. But this requires a highly organised and costly engineering department with advanced inspection and data-analysis facilities.

For the engineering department of a big airline a computer is a necessary investment. There are so many components with different and variable inspection lives, and highly paid staff to be employed efficiently and at times when the customers do not want to fly, that record-keeping and condition-monitoring get beyond the capacity of charts and chalk. The computer keeps a check on component failures and helps more scientific analysis of component reliability and condition, and hence inspection times, spares investment, overhaul lives, and safety.

The ultimate is "on-condition" or let-well-alone maintenance. The routine stripping and rebuilding of components can actually induce failure. On condition maintenance demands, to be safe, not only thorough and expensive inspection but also computer records of each component's behaviour. There must be the closest co-operation between the airline, the manufacturer and the airworthiness authority.

The priority objective of maintenance is safety. The economic objective is to achieve the highest safety standard at the minimum cost, including the loss of revenue when the aircraft is on the ground. Both demand the highest component reliability.

The airline accountant's favourite failure is the "allowable deficiency," the defect which does not ground the airliner and which the airworthiness authority will allow to be fixed at the next convenient check or on return to base. If an airliner has three inertial platforms for its navigation system, can it depart with one found to be unserviceable during the pre-flight check? The answer may be yes if the mean time between failures (MTBF) of the particular platform is high enough for a second failure to be unlikely. This is a safety judgement, and it requires MTBF records which call for a highly developed and expensive engineering department.

Specialist maintenance companies and other airlines will do contract maintenance for airlines which are yet too small for an elaborate engineering department. But the economic case for engineering independence becomes strong quite early in an airline's growth.

Most big airlines overhaul almost every component, including engines and instruments, and have facilities such as engine test beds, clean rooms, laboratories and electronic test equipment of factory standard. Only the most specialised electronics go back to the manufacturer.

As self-maintenance increases so does the spares stock. A small airline may carry spares worth 20 per cent of, say, a three-ship fleet, though an airline with 100 aircraft of the same type will need only about 10 per cent.

A typical spare-engine holding for an airline that does its own engine overhaul is one for every five installed. Costing £½ million or more per unit for the big subsonic airliners and more for supersonic airliners, engines have to be stocked sparingly. Their design and installation are such that a change can be done by ten men in two hours. Modular construction permits whole sections like turbines or compressors to be drawn out and changed on-wing.

Spare engines cannot be positioned at key stations all round the world, as they were in the early days. If an aircraft is stranded down the route it is usually more economic to transfer the passengers to another flight or even to another airline. Engine-out ferrying of empty aircraft back to base is not recommended. The airline usually flies out a spare engine from base. If the airline is a member of a spares club, it may call upon the nearest member for help.

Parts pools are becoming more common as spares of all kinds get costlier. Spare engines are moved around the world by specialist air-cargo operators, with which airline companies have contracts, or they may be clipped under the wing of the next company aircraft scheduled down the route. The sight of "five-engined" 747s, 707s or DC-8s is quite common.

INDIRECT COSTS are more difficult to quantify. They include station costs, passenger services, ticketing, sales and promotion, administration and general. These include the areas in which economy measures are applied when times are hard. In times of inflation especially, "frills" must give way to safety costs and holding fare levels.

Station costs are a major item, accounting for about 20 per cent of a short-haul airline's total expenses, though they are not such a high proportion of a long-haul airline's costs. Much depends on the quality of service given to the passenger and cargo shipper. It may be cheaper to sub-contract traffic and baggage handling to specialist companies at the airport; but this becomes uneconomic if the airline has to employ supervisory staff to maintain customer-service standards. There is a point at which the job can be done more cheaply and better by the airline's own staff. Some airlines feel strongly that the airport's role should be merely that of landlord.

Some airports prefer to provide all apron services. Other airports, especially in the USA, encourage airlines actually to design, build and operate their own terminal buildings. New York Kennedy, for example, has a dozen private airline company terminals. Given the traffic volume and service frequency, airlines which handle their own traffic services are generally the ones with the lowest levels of station cost and highest standards of customer service.

Passenger services The cost of all staff and facilities directly concerned with passengers comes under this heading. So does the cost of in-flight food, and of hotels and transport when flights are delayed.

Passenger-service costs can account for anything up to ten per cent of an airline's total costs. An airline may spend perhaps £3,000 per stewardess on safety training, a cost which has to be amortised over the average girl's career, which is typically two or three years. Several incidents involving emergency evacuations and hijackers have proved the value of investing in well trained cabin crew.

Ticketing, Sales and Promotion account for at least 15 per cent of an airline's costs. Ticketing and reservations staff, like cabin and traffic personnel, are the first guardians of an airline's goodwill, and have to be paid for. Commission on tickets sold by travel agents usually comes under this heading. Probably 60 per cent of the airline industry's tickets are sold by agents, although some US airlines sell nine out of ten of their tickets themselves. Commission is typically 5 per cent for domestic scheduled services and 7-7½ per cent for scheduled international tickets. "Commission wars" have unofficially increased these to as much as 15 per cent on routes like the North Atlantic.

The scheduled airlines have big advertising budgets to persuade the public to buy tickets. Because fares and airliners are always much the same, airline advertising has to be ingenious to differentiate the product. Anything up to 15 per cent of the price of a scheduled-service ticket is accounted for by advertising and promotion.

Administration Under the heading Administration and General, accounting for about 5 per cent of total operating cost, go all the expenses incurred in the general administration of an airline. None falls specifically under any of the foregoing headings. Such costs include headquarters buildings and office equipment, management information services, personnel, accounting and medical services, board members' salaries and expenses, legal representation, subscriptions to trade and professional organisations like Iata, and corporate rather than operating costs.

CAPITAL An airline obtains its capital from private shareholders, banks, governments, or from combinations of these sources.

Nearly a third of Iata's 100 or more members are wholly owned by individual shareholders or banks; over a third are wholly State-owned; and the rest are of mixed ownership.

The privately owned members of Iata include all the American international airlines, all but one of the Canadian companies, and a number of Latin American operators. The European international members of Iata which are wholly privately owned are few: they include British Caledonian and Icelandair. Swissair is more than half privately owned. Significant non-European private Iata airlines are Mexicana and Philippine Airlines.

Among the best known international airlines with mixed ownership — though with a majority of State capital — are Air France, Alitalia, Lufthansa, Japan Air Lines, KLM, Sabena, and SAS.

The wholly State-owned members of Iata include Aer Lingus, Air Canada, Air-India, Air New Zealand, British Airways, East African Airways, Iberia, Iran Air, Iraqi Airways, Qantas, South African Airways, New Zealand National Airways, and Trans-Australia Airlines.

The capital in Iata is mainly private because of the predominance of the US members. But the majority membership numerically is State-financed. The 400 or more other world airlines which are not members

180

of Iata — some of them big — are mainly privately financed. Taking the total world air transport effort, the majority of finance, perhaps 75 per cent, is still from private sources, though the trend is towards State participation.

Whatever the source of capital the same financial disciplines theoretically apply, though the normal yardstick of return on investment does not fairly measure the performance of an airline which is operated, as many are, to provide a public or national service, to fly routes which do not have enough traffic to attract private capital, or to show the flag.

Airlines raise their capital, as do other industries, by means of equity or debt, or both. Equity capital is obtained by internally generated funds or by selling shares (or stocks as Americans call them) to investors. Ordinary shareholders receive a dividend decided by the company's board according to profits and trading conditions. In good years the dividends are high, and the company is in a strong position to raise more capital for expansion by issuing more ordinary shares.

Equity Capital in effect decides ownership. Shares may be held by members of the public, corporate investors such as insurance companies, or by governments. Equity capital is not recoverable by the investor from the airline unless it goes bankrupt and is wound up, when what is left after payment of debts to creditors is distributed to investors.

Loan Capital is raised by borrowing at fixed-interest rates. The biggest lenders in the airline business are banks and governments. The terms on which they lend vary widely. In general the lender wants interest and security. The borrower wants terms which allow him to buy the aircraft of his choice and to make a profit operating them while accepting that he must pay the fixed interest regardless of trading conditions.

Commercial lenders often retain the title to aircraft as security. The airline might even mortgage other property, or obtain government guarantees of their loan. Lenders do not want ownership or control, though in practice they can strongly influence management, especially if they hold the title to the fleet. Aircraft are a sound investment for lending institutions, and can usually be sold or leased profitably. Loan capital may also be raised by preference shares or debentures or other fixed-interest stock on which the lender has first call in the event of bankruptcy.

Lenders will often insist on a certain level of working capital — cash in hand or which is realisable in the short-term — and on maintaining a balance between Equity and Debt Capital as a condition of a loan.

The Equity/Debt ratio in the airline business rises and falls with the re-equipment cycle, debt exceeding equity as each new generation of airliner is financed, introduced, and paid for. Taking one decade with another the Equity/Debt ratio should not exceed 1:1, but it is becoming nearer 1:2. The traditional airline-industry ratio between Capital and Turnover of 1:1 is also changing. By the early 1970s some of the bigger airlines were finding it difficult to turn their capital over once every two years.

Capital costs are steadily increasing, not only in absolute terms but also relative to revenue. The revenue-earning power of the airliner is diminishing in relation to its capital cost, and airlines are having to invest more and more capital in many other kinds of equipment — reservations computer systems, electronic maintenance equipment, training simulators and so on. Capital for this type of equipment tends to be less realisable, and hence more expensive, than for airliners.

A Capital Turnover (capital divided by revenue) of about 1.5 is normal in the airline business. The industry is not as highly capitalised as some. For example, electricity is about 16, rail 15, shipping 6, road passenger transport 2.5, iron and steel 1.5, general manufacturing industry 2. Capital turnover is not to be confused with Operating Ratio, the relationship between revenue and expenditure.

Aviation's below-average capitalisation may appear surprising considering the high cost of aircraft, the industry's main equipment. But the revenue-earning capacity and resale values of well maintained airliners are high — a fact, incidentally, which attracts newcomers to the business, especially as aircraft, crews and maintenance engineers may usually be hired easily. An airliner should be able to earn much more than its value in revenue a year. The air-transport industry taken as a whole — including airports and air traffic control — is more highly capitalised, probably to the order of 2.

A simplified Balance Sheet for a hypothetical big, efficient and profitable airline with international and domestic services might look like this:

ASSETS *(what has been financed)*		LIABILITIES *(how it has been financed*	
	$ million		$ million
Working capital	129.10	Debt	309.60
Aircraft	503.90	Equity (including accum-	
less depreciation	–157.70	ulated profits)	190.40
	475.30		
Other long-term assets			
(depreciated)	24.70		
	500.00		500.00

Much more detailed is the Balance Sheet standardised by the International Civil Aviation Organisation (Icao's Reporting Form E). It may be regarded as typical of good accounting practice. Simplified, it might be as follows for the same hypothetical, efficient big airline with international and domestic services:

ASSETS	$ million	LIABILITIES	$ million
Current assets		**Current liabilities**	
Working capital: cash, short-term money receivable (i.e. within a year), shop materials, consumable supplies	84.60	All money due out — salaries, wages, interest, ticket balances to other airlines	57.70
Equipment purchase funds		**Unearned transport revenue**	
Money set aside for buying aircraft and other equipment	44.40	Money received for transport not yet provided	7.70
Other special funds		**Deferred Credits**	
Pensions, self-insurance	0.10	Unpaid interest on long-term debts and other accounts	100.50
Aircraft (including all equipment and spares)	503.90	**Reserves**	
Less depreciation	−157.70	Generally broken down into: operating reserves, e.g. money set aside for aircraft modification, insurance and other reserves	30.30
	475.30		
Ground Property	46.60		
Less depreciation (everything other than aircraft) — equipment for passenger services, airports, vehicles, met. services	−27.20	**Advances from affiliated companies**	
	19.40	Any money lent by wholly owned subsidiaries	3.00
Land	0.30	**Other liabilities**	
Investment in affiliated companies		Any other debts not otherwise provided for	3.00
Affiliated companies, sometimes known as subsidiaries, are those wholly owned; associated companies are those in which the airline holds stock without control	0.20	**Long-term debt**	
		All borrowings — debentures, bonds, trust certificates, mortgages	107.40
Deferred charges		**Capital stock**	
Mostly the cost of training for a new fleet and other costs properly chargeable to the future	2.70	The par value of all equity in the hands of the public or governments	67.40
Intangible assets		Capital surplus	
Goodwill, patents	0.10	Excess over par value of shares sold	22.30
		Retained profits	
		From the Profit and Loss Account (after tax)	

183

Other assets			plus accumulated profits	
Includes investments in			from last year's balance	
associated companies	2.00		sheet	100.70
TOTAL ASSETS	500.00		**TOTAL LIABILITIES**	500.00

Finally, the standard Icao Profit and Loss Statement†, which shows the year's operating result, may be simplified as follows:

PROFIT AND LOSS

Revenues

Scheduled services
Passenger
Excess baggage
Cargo
Mail
Non-scheduled services
Incidental

TOTAL OPERATING REVENUES

Expenses

Flight operations
Flight crew
Fuel
Insurance
Rental
Crew-training
Other flight expenses
Maintenance and overhaul
Depreciation and amortisation*
Station and other ground expenses**
Passenger services
Ticketing, sales and promotion
General and administrative
Other operating expenses

TOTAL OPERATING EXPENSES

Operating result

After further non-operating items, of which one of the most important and interesting is Direct Subsidies from Public Funds, the profit and loss before and after tax is stated.

---

*A separate statement is required by Icao covering flight and ground equipment, and amortisation of development and pre-operating costs including crew-training.
**Including landing and en-route charges.
†Icao Air Transport reporting Form F, simplified.

SUBTLE CORPORATE INCAPACITATION The relationship between the safety of an airline and its economic strength cannot be proved by accident statistics. There is some evidence that airlines suffer accidents after prolonged financial distresss (for example, Pan American in 1973 and 1974). The airline industry knows that safe airlines are financially strong airlines. Financial weakness rarely affects safety directly. Even "cowboy" operators, of which there will always be some, know that crashes hurt business — not to mention their own necks. Owners who "cut corners" — who tear out Technical Log defect reports instead of fixing them and who push pilots to carry Class A ("no-go") snags or to exceed duty times — are the cowboys who have always flown that way, and got away with it. Financial weakness has a more subtle effect on the professional airline and in fact might be described as "subtle corporate incapacitation".

An operator enters the business with a loan, perhaps from a bank or tour company. Ticket deposits at the start of the season help to finance the operation, including staff wages. The aircraft rent, maintenance and fuel bills, airport landing fees and so on, down to the office cleaners, will be fully paid at the end of the season at the latest. All is well while business is good. But if traffic falls short of expectations, working capital has to be raised on the more speculative expectation of the following year's traffic.

Now the bank or tour operator starts to demand a bigger say in the running of the airline in which it has so much at risk. It calls for cuts here and cuts there, with little understanding of the operation. The staff, especially pilots and engineers, sense trouble. Morale declines. Management becomes more and more evasive and preoccupied with the commercial crisis, leaving the safety professionals increasingly unsettled about their problems. Staff start to leave, and management refuses to replace them. As a result heads of departments such as flight operations and maintenance come under ever greater stress. Maintenance, crew-roster and training schedules and records become disordered. Accounts fall further and further behind. A general atmosphere of shambles pervades the operation. Morale and discipline, on which safety so much depends, decline. Auditors, creditors and government safety inspectors become less and less tolerant.

This is the atmosphere in which financially weak airlines can become vulnerable to accidents. But financial weakness does not always affect safety. Even airlines which have gone bankrupt have remained operationally immaculate until the last. Many pilots and engineers who have actually experienced the financial demise of an airline will testify that safety was never allowed to become the victim of subtle corporate incapacitation.

19 The Airline Pilot

In a letter to *The Times* (September 23, 1975) an airline captain — in a controversy about psychiatric tests for pilots — writes:

> I am an airline pilot and I like my job. Twice a year I have to be medically examined, each time with an ECG and all at my expense. This I accept. Twice a year I have to demonstrate my professional competence in normal and emergency conditions. This I accept.
>
> I can expect a spot check, either by a CAA inspector or a training captain on any flight, specifically to report on my competence. I have a co-pilot whose duty is to monitor all my actions and vice versa. All my radio transmissions are on tape and cockpit voice recorders are on the way. I have been called to account for a certain decision (correct as it happened) picked up a month later during a random check of a flight data recorder.
>
> I have a *legal obligation* to assess and not to fly if I am suffering from fatigue. I am not allowed, rightly, to drink at any time during my working period nor in the eight hour period before it. Failure on my part medically or professionally, at any time, will leave me without a livelihood.
>
> Lastly, I have to retire ten years earlier than anyone else, at age 55, so that there can be no question of an "old dodderer" being in charge, insisting that he can still operate...

SELECTION As pilots reach retiring age, normally 55, a great deal of irreplaceable safety — the safety which simulators cannot supply — is lost to the airline industry. Training, however good, cannot give a pilot the airmanship which comes only from a lifetime spent flying all types of aircraft in all conditions. But today's young pilots are generally as good technically as their 20,000 hour fathers in the left-hand seat. They learn fast and work hard, and their technical training is generally admitted by the older pilots to be better, especially their knowledge of aircraft design and engineering. Knowing what to do in a bad moment comes from such technical knowledge as well as from airmanship and experience.

An exceptional pilot takes about 15 years to achieve captaincy of a big jet airliner. Starting training at about 18, he typically attends ground and flying school for two years, flying light piston-engined twins and singles. He may start flying the line as P3, as Second Officer in the third seat, gradually obtaining the experience to become a First Officer and P2. Having graduated to First Officer and co-pilot of the larger jets he may spend perhaps seven or eight years before he achieves captaincy and command, usually of a smaller airliner.

Military processes of selection and training produce pilots of the highest calibre almost regardless of cost. Air force selection procedures, and the psychological and physical aptitude tests, are particularly demanding. In some countries, though not in Britain, the air force is a major source of pilots, Israeli and Swiss pilots fly for both the national airline and the air force. But the college-trained civil pilot is good too. There is usually no difference between an ex-military pilot and an *ab initio* civil colleague within three or four years. Military pilots have to "unlearn" in the civil cockpit, especially if they have been in combat rather than in transport squadrons.

"We are selecting potential captains," says a senior British Airways captain, "and they have to be good even to begin flying at Hamble." The Hamble course lasts about 19 months and takes the man to CPL and instrument rating, but he can be "scrubbed" on his conversion course within the airline.

The cost of training a pilot from selection to first revenue-earning operation is nowadays about $50,000.

CREW RISK How hazardous is the job of airline pilot? Although the world's leading insurance companies no longer increase premiums for those who travel by airline, airline crews are still considered a slightly higher than average risk by most of the insurance world. The crew fatality rate for eight selected leading airlines is 0.8 per million aircraft hours flown. This represents a threefold fall since 1960.

Assuming that the average crew-member flies 10,000 hours in his or her career — more for flight-crew, less for cabin-crew — the life-time risk is therefore just under 1 per cent, flying for a leading airline. The risk rates of jobs generally accepted as hazardous are coal-mining, 2 per cent; building construction, 5 per cent; trawler-fishing, 5 per cent.

On world scheduled airline services between 50 and 100 crew-members are killed each year. The actual number has tended to come down from just under 100 in the early 1960s to around 75 in the 1970s, despite more flights. The annual number of crew injuries on scheduled services averages about 20. Up to 30 per cent of the crew members on average survive an accident. This survival rate is tending to improve.

The distance flown by a crew member before he or she becomes a statistical fatality is increasing each year, approaching 75 million km in the 1970s compared with 30 million km in the 1960s. The crew-member's chances of being involved in a fatal crash, though he may not be killed himself, diminished from 1 in 150 million km in the 1960s to 1 in 300 million km in the 1970s.

In terms of sectors flown, crew deaths approach an average of 1 in 90,000 in the 1970s compared with 1 in less than 60,000 in the 1960s. Sectors flown per fatal aircraft accident (not necessarily killing the crew) are around 400,000 in the 1970s compared with 200,000 in the 1960s.

Hours flown by a crew-member before a fatal crash went up from over 500,000 in the 1960s to 600,000 during the 1970s. This is a fatality rate of about 1.6 per million hours, or double that achieved by eight leading airlines (see above). Nevertheless, taking the world's scheduled airlines as a whole, if a crew-member averages 600 hours of flying time a year he or she can expect to be involved in a fatal crash — not necessarily killed — once in 1,000 years.

TRAINING Those responsible for air safety are finding it more and more difficult to define major areas for remedial action. The machine becomes more and more capable, reliable and foolproof, and yet the human being is still the same old Mk 1 model. His relationship with the machine is far from understood. We are told that machines can eliminate human error, but we know that this is not true. Aircraft continue to fly into the ground — extremely rarely, but with disastrous consequences when they do.

The trouble is not with machines, but with men, and especially with their training. The accident statistics illustrate the truth of the dictum that an airline's best safety investment is a well trained pilot. Of 250 accidents to five types of subsonic jet transport in about 25 million flying hours, half have been attributed to pilot error. Pilots often feel that design error or the failure of the aircraft or air traffic control system contributes to their mistakes. Just over a further third of the 250 accidents surveyed were caused by engineering failure, design deficiency (the majority) or maintenance fault — though accidents are difficult to categorise because they are almost always caused by a combination of failures.

Pilot fatigue usually does not appear in any of the usual accident lists. It may sometimes be a contributory cause, especially at the end of a difficult and long flight.

The percentage of accidents attributed to "pilot error" appears to diminish with experience of an aircraft type, falling from about 80 per cent of all incidents during the first two years of a new type's service career to 30 per cent after ten years. The average rate of pilot error remains at least 50 per cent.

The approach and landing are still the most vulnerable phases of flight, and by diminishing the human element automatic landing systems are theoretically reducing the risk of human error. But care has to be taken that pilots do not become bored machine-minders who, when the machine fails, are at a loss.

SIMULATORS have become a technology of their own, capable of duplicating not only the cockpit layout but also motion, turbulence, sink, wind shear, terrain, approach lights, snow and ice on the runway, engine note, and even the bump of the wheels and braking deceleration on touchdown. The simulator is so like the real thing, and so readily capable of "action replay," that airlines and safety authorities now accept it as a better trainer in most — but not all — respects than the aircraft.

Simulators are a good safety investment, taking pilots to performance limits such as a double engine cut which, in the air, would risk structural failure or loss of control. The simulator can actually give the pilot a more realistic impression of the asymmetric control forces; idling thrust after a power cutback in the air produces less of a shock than a real power failure.

The first man to set foot on the Moon, Neil Armstrong, afterwards said that the approach and landing were "just like the simulator." The final airline type-conversion flight, especially engine-out take-offs and landings, gives the pilot confidence and adjusts him psychologically to the fact that it is indeed "just like a simulator."

Another advantage of simulators is that they do not disturb airport communities. If all simulator training suddenly stopped, airport-base training would dramatically increase aircraft movements, and hence noise, to the point at which public protest would be militant against all operations. By their nature training flights are noisier than routine services, involving go-arounds, overshoots and repeated circuits and approaches. Fuel consumption would also be unacceptable and the effect of training on the aircraft structure (stalling, for example, causes the airframe to shake quite violently) would seriously reduce fatigue life. All this is in addition to the cost of keeping expensive airliners off revenue-earning operations.

Crosswind training may be delayed for days and even weeks waiting for the right winds to blow: in the simulator crosswinds can be fed in on demand, and can be much stronger than the 10kt or so which is a typical requirement on the actual aircraft. On the simulator starting at 15kt and going up to 30kt on a "slippery" runway is possible.

Another type of training done more and more on the simulator is the abandoned take-off or "accelerate-stop." A typical requirement is for the trainee to accelerate to V_1 (the "decision speed" below which the take-off must be abandoned if there is an engine failure) and immediately before V_1 to have an engine failure (one engine being throttled back by the instructor). There is debate about the meaning of "immediately". Should it be 1kt before V_1 or 10kt? The cloer to V_1 the more realistic the experience, but the greater the hazard and the wear and tear on wheels, tyres and brakes in the actual aircraft.

The higher the braking speed and aircraft weight the higher the energy absorbed by the brakes. A graph plotting braking speed against weight for the Boeing 707, for example, shows that anything up to 15 million ft/lb requires seven minutes' cooling for each million ft/lb. Anything up to 18m requires a minimum of 1½hr cooling followed by an inspection. After 18m the fire service must be called; and fire or not, all tyres and brakes must be changed.

Pilots argue that even V_1 minus 10kt is hazardous and that all accelerate-stop training is better done on the simulator. The object is in any case to test the student's reaction time, not the strength of his calf muscles or of the aircraft brakes.

Lufthansa's training procedure is to check all pilots six times a year in the simulator and in the aircraft. Pilots have two checks down the line, two base checks, and two simulator checks. The West German airline's view is that the pilot who is perfect in the simulator is perfect in the aircraft. Lufthansa's chief pilot considers that nowadays the comprehensive simulator with visual aids "gives it all — even better than the aircraft itself."

British Airways European Division (ED) used to hold the view that a pilot should be able to demonstrate his ability to handle an aircraft in any situation that he might ever have to face — flapless landings, two-engine-out approaches, and so on. But, says a senior captain, "if we do practise them on the aircraft we will sooner or later have an accident. Anyone can do an emergency descent, but if you keep on doing it somebody is one day going to hit something and he will become a statistic. We used to do three-engine training with one feathered. Of course one day somebody pulled back the wrong engine."

TriStar captains convert from the Trident after about 16 hours on the simulator and a four-hour check of "normal emergencies" in the air. Base checks include one-engine-out approaches and landings, but even stalls are now done on the simulator together will all two-engine-out situations, Dutch rolls, and emergency descents. The stall can be taken further on the simulator than in flight, well beyond the stall warning.

INCIDENTS AND WARNINGS Each airline has its own incident-reporting procedure, voluntary as well as compulsory. Each airline, and especially its flight crew, has views on the value of cockpit warnings.

Lufthansa requires its pilots to report all incidents, but is not in favour of anonymous reporting. The chief pilot wants to know who the pilot is, especially if a human problem is involved.

The West German airline believes in the use of the flight-data recorder (FDR) as a source of incident information, but is careful to avoid giving pilots the feeling "of a big electronic brother watching over them." FDR results give information about, for example, descent rates of more than 1,000ft/min at four miles or closer to the runway. FDRs can establish trends, and warn pilots about them without losing their confidence and provoking fear of discipline. Lufthansa is wary of relying on too many warning systems in aircraft. It advises pilots that, as aircraft become more and more technically reliable, the crew must be aware that aircraft systems can still go wrong.

Pilots should not depend solely on warning systems. The Ground Proximity Warning System (GPWS) (see Chapter 20) can lead to complacency about descent and terrain-checking disciplines, in Lufthansa's view.

On the old piston-engined airliners there was almost certain to be a snag of some sort on every flight. Nowadays pilots have to guard against assumptions of technical infallibility. The airline industry as a whole, feels Lufthansa, must find ways of making pilots more aware of the need to be alert, and to have a healthy mistrust even of perfect aircraft.

Are there nowadays too many warnings? Are pilots being lulled into a false sense of security by the reliability of the modern machine? A senior British Airways captain feels that the best way to guard against this "is to ensure throughout training that pilots keep their minds on the basic airmanship virtues — watching attitude, speed, horizontal situation — all the things that will keep you out of trouble."

On warning systems in general British Airways is concerned about the number of different sounds — for example, 12 different kinds of horn and chime. This can saturate the pilot's senses, making it difficult to remember which warning is which. "The single master warning system is essential, with perhaps one or two 'discrete' tones, perhaps for fire or autopilot disconnect. There is still a lot of work to be done under the general heading of ergonomics," says a senior pilot.

In general, visual systems are easier to disregard, "though aural warnings which can be cancelled can degrade safety." It is debatable whether warning systems that can be cancelled are in fact true warnings. A classic example is the undercarriage warning horn which can be cancelled and also confused with a different warning. One British

Airways captain has even seen a manufacturer's test pilot attempt to cancel an altitude alert chime which he had mistaken for an undercarriage warning horn. "If the GPWS cries wolf it will be disregarded, like the stick-shaker warning or the configuration warning light."

British Airways has a formal procedure for reporting incidents to Group Air Safety, an office independent of flight operations and engineering which investigates the incidents, presents the results and makes recommendations. In addition European Division has an anonymous incident-reporting procedure. A senior captain says: "We take no steps to discover the identity of anonymous reporters, because the system produces information we wouldn't otherwise get." British Airways European Division's air safety adviser admits that anonymous reports can sometimes pose a problem because they are "uninvestigatable"; but he agrees that the advantages of the anonymous incident-reporting system outweigh the disadvantages.

There is a senior ED captain for each aircraft type. To him the line pilots can write or talk in confidence about incidents, knowing that their names will not be revealed in any circumstances to the flight manager. There is a code of honour about this which applies even if the incident was a serious one. No pressure is put on this "father-confessor" captain to disclose names. There is nothing too watertight about the system; no form-filling is involved, and the important thing is that "we don't break faith."

The value of anonymous reporting must not be got out of perspective. British Airways considers that "exceedence" reports from flight data recorders (FDRs) can be of the greatest importance.* Agreement has been reached with the pilots' union Balpa that no disciplinary action will be taken solely on the basis of FDR, though it can be used as back-up evidence in disciplinary cases. Cassettes do not have pilots' names on them. "FDR has sometimes been used actually to make the case," says a senior captain, "but this is not the way to use it."

He believes that the bulk of pilots accept FDR monitoring, especially the younger ones. "They know that we are looking for trends — heavy landings, high sink rates, and so on. The FDR information is more than fascinating, especially when you can see the reactions to measures we have taken. You can see the effect of a change in procedure after a few months by watching FDR. An example was when we changed the Gibraltar approach procedures. FDR, in my view, is one of the most promising incident-reporting areas, and we are still learning."

But FDR-monitoring cannot work if there is ever a suspicion that it

*Computer print-outs each day of each aircraft FDR underline any limits which may have been exceeded.

will be used as a "cudgel, a sort of electronic big brother." British Airways gives FDR presentations to pilots. "FDR gives us a sort of route check of every flight. It helps us to know the state of the airline."

FLIGHT-TIME LIMITATIONS The law of each State is defined to ensure that no crew-member engaged on a flight for the purpose of public transport is subjected to excessive fatigue. The law requires the aircraft operator to include in his manuals details of flight-duty limitations, taking into account the particular circumstances of his operation.

Rest and duty periods vary widely from state to state, from airline to airline, and even within airlines. Obviously, a pilot who makes half a dozen or more landings a trip in bad weather or in darkness is likely to get tired more quickly than a long-haul pilot making perhaps one or two landings a day assisted by a crew.

Typical of flight-time limitations are those of the British and Americans, whose pilots are represented by strong unions, and whose airline operations are the most varied. In general the British require a minimum rest period of 10 hours for a duty period of 10 hours preceding it. Thereafter duty-rest cycles are "half-an-hour per hour." After a duty period of 18 hours a 20-hour rest is required, and so on up to 24 hours, after which a 32-hour rest is required.

Various factors have to be taken into account by the airline's planning department, and by crew members themselves, to ensure that the normal human 16-hour/8-hour/16-hour waking/sleeping/waking pattern is not grossly disrupted, bearing in mind the irregular nature of an airline crew's work, involving "unsocial" hours. Allowance must be made in planning for the time-zone changes which mean that crews have to sleep outside the sleeping time of the local community. Quietness is then a difficult condition to achieve, and special importance is attached to the selection of quiet accommodation.

Human beings are conditioned to a 24-hour body rhythm normally related to local time. Adapting to changes of local time following eastward or westward air travel — so called "jet lag" — takes place fairly slowly, some days being required for complete adaptation to changes of more than a few hours. Disturbances of body functions occur, and sleep is difficult. Special rearrangement of the waking/sleeping/waking cycle is necessary to adjust the crew members' "body time" to the local time. Where airport-to-hotel travelling times exceed one hour each way away from base, rest periods of up to 12 hours should, according to British regulations, be increased by the excess amount.

The aim should be to roster crews so that they have a clear break of at least 36 hours, including two nights, at least once a week. A time-zone change of four or more hours should, under British regulations, be followed by a rest period of not less than 12 hours. In general, crew-members should not be scheduled for more than two successive night-flying duty periods (that is to say flights ending after 0030hr local time) unless they have rested for at least 24 hours before the first of the two night-duty periods.

Single-pilot crews of smaller airliners are limited to a maximum period of 10 hours, with the statutory limit at 11. These periods can be increased by two hours if a continuous break of at least five hours is taken.

In the case of crews with two or more pilots, flight-duty periods are limited to a maximum of 15 hours with an absolute limit of 16 hours.

Allowances are made for the number of sectors flown, typically one hour for up to six sectors. Allowances may be reduced where a crew-member's workload is relieved by another crew-member.

A British pilot may not fly an airliner if he has flown more than 100 hours in the previous 28 consecutive days; and he may not fly if he has exceeded 900 hours in the previous 12 months.

Operators are required to keep detailed particulars of all crew flight-times.

An American airline pilot may not fly more than 30 hours in any seven consecutive days; more than 100 hours in any calendar month; or more than 1,000 hours in any calendar year. A pilot who has flown more than eight hours during 24 consecutive hours must have at least 18 hour rest.

The above rules apply to one-pilot or two-pilot crews; if there is an additional flight-crew member a pilot may fly up to 12 hours in any 24 consecutive hours, but may not fly more than 120 hours in any 30 consecutive days.

Captains are allowed discretion to continue or to cancel a flight depending on circumstances. As in ordinary life, fatigue is a matter of sense and personal discipline. Flight-time limitations are based on the commonsense fact that after a 16-hour day a man is ready for eight hours sleep, or more if his day has been tiring, or if meals and sleep have been disrupted by time-zone changes.

The Icao standards usually form the basis of national laws. States in turn usually delegate to the airline, through mandatory flight-time limitations, the maximum legal working hours. These are not the hours which pilots actually work. The limits may be reached for short periods, but over the whole year an airline pilot's average duty hours will rarely reach half the, say, 1,200 hours typically permitted.

Some airlines permit their pilots to free-lance as air-taxi or commuter-airline pilots in their time off, provided they "log" their times and include them in the total limits.

CREW COMPLEMENT Crewing requirements of public transport aircraft are generally related by law to their maximum weight. Typically, airliners below a take-off weight of 5,700kg, 12,500lb, may be operated with one pilot. All others must be operated with two or more. Usually only short-haul aircraft — say those operated over sectors of 1,500km — will be operated with a crew of two, both qualified as navigator and radio officer. Longer-haul aircraft will carry a crew of at least three and usually four, including a specialist flight engineer.

The specialist navigator is gradually being replaced by automatic navigation systems operated by the pilots. Pushbuttons, selectors, displays or even maps are packaged in small units on the pilot's instrument panel.

The specialist flight engineer also is being displaced by automation. The engineering content of each new airliner gets more complex, but technology and the computer have simplified the control function to the point where more and more of the flight engineer's job is being done by pilots. Electronics technology in particular has greatly extended human control, making systems more reliable and controls simpler. Check-lists can be done automatically, thanks to the computer, which can also find and diagnose systems faults. It can even check itself. Cabin air-conditioning, pressurisation, engine control and fuel management are becoming largely automatic.

Whether or not a flight engineer is carried is a company decision. The airworthiness authority may merely specify that the officer operating the engineering panel has to be qualified. Thus he may well be a pilot rather than a specialist engineer — though he will not have had the engineering background which the flight-engineering profession insists is indispensable. Concorde's crew includes a full-time professional flight engineer.

The case for a flight engineer was strongly argued by the profession after a very heavy landing in Cyprus by a three-pilot Boeing 707. Inspection revealed damage. The local station engineer declined to agree that the aircraft was fit for flight. But it was flown, the incident being entered in the Technical Log as a "firm" landing. This could never have happened if a flight engineer had been included in the crew complement, argued the profession.

As technology makes the job of flight engineer and navigator increasingly that of monitor, economic pressures force crew numbers down. Yet the value of specialists may be apparent on the long-haul airliner, which may operate in areas where navigation aids are sparse and overnight check facilities limited. Manufacturers recognise the competitive operating-cost savings of cockpits laid out for two-pilot crews, even in the bigger long-haul aircraft. Boeing has estimated that a two-pilot flight crew can reduce direct operating cost by up to 15 per cent. This is a big and tempting economy — as great as was the turbofan when it replaced the turbojet in the 1960s.

The flight engineer will probably outlast his fellow specialist crew members, the radio officer and navigator. While technology has simplified the cockpit, and the pilot has been trained to know what to do in the event of failure, a specialist systems engineer may diagnose faults and prescribe the correct action more quickly in an emergency; and he can be much more valuable down the route, far from home base, when an unusual technical problem develops.

Will the pilot himself ever be replaced? This is feasible now: unpiloted machines have been landed on other planets. But it is probable that the airline passenger will always feel safer if there are human beings up front monitoring the technology which has made flying so reliable and safe, but which can still go wrong.

CREW HEALTH The safety objective has been defined by aviation doctors as a probability of human medical failure not greater than 10^{-8}, or one in 100,000,000. This could be achieved with present medical knowledge, even though 10^{-8} is ten times more severe than the airworthiness requirements governing the probability of aircraft failure. But this sort of medical safety level could be achieved only by "scrapping" every pilot who had anything the matter with him. This is unacceptable socially and operationally. Airlines cannot afford to throw out experienced and highly trained men without extremely good cause.

Cardiovascular disease is the commonest cause of lost licences, followed by disorders of the mind. Dr Geoffrey Bennett of the UK Civil Aviation Authority believes that mental disorders which come to the doctors' notice is only the tip of the iceberg. "All operations people", he has said, "know the pilots who are having acute domestic crises, and the effect these have on their performance and their liability to make mistakes."

The job of an airline pilot can be very unsettling for a wife, who may dislike the irregular social life, and imagine a threat from the young stewardesses.

Alcohol is a common tranquilizer, as in many walks of life. As a drug it calms the nerves and is often used to help sleep, particularly by aircrew who have to find their rest at all sorts of abnormal hours. The rule in most airlines is that more than 12 hours must elapse between drinking and flying, though an eight-hour period is usually acceptable after moderate drinking. Many doctors say that performance is still affected even 24 hours after heavy drinking; there may be no apparent drunkeness or alcohol on the breath, but reactions are slower. The airline industry has to be more concerned about alcohol than many others. In other jobs a man who achieves nothing in the afternoon after a heavy lunch in the pub, or who arrives at work in the morning with a headache, does not help the company — but he is not a hazard to life.

In general the airline pilot is an extrovert who has always been a social drinker. He has easy access to duty-free liquor, and between flights away from home he may know many hours of boredom. Dr Geoffrey Bennett of the UK Civil Aviation Authority has estimated that about 2 per cent of the world airline industry's employees are alcoholics in the usually accepted sense — people whose social or professional lives are actually impaired by drinking. The mild alcoholics are usually protected by colleagues who will loyally conceal the trouble for long periods. Eventually the man may turn up on duty quite obviously drunk, indicating in a professional that he has become completely careless about the consequences of his drinking. By then it is usually too late to save him.

The airline industry's company doctors fly down the routes with crews and "keep their stethoscopes on the pulse of the airline." They show sympathy for pilots who come to them with personal drinking problems, and give help tactfully and in confidence.

EMOTIONAL DISORDERS There is a relationship between accidents and "life changes", according to work done by the University of Washington and the US Navy. The worst emotional disturbance — weighted as 100 LCU (or Life Change Units) — is the death of a spouse. Of those persons amassing 150-199 LCUs in a given period, more than a third had illnesses within two years. Of those with between 200-299 LCUs, more than half reported health changes; and of those with over 500 LCUs, more than three-quarters had nervous illnesses. On average, health changes followed a personal crisis by one year.

It has often been found that crashes involve outstanding aviators who had been top of their respective classes, but who had been found after accidents to have lost friends, or had problems with wife or sweetheart. The LCUs accumulated in a six-month period prior to their accidents were more than 300 for one pilot and more than 200 for another.

A US Navy psychiatrist has described the typical accident-prone pilot as "quick, decisive, active, impulsive, independent and adventurous — in short the kind of pilot who would impress his flight instructors." The accident process, according to this source, is manifested by errors in all areas — personal, social and professional. A strong moral upbringing, according to the US Navy, produces perfectionist pilots who may be "over-achievers." Such pilots tend to push themselves to the limit, but may not realise that their limits have changed. It is important that their supervisors should know something about their personal lives, and be able to judge the moment to say to such pilots, to avoid offending them: "We know you are good, but do not confuse ability to fly with fitness to fly."

PILOT MEDICAL POLICY "Heart test again fails to avert a fatal air crash," ran the headline. The accident involved an air-taxi aircraft which crashed taking off from Leeds, Bradford, killing eight people. The pilot was found to be suffering from heart disease. So was the captain of British Airways Trident Papa India which crashed near Heathrow in June 1972 with the loss of 118 lives, although nobody will ever be sure that heart disease was a cause of the accident.

The controversy about heart testing is whether pilots should be subjected to a stress electro-cardiograph (ECG) examination as well as the conventional resting ECG. The view of British Airways is that while a stress ECG can be useful in certain circumstances, experience and research show that a good stress ECG result can be proved just as wrong as a bad one. To be of most value a stress ECG requires that the person be "puffed out," on exercise machines and in other ways. This can be unwise and even dangerous under certain circumstances.

MEDICAL LICENCE-TERMINATIONS, BRITISH AIRLINE PILOTS

	1964	65	66	67	68	69	70	71	72	73	Ten-year Total	%
Cardiovascular	9	14	8	12	3	15	20	29	22	41	173	50.0
Cancers	0	2	2	1	3	1	1	2	5	4	21	6.1
Endocrine & metabolic	5	2	0	0	2	1	1	1	0	1	13	3.7
Digestive	0	0	0	3	0	2	1	1	0	0	7	2.0
Musculoskeletal	3	2	0	2	3	0	1	1	1	1	14	4.0
Genito-urinary	0	0	0	0	0	0	0	0	2	0	2	0.6
Nervous	1	2	0	1	1	2	3	7	5	6	28	8.1
Eyes	1	1	0	1	2	2	0	1	2	0	10	2.9
Ears	1	3	1	2	1	0	1	5	4	1	19	5.5
Mental	7	2	0	1	2	3	3	3	6	10	37	10.7
Respiratory	1	0	2	1	0	1	1	1	1	4	14	4.1
Unclassifiable	0	1	2	4	0	1	0	0	0	0	8	2.3
Licences lost	28	29	15	28	17	30	32	51	48	68	346	
Licences current	4,093	4,486	5,506	5,705	6,359	6.791	7.194	7.684	8,120	8,245		
Incidence per 1,000 pilots	6.85	6.50	2.95	4.90	2.65	4.40	4.445	6.65	5.90	8.25		
Incidence per 1,000 pilots (cardiovascular)	2.20	3.10	1.60	2.10	0.50	2.20	2.80	3.80	2.70	4.95		

Source: British Air Line Pilots Association

There are some unquestionably conclusive ECG readings — a bad resting ECG, for example. But stress ECGs are as yet too inconclusive to ensure 10^{-8} medical integrity, especially when a man's livelihood and a substantial airline investment in irreplaceable experience are at stake. The stress ECG brings up false positives, and other evidence and techniques can be more important — blood pressure and blood chemistry tests, and studies of family history, for example.

British Airways is taking a great interest in the research of the world's most distinguished bodies in the field, including the Royal College of Physicians and the United States College of Physicians. The airline is co-operating with both and providing data to the International Air Transport Association's medical advisory committee. Nothing is emerging to suggest that a stress ECG is essential. This is apparently also the view of Britain's National Heart Hospital, which reads all the airline's ECGs.

Autopsies by US Army doctors on young soliders killed in Korea and Vietnam showed that a surprising number had advanced narrowing of the coronary arteries. Royal Air Force doctors have found a surprising incidence of heart disease in young pilots killed on active service, and pathologists in British general hospitals have also found similar evidence in young people killed in accidents. One theory is that, because there is no similar evidence in eastern or southern races, diet or heredity cause heart disease in western races.

An airline has by law to ensure that each of its pilots has a six-monthly medical. British Airways does not, as a matter of policy, carry out licence medicals itself. These are done by doctors approved by the Civil Aviation Authority. British Airways doctors believe, and so undoubtedly do most of the airline's 3,400 pilots, that the doctor-patient relationship within the airline would change if the company had the power to take away a pilot's licence and livelihood. They are protecting the "total medical knowledge concept," which is another way of saying that the airline will find out more about its pilots as a whole, and as individuals, if they can talk about their aches and pains without fear of losing their licences.

It is true that some pilots never go to the British Airways doctor, or indeed to any doctor, and this is the negative side. The only doctors who see such pilots formally are the CAA-approved examiners. The Papa India crash made the British Airways Medical Service really question its policy of informality. It decided that the balance of advantage was in favour of the present system.

The informal doctor/pilot relationship is fostered by appointing medical officers to each flight in each division of the airline — Overseas, European and Regional. They are highly experienced in aviation medicine and establish personal rapport with the crews. They fly as supernumerary crew and become accepted in the way the squadron doctor is in the Services.

All pilot recruits are given the most thorough medical before being accepted. The recruiting medical goes deep because on it depends a 30-year-plus investment decision. No medical can ever insure against an unexpected deterioration of vision, blood pressure or hearing; nor can the electro-encephalograph (EEG) test of brain activity necessarily detect any latent epileptic tendencies, although one in about 200 EEGs may in fact show such trends. But if a blackout should occur during a pilot's career the recruiting EEG provides the baseline from which a positive conclusion may be reached.

In addition to the CAA medical British Airways provides facilities for full medical checks on a routine basis, always after sick leave (when a licence automatically lapses after 20 days), and after an accident, at home or at work, or any high-stress experience such as a hijack.

About a dozen British Airways pilots a year lose their licences for medical reasons before normal retirement at 55 — a rate of about 0.3 per cent. Of these dozen just over half are pilots with heart trouble. The British Airways doctors may give the pilot a personal second opinion, but only very rarely is there a successful appeal against the findings of the CAA. The retirement age recommended by the International Civil Aviation Organisation is 60 for the first-class air transport pilot's commercial licence. Pilots of lighter commercial aircraft can continue to hold licences beyond that age.

The British Airways licence-loss rate from heart trouble is claimed to be among the lowest in the airline industry, and is below the general average for men between 40 and 55. This is a good measure of the quality of the selection medical. In fact the UK national average is more like 0.9 per cent — three times the British Airways rate. Nevertheless, to get the rate down even more, research goes on right into retirement as well as in operation. British Airways is studying the health of about 1,000 pensioner pilots. They are regularly contacted, so that 30-year medical data on pilots is available.

In day-to-day operations eight pilots are being monitored during automatic landings. This is part of a long-term programme to find out more about the relationship between man and machine — perhaps the one big remaining area of air safety improvement. Just how aware is the pilot of what he must do in an emergency? How much does he know from one moment to another about his speed, rate of descent, attitude, height and so on? Would he do the right thing in an emergency? Does he have enough information? What is his level of "arousal"? Heart rates and hand tremor are monitored before and after the approach and landing.

An incidental benefit of this automatic-landing research is the light it throws on crew duties. Is P2 overloaded or not? Nobody has ever really produced data on which sensible answers can be based. Crew members complete special check cards, and their voices as well as heart rates are recorded and studied. The general objective, to use the jargon, is to learn more about "human factors and the man/machine interface in the approach and landing phase." This in plain language is where half of all airline accidents occur, and it is the critical area for human research, the single biggest area left now that man has got machines so efficient and reliable. There may actually be insufficient stress during an automatic landing so that, in the 10^{-7} event of systems failure, reactions might be slow or ineffective.

All staff handling cabin food are subjected to rigorous hygiene tests before selection. This requires a comprehensive pathology laboratory. Catering hygiene is not just good business; it is safety too. The rule is that the captain's and co-pilot's meals must be different; and certain types of food — including shellfish — have been banned altogether since the occasion some years ago when 22 crew-members in the Caribbean area contracted food poisoning, almost grounding the airline's entire operation in that region. The trouble was traced to a particular source of oysters.

PILOT INCAPACITATION In the USA, where records are kept, 16 airline pilots of average age 44 died in flight in 15 years. All deaths were caused by heart attacks. Three of the 16 deaths occurred during the approach and landing, when heart-beat rates were relatively high. Seven took place soon after landing. In the world as a whole only two fatal accidents involving passengers can definitely be attributed to pilot heart attacks.

All the best airline pilot-training drills include incapacitation simulations and — particularly since the BEA Trident crash at Heathrow in 1972 — a simulation of the "subtle incapacitation." The findings of the inquiry into the BEA Trident crash at Heathrow soon after take-off were that the crew made an error of judgement, perhaps as a result of the captain's abnormal heart condition.

There is a tendency for the number of in-flight incapacitations to increase as the air-transport business grows, and as the percentage of pilots in their fifties increases. In 1972 just over 25 per cent of American airline pilots (5,600) were in their fifties; in 1987 this figure may be over 40 per cent (8,600).

Incapacitation is one of the safety drills carried out by the best airlines during simulator training, especially with two-man crews. The worst case was thought before the Trident accident to be a pilot falling on to the controls or throttles in a two-crew aircraft during the landing or, potentially even more dangerous, during an overshoot. The "subtle" incapacitation is seen to be potentially just as dangerous.

There is evidence to suggest that heart disease is less common among airline pilots than it is among other men. The statutory regular medical examination, and the prospect of losing licence and livelihood, are incentives to pilots to keep themselves fit.

The commonest causes of complete incapacitation, according to a survey of 5,000 members of the International Federation of Air Line Pilots Associations, are not heart disease but stomach complaints and other alimentary disorders. The well trained pilot is not least the one who recognises impending incapacitation in himself and his colleagues.

FATAL CREW INCAPACITATION (PRIME CAUSE OR POSSIBLE)

Date	Aircraft	Carrier	Location	Type of flight	Fatalities		Occupants		
					Crew	Pass-engers	Crew	Pass-engers	
May 24, 1961	DC-4 (VH-TAA)	TAA	Queensland	SF	2	—	2	—	Heart attack
Dec 14, 1962	L-1049H (N6913C)	Flying Tiger	Hollywood	SF	3	2	3	2	Heart attack
Jan 28, 1966	CV-440 (D-ACAT)	Lufthansa	Bremen	SP	4	42	4	42	Stall at low level, possibly after pilot incapacitation
April 22, 1966	Electra	American Flyers	Ardmore, Okl	NSP	5	78	5	93	Heart attack
Aug 5, 1966	DC-8 (PH-DCD)	KLM	Tokyo	SP	1	—	11	53	Captain died during the approach. Aircraft landed by co-pilot
May 13, 1967	Viscount (ZS-CVA)	South African	East London	SP	5	20	5	20	Possible heart attack (crashed into sea)
June 18, 1972	Trident (G-ARPI)	BEA	Staines	SP	9	109	9	109	Heart condition listed as "underlying cause"

SP, Scheduled Passenger; SF, Scheduled Freight; NSP, Non-scheduled Passenger.

United Airlines has made a training film of pilot incapacitation. The following is an extract from a letter written by a US Federal Aviation Administration flight inspector to the senior vice-president, flight operations, of United.

"I was conducting flight checks on an American Airlines DC-10. The first officer was flying, and we had just made our take-off rotation when he suffered a fatal heart attack. The check airman in the left seat had given him the command 'start your left turn to 130° and maintain 1,000ft.'

"There was no response either visually or aurally. I feel we both recognised a problem, then observed the first officer who was experiencing difficulty breathing. This incident was so similar to the United Airlines film, and I know my actions were automatic.

"The captain took over the controls, the flight engineer and I restrained the first officer pitching forward on the control column. We slid the seat aft and removed him from the seat. We started emergency oxygen and heart massage. Unfortunately we did not save him.

"We were in a critical phase of flight, at night, with a turn-out over water, at low altitude. The crew did an excellent job and we landed safely... Thanks again for the training film."

The reason for two pilots is to achieve what, in the engineering world, the systems designer calls redundancy. If one part of the system is incapacitated, the other backs up and takes over.

The object of the operations manual is to ensure that neither pilot is singly responsible for one critical function, such as checking an altimeter or a navigation beacon. In systems engineering, an undesired event — for example, loss of elevator power — will occur only if both A and B elevator actuators fail. On the other hand, either A or B actuator will fail if any one of its elements — electrical, hydraulic or mounting — fails. If the two actuators are independent, and the failure rate of one of them is 1 in 1,000 hours, then the rate applying to both is 1 failure in 1,000,000 hours. But if the actuators are not independent, and have perhaps a common mounting or electrical supply, the failure rate becomes 1 in 500.

The relationship between the pilots, that of commander and subordinate, can sometimes defeat the objective of an operations manual aimed at completely independent pilots. The copilot may, for example, suspect that the captain has made or is about to make a mistake; but he may not be sure, and if he is "fresh out of college" he will perhaps not dare to challenge the captain's action.

Safe airlines and safe captains are the ones who accept that authority must be challenged. Procedures are there to be followed, so that one pilot is always checking the other, ensuring that the aircraft does not fly into the ground while both pilots are checking a beacon, a map, or a warning light.

The relationship between captain and copilot has been the subject of a penetrating article by a senior TWA pilot:

"From the dawn of time until today, from the epic adventure of the *Bounty* through Captain Queeg's USS *Caine*, the sovereignty of the captain has stood... In the short time since man has taken to the air, the concept has been applied to those who command aircraft, as logical extensions of the nautical experience."

The article goes on to quote from the US National Transportation Safety Board accident report:

"The concept of command authority, and its inviolate nature except in the case of incapacitation, has become a tenet without exception... This has resulted in second-in-command pilots reacting differently in circumstances where they should perhaps be more affirmative. Rather than submitting passively to this concept, second-in-command pilots should be encouraged under certain circumstances to assume the duty and responsibility to advise the pilot-in-command that the flight is being conducted in a careless or dangerous manner."

The TWA author continues:

"The day when the first officer was an empty suit in the right seat, a gear-jerking apprentice for a captain upon whose shoulders rests sole responsibility for the conduct of the flight, are gone for ever. The first officer is a fully qualified pilot, capable of assuming command in the event of incapacitation of the captain. As such, he shares in the responsibility of the captain and must always be fully aware of the safety environment of the flight...

"The first officer is the planned safety factor... the fail-safe man in the cockpit. He must speak out loud and clear while there is time... He may have to make a control input to prevent disaster.

"Regardless of understandable reluctance to act due to protocol, embarrassment, fear of being castigated and the like, times arise when action is necessary."

The best captains, according to the message of that article, are those who accept a copilot's challenge to their authority, even when the copilot proves to have been wrong.

"THE LAST FRONTIER" The Director-General of the International Air Transport Association (Iata) has described human reliability as "the last remaining major problem of airline safety." More than three-quarters of accidents occur during take-off and climb or during the descent, approach and landing; and analysis of these accidents by Dr Shaw, technical director-general of Iata, shows that almost the same proportion was found on investigation to have had "human factors" — what used to be called "pilot error" — as a key element. Shaw says: "It is clear that until we can make a real breakthrough in this area of human reliability — the last frontier — we cannot look forward to a significant resumption of the downward trend in aircraft accident rates."

Shaw suggests that the loss rate of jet airliner hulls, having declined up to the mid-1970s, began to increase thereafter. The rate fell from more than 20 hulls lost per million flights in 1960, soon after the start of the jet age, to below three by the end of the 1960s, and to nearly two by the early 1970s.

Pilots are susceptible, like all human beings, to believing what they see. Sometimes, as we all know, optical illusions can deceive. As Shaw says, a sloping runway can produce false illusions during the approach of height above the ground. The pilot will tend to overshoot an up-sloping runway, and to undershoot a runway sloping away from the approach direction. Variations in runway length and width can have the same effect. The narrower the runway, the more the illusion of overshooting and the stronger the temptation to increase the rate of descent. Again, sloping terrain ahead of or beyond the runway can lead to height illusions. Lack of any sight of terrain ahead of the runway will produce an illusion of height (the "black hole" illusion) causing a considerable number of undershoot accidents. According to Shaw at least one airline routinely prints data on runway slope and width on its approach charts to help to alert pilots to these illusions.

Runway and approach lights when obscured or diffused by rain, fog or cloud can also cause false illusions of height. This phenomenon is particularly dangerous, according to Shaw, if there is a change of lighting intensity, as for example when landing into low scud, fog patches or intermittent rain. This can create the overwhelming illusion that the aircraft is gaining height and a compulsion to push the stick forward to correct this illusory climb (known to World War Two pilots as the "pushover" illusion). This still causes accidents. Pilots should develop an ingrained instinct to distrust their physical senses and to place a strict reliance on instruments and procedures.

One solution is the monitored approach, whereby every instrument approach is monitored by at least one member of the crew, whose job is never to take his eyes off the instruments. In fact, most airlines now demand that the aircraft be flown automatically coupled (or autocoupled) to the ILS down to Decision Height.

The trouble with the human brain is its capacity to switch off inputs which it does not want to believe. For example, voice-recorder playbacks after many accidents show that the pilot totally ignored not one but several warnings that he was too low. As Shaw says: "When in the grip of a powerful and compelling visual input in a critical stage of flight it may be that the pilot flying the aeroplane is effectively stone deaf."

This calls into question the effectiveness of all forms of warning, including the Ground Proximity Warning System in which a recorded voice in the pilot's headphones warns him that he is too low. There may be so many dings, dongs, bleeps and buzzes that the crew mentally switch them off, particularly during busy periods. This is particularly true of the altitude alert. Warning devices do not necessarily solve the safety problem.

The propensity of the human brain to see and believe what it wants to see and believe makes it essential, in Dr Shaw's opinion, to require the second pilot, or the pilot who is on instruments, to take over control and to initiate an overshoot if the instruments show the aircraft to be below the specified flight-path.

This is why strict adherence to Standard Operating Procedures, or SOPs, is absolutely critical. At times of heavy cockpit workload SOPs can sometimes be overlooked. Paradoxically, this can happen at times of light work-load and boredom. Not unknown on the flight-deck of a modern airliner, which nowadays operate so reliably and without incident for hours at a time, is the problem of low pilot "arousal". In Dr Shaw's opinion this is largely a matter for pilot self-discipline. It is up to the captain and his crew to "keep on their toes" in spite of every temptation to succumb to boredom. The problem of low "arousal" can be tackled by the use of films, seminars and flight-crew magazines. The dissemination of information about other people's accidents also helps.

Complacency in flight-operations management is "at least as great a danger as complacency in the flight crews themselves", according to Shaw. The design of SOPs puts a heavy responsibility on the flight-operations management which designs the procedures so vital to safety. Approach charts (otherwise known as approach plates) are a good example. Says Shaw: "The total system must be subject to continuous audit and review."

Checklists, charts and approach plates must be unambiguous and vital information must not be concealed by irrelevant details. Most important, as Dr Shaw says, is the existence of methods continuing to test the validity of SOPs.

Captain, after trying a new flight simulator: "It sure doesn't feel like a toupé."

---

20 The Last 1,000ft

Six in ten airliner accidents occur during the approach and landing. It is statistically debatable whether the accident rate in the approach and landing phase — in "the last 1,000 ft" — is improving.

In the mid 1960s the number of airliners lost in the approach and landing phase was between two and three per million flights. In the early 1970s this was down to almost one; but by the mid-1970s it had returned to between two and three.

The steadiness of the overall accident rate shows how safe air transport has become in all other areas, and how important it is to concentrate safety effort on "the last 1,000ft," and especially on human error in this phase of flight. Of 39 approach accidents to airliners lost in the three years 1972-1974, 35 were attributed to human error.

Altitude awareness is perhaps the professional pilot's most highly developed facility, instilled into him from the first hour of training. But in the first half of the 1970s there were more than 80 fatal approach accidents to public-transport aircraft, with the loss of over 2,600 lives. Most of these accidents were caused by the crew's unawareness, until too late, of their proximity to the ground. The record shows that the probability of an approach accident at night appears to be two and a half times greater than in daylight; and the probability of an approach accident is nearly four times greater in reduced visibility.

The old adage that "aeroplanes should land slowly" is borne out by safety experience. A study by the United States Air Force of its accident record shows that it experiences 7.75 landing accidents per 100,000 landings when touchdown speed is 150kt or more; 4.5 when 125kt; and 2.3 when 100kt.

About 2.5 in a million landings end with the aircraft overrunning the runway. In just over 75 per cent of such incidents the aircraft overrun by up to 150m, and in almost 50 per cent by up to 60m. Just over 2.5 in a million landings involve an undershoot — more than 50 per cent within 50m of the threshold, and 80 per cent within 150m.

Time and again, even at the end of precision ILS approaches, and even with the runway in sight, sudden rain, snow, fog or wind-shear, illusory ground lighting or some cockpit distraction results in an "inadvertent descent below the minimum descent altitude."

When the air-safety professionals gather together many and varied are their suggested reforms. A frequent finding is that descents below the glidepath ("duck-unders") occur when both pilots are looking outside the cockpit for the approach lights.

The need for one pilot continually to monitor the instruments and call out heights while the other looks for the lights calls for a high degree of discipline, training, checking and supervision. United Airlines, for example, requires the copilot to monitor the flight instruments down to below Decision Height — even to touchdown, rollout and, if called, go-around. The American Air Line Pilots' Association, Alpa, recommends in general that the "flying pilot" should be required to monitor the instruments continuously until RUNWAY IN SIGHT has been called.

The highest risk appears to exist in reduced visibility during a non-precision approach. This is defined as "a standard instrument approach in which no electronic glideslope is provided" — for example, an approach using a VOR-DME or a non-directional beacon to runways not provided with full Instrument Landing System (ILS). Most of the "pilot-error" accidents occur during so-called non-precision approaches. There is an "altitude awareness gap," which has trapped many pilots between the time the approach lights become visible and the moment the end of the runway is sighted.

Glideslope guidance, sometimes called vertical guidance, is needed at all public-transport airports. It can be provided by Instrument Landing Systems (ILS) or, more in the future, by Microwave Landing Systems (MLS). Visual Approach Slope Indicators (Vasis) are essential at airports with or without — and especially without — electronic glideslope guidance.

For approaches without an electronic glidepath it is technically possible to provide an electronic "descent fix" at the point where, say, the prescribed descent path to the aiming point on the runway intercepts Decision Height.

The calculation of Decision Height* (DH) may need to be more

---

*There are various definitions of Decision Height, a term which confuses even some professionals. According to Icao, it is the height below which an aircraft on an electronic glideslope may not descend, and at which an overshoot must be initiated, if there is no visual reference.

clearly defined. Some airline pilots have difficulty understanding the criteria for establishing DH. Approach lights do not always provide good vertical guidance, and it is not necessarily safe to descend below DH just because the approach lights are in view.

A sudden fog-bank can be dangerously disorientating. Until DH is more rationally defined it can be argued that descent below Decision Height must be prohibited unless the actual runway lights — not just the approach lights — are in view. Visibility limits should be sufficient to ensure that the runway will in fact be in view at the specified DH.

Minimum Descent Altitude (MDA) is not to be confused with DH. It regulates instrument approaches where no electronic glideslope is available.

GROUND PROXIMITY WARNING SYSTEMS The US National Transportation Safety Board, which investigates accidents and acts as a check on the FAA's safety regulations and enforcement, first argued the need for Ground Proximity Warning Systems (GPWS) in 1970. Its recommendation was re-emphasised in February 1972, after the "Martha's Vineyard" crash. Happily not fatal, this involved a DC-9-31 en route from New York on June 22, 1971. The aircraft struck the water about three miles short of runway 14 while descending for a landing at Martha's Vineyard. The crew suddenly saw the water close below them, added power and raised the nose; but the tail struck the water hard before the aircraft began to climb. The undersides of the engines were damaged, but the aircraft landed safely at Boston with no injuries.

The NTSB determined that the probable cause was "lack of crew co-ordination in monitoring the altitude during a non-precision instrument approach; the misreading of the altimeter by the captain; and the lack of altitude awareness on the part of both pilots." Such words have occurred, before and since, depressingly frequently in accident reports.

As a result of accidents and incidents mainly involving non-precision approaches, NTSB investigators examined the use of existing altitude-alerting devices. They came to the conclusion that such devices were not generally used by the airlines; crews were not well trained in the use of altitude-alerting equipment; and crews complained that audio and visual alerting systems were distracting and therefore counter-productive. The NTSB was surprised how many surviving crew-members indicated that they were unaware of their altitude until too late in the approach.

The Ground Proximity Warning System was recommended as a device which would not replace crew disciplines or existing warning systems. It would additionally warn crew members of potential danger

209

resulting from combinations of low altitude, sink rate and terrain — including high ground ahead of the aircraft.

The Federal Aviation Administration decided to make GPWS mandatory in a Notice issued in December 1974. The amendment to Federal Aviation Regulation (FAR) 121 made it illegal for any large turbine-powered aircraft to be operated without a GPWS after December 1,1975. The GPWS must:

(1) Operate at any height less than 2,500ft above the ground;
(2) Provide both visual and aural warnings which
    (a) initiate simultaneously and are distinct from other warning devices;
    (b) initiate automatically without any crew action;
    (c) operate continuously until the hazardous condition no longer exists;
(3) Provide warnings based on
    (a) the rate of descent (including any negative rate of climb after take-off) in relation to height above the terrain directly beneath;
    (b) the computed height above the terrain along the projected flight path;
    (c) landing gear and flap positions;
    (d) the performance of the aircraft.

A typical GPWS warns the pilot of his proximity to the ground. There are five modes:

Mode 1: Excessive rate of descent or sink When sink rate is 3,500ft/min at a height of 2,450ft above ground level, or 1,300ft/min at 50ft;
Mode 2: Rising terrain ahead When the ground rises beneath the aircraft at rates of from 3,800ft/min at 1,500ft to 2,000ft/min at 50ft;
Mode 3: Sink rate after take-off When sink rate after take-off exceeds 100ft/min until the aircraft is 700ft above the ground;
Mode 4: Too near the ground When the aircraft flies below 50ft above ground level with the undercarriage up. With undercarriage and flaps not in the landing position a warning is given which varies from 500ft with sink rates greater than 50ft/min, down to 200ft with sink rates less than 600ft/min;
Mode 5: Descending below approach path When the aircraft inadvertently "ducks under" the instrument glide-slope in excess of a predetermined margin.

All GPWS altitudes are computed from the aircraft radio altimeter and generally use the central air-data computer.

The FAA emphasises that the system must provide not only warnings based on the rate of descent and height of the aircraft directly above the terrain below it, but also on the terrain along the projected flight path. In other words the GPWS, unlike a radio altimeter, must warn the crew that it is flying into mountains. Thus is the technology of military terrain-following radar and computers being transferred to civil aviation.

QFE/QNH Altitude awareness also means awareness by the aircraft designer of the barometric altimeter's limitations, for example in certain rain and icing conditions. The radio altimeter measures QFE — height above the terrain immediately below it. Because the radio altimeter does not depend on barometric pressure, it helps to avoid atmospheric errors. Though it works only near the ground, this is the critical part of the flight. Instrument and automatic approaches in fact depend on radio-altimeter data. When the aircraft reaches the pre-set Decision Height (DH), the radio altimeter can be arranged to set off an alarm which cannot be cancelled below that height. This is not generally popular among pilots, who do not like to be distracted during a busy approach and landing.

European airlines generally use QFE altimeter settings (height above the ground). Nearly all American airlines use QNH (altitude above sea level) although they and their safety authorities are aware of the advantages of QFE. Its main advantage is that it relieves the pilot of the need to make a mental calculation of the height in relation to the airfield. QFE is more fail-safe: to be higher by mistake is usually better than to be lower by mistake.

To avoid QFE/QNH altimeter setting mix-ups some airlines recommend the use of numbers one and two altimeters (pilot and co-pilot) set on QFE (or zero altitude for landing) with number three altimeter visible to both pilots set on QNH for air-traffic control purposes. Eastern Airlines, for example, believes that all airlines should use both QFE and QNH.

RUNWAY VISUAL RANGE (RVR) Runway visibility or runway visual range (RVR) represents the horizontal distance an instrument can "see" along the high-intensity lights of a runway. It is measured by a "transmissometer" located near the touchdown point. This consists of a light projector and a photometer receiver separated by a known distance 200ft, 500ft or 700ft. The light is projected at a constant intensity, and its strength measured by the photometer. This reading is calibrated by human observers to give the tower a measure of RVR in hundreds of feet. An RVR reading of 1,200ft is considered to be the absolute safe minimum for a visual, as opposed to a fully automatic, landing, providing a marginal visibility for a safe landing in low cloud. At a decision height of 100ft a pilot would in practice have a visibility of only 600-800ft because of the obstruction of the view by the aircraft nose.

Even if the approach lights have been sighted after a normal instrument approach, the sudden shallow fogbank drifting across the approach path has deceived many crews in the last critical few hundred feet. It will not have been forecast by the runway visibility meter, or RVR transmissometer. The aircraft is still between 100 and 200ft — too high to land but too low and descending too fast to overshoot successfully. The aircraft descends below the glidepath before power is applied and hits the ground short of the runway.

One of the biggest traps is the rate at which RVR changes. At Heathrow, for example, RVR could be 1,000m until 1730hr but down to 100 and back up to 1,000 within 15 minutes. And RVR is not the same as SVR (Slant Visual Range). An RVR of 400m is an SVR of, say, 150m in fog and the chances of seeing anything in a 1,200ft RVR are, at the most, 80 per cent.

CLOUDBASE can be measured by a ceiliometer, a light projector which moves like a metronome in the vertical plane. Between 300ft and 1,000ft away a photometer detector reads the reflected light as it touches the base of the cloud. At that moment the angle of the projector and the known distance to the detector are calibrated to give, by triangulation, the cloudbase or ceiling. Continuous readings are available in the tower, as with RVR.

ILLUSIONS If the visibility deteriorates, either through fog drifting in or the structure of the fog (radiation fogs in the formation phase are thickest near the ground) the pilot will have the illusion of "pitch-up." The instinctive reaction is to push forward on the control column, and the aircraft is into the ground. The "push over" (see page 205) can come from the sudden reduction in the number of approach lights the pilot can see; this is unfortunately the same "visual input" as if the nose had risen rapidly. The illusion can be aggravated by errors in the pressure-sensitive flight instruments, because of transient effects from aircraft attitude changes, ground affect and configuration changes. (In most aircraft these have not been investigated.) The end result is that even if the pilot does not dive into the ground, his flight path may become divergently unstable and he will subsequently do so.

INSTRUMENT LANDING SYSTEM (ILS) is a descendant of the German Lorenz Standard Beam Approach (SBA) of the 1930s. That was an audio aid, dots and dashes telling the pilot whether he was "on the beam".

Another ancestor of ILS was the British World War 2 system Babs, which used the same airborne equipment as did Rebecca/Eureka (see

Chapter 13) but which was not much favoured by pilots as it was navigator-interpreted.

The early type of straight-in ILS has two beams. One, the Localiser, comes from a VHF transmitter at the far end of the runway on the centre line. The other, the Glidepath, is to one side. The localiser is a thin beam in the vertical plane which keeps the pilot on the centreline. The pilot sees it as a vertical needle on his ILS instrument. The glidepath or glideslope is a thin beam in the horizontal plane which keeps the pilot on the correct descent path. He sees it as a horizontal needle on his ILS instrument. By flying the aircraft so that the needles are exactly crossed — "locked on" — the pilot or autopilot keeps the aircraft on the correct landing approach up to the moment the nonflying pilot calls out APPROACH LIGHTS, when the landing may be completed visually.

In practice, raw ILS information is rarely used by airline crews; in the early 1950s the concept of the director instrument was born — the Sperry Zero Reader being among the earliest production systems. Raw information is fed through a computer and presented to the pilot in the form of "how to get there" rather than "you are here". The same computations can be fed through the autopilot to give a complete flight system and there is a choice of ways of presenting the information to the pilot; all amount to "flying the bug".

The problem still remains with ILS that there is one part of the system which has relatively low integrity, namely the transmission path, partly because it is a single path. For this reason it seems unlikely that we shall have operations below Category 3(a), or very poor visibility (see below). Even in the best ILS installations the integrity of the transmission path cannot be completely guaranteed.

VASI, or Visual Approach Slope Indicator, helps the pilot to keep the aircraft on the correct approach path after completing an instrument approach. Vasi should be fitted at all public-transport airfields whether or not equipped with ILS.

In one form, bars of red and white lights on each side of the runway are so beamed by reflectors that when the pilot is too low he sees all red lights; when he is too high he sees all white lights; and when he is on the correct approach path he sees red and white bars one above the other.

Another type is T-Vasi. If an airliner is on the correct 3° glideslope only the crossbars of the Ts will appear on each side of the runway. If the full Ts appear with the legs towards the aircraft it is too low. If the legs are red the aircraft is very much too low, and about to undershoot grossly. If the legs of the Ts are away from the approaching aircraft, the pilot is too high and should descend until only the white cross-bars are visible.

213

An advantage of the T-Vasi system is that it can be used by Boeing 747s and other very big aircraft to provide safe wheel-height clearances on arrival over the threshold. The pilot might, for example, fly the T-Vasi so that two lights of the "away" legs show; he would then be safely on the high side throughout his approach. The standard Vasi system described earlier needs to be used carefully by 747 pilots, and may need additional wing bars for safety.

Vasi is useful after completing an instrument approach and seeing the approach lights. In the dark or in poor visibility descent rate is difficult to judge. Like the mirror landing sight invented by the Royal Navy for its aircraft carriers, Vasi is a very useful pilot aid, especially when the ILS or approach lights are inoperative, or not installed.

Head-up displays, sometimes known as Airborne Vasis or Visual Approach Monitors, are still in the development stage for civil airliners. In the opinion of some experienced pilots, including some of those who have tested it in airline service, the head-up display is a preferable alternative to ground-based Vasi.

HEAD-UP DISPLAY (HUD) This is an instrument which projects instrument readings like airspeed, ILS and height "into the windscreen". The image is focussed on the windscreen coaming. The pilot who is looking for the runway lights to appear out of the darkness or mist does not want to have to keep looking down at his instruments.

The HUD was introduced in the mid-1960s to assist combat pilots attacking ground targets. It was tested by the airline industry in the early 1970s but has not yet been widely adopted, mainly because pilots prefer the disciplines of calling out speeds and heights, and of one monitoring the other.

MICROWAVE LANDING SYSTEM (MLS) is the successor to ILS. While ILS operates in the VHF/UHF bands, MLS uses waves of 50 times higher frequency. This reduces interference from trees, airport buildings and other aircraft from which ILS can suffer. Further, the microwave signal will scan through very wide angles, affording a wider selection of approach paths (60° to each side of the runway compared with 2°) and descent paths (20° compared to 2°), enabling steeper or even curving approaches to be made, and easing the air traffic controller's job of mixing slow and fast approaching traffic.

MLS will allow air traffic control to bring aircraft in from other points of the compass, instead of along a narrow approach path for landings. It can take fuller advantage of RNav (Chapter 13) or area navigation, and should help noise-abatement procedures. Compared with ILS, MLS is also more accurate for automatic landing. MLS will help to increase the capacity of the air traffic control system, though MLS and ILS will continue to operate together for many years.

According to the US National Transportation Safety Board "MLS has considerable potential as a new concept in landing guidance... it requires no external energy, and is virtually maintenance- and interference-free."

AUTOMATIC LANDING or blind landing depends on the quality of the ILS on the ground and of the autopilot in the aircraft. Only a few ILS transmitters are cleared for Category 3 automatic landing — completely blind down to 100ft and including automatic touchdown. Very high standards of ILS beam accuracy are required for Category 3 weather conditions.

Automatic landing came into regular passenger service in the early 1970s, some 40 years after the first experiments in the 1930s. In Europe and America autopilots were coupled to ground radio beams and hands-off landings were demonstrated. Development to the exacting standards of safety required for routine public transport began in the 1950s.

The system had to demonstrate that it was not only fail-safe but fail-operational. In the unlikely event of an autopilot failure at the critical height, a failure had to be automatically detected and the reserve or standby autopilot smoothly and instantly switched in without disturbance of the approach path. The standards of engineering integrity required of the autopilot and the ILS electronics are such that they have to meet a theoretical "acceptable" failure rate of not more than one per ten million landings. This requires flying controls with back-up systems for the back-up systems.

Aircraft are certificated for blind landing according to various weather minima categories. These are laid down by the International Civil Aviation Organisation (Icao). They assume full approach and runway lighting, and relate to the cloud-base height and forward visibility below which a pilot must divert to another airfield:

CATEGORY 1 Operation down to a decision height of not less than 200ft, 60m, with a forward visibility of not less than 2,500ft (½ mile) or 800m runway visual range (RVR).

CATEGORY 2 Operation down to decision height of 100ft or 30m, with a forward visibility of not less than 1,200ft (¼ mile) or 400m RVR.

CATEGORY 3a Operation down to decision heights of below 100ft with a forward visibility of not less than 700ft or 200m RVR.

CATEGORY 3b As 3a, with an RVR of 150ft or 50m (enough for taxiing).

CATEGORY 3c Zero-zero (zero cloudbase and zero visibility).

SPOILERS A number of accidents, including one to a DC-8 in which 109 people were killed, have been caused by premature operation of wing-lift spoilers. Also known as lift-dumpers, these are intended for operation on the runway to get the full weight of the aircraft as quickly as possible onto its wheels so that the brakes can be fully effective, especially on wet runways. Spoilers are sometimes coupled to reverse engine thrust, and on some aircraft it is possible to extend them in the air; on others they are automatically extended when the wheels spin or the nosewheel strut compresses.

Accidents have happened when, during an overshoot, the spoilers have retracted too late for the wings to generate lift; or on the approach, when the spoilers have extended, causing a sudden uncontrollable descent. In one case the aircraft landed so hard that the undercarriage broke and an engine fell off, causing a fire. The pilot attempted to take off again, but the asymmetric power and spoiled lift combined with the fire were too much for the pilot to control. The aircraft rolled onto its back and crashed a few moments after the landing with heavy loss of life. The cause of that accident, according to the cockpit voice recorder, was premature in-flight application of the spoilers by the co-pilot.

Modifications to inhibit in-flight application of spoilers, by making their operation dependent on compression of the wheel legs, can compound the hazard: a pilot does not want sudden spoiler drag during a bounced landing or when — as often happens in a crosswind — one wheel-truck touches first.

One authority finds that lack of crew co-ordination accounts for 38 per cent of approach and landing accidents. According to another, in 20 years more than 150 airliner approach and landing accidents, and an unrecorded number of incidents, have occurred in VMC (Visual Meteorological Conditions) to crews who have seen the runway. They either touched down much too short, or overran, or bounced hard enough to cause damage.

APPROACH SPEEDS A graph of drag plotted against airspeed shows a U-shaped curve. The bottom of the U is known as the minimum drag speed or Vmd. There is a steep increase in drag as speed falls towards the stalling speed Vs. Care must be taken during the approach to avoid letting drag increase above the available thrust — "getting on the back side of the drag curve" — especially in the case of an approach with a failed engine.

The airliner approaches at a speed safely above Vs, typically 1.3 Vs. The closer the speed to the stalling speed the poorer the stability of the approach. The aircraft, because of its weak speed stability, can be vulnerable to wind-shear, that is to say to any changes in speed and direction of the wind — in a word, turbulence. Pitching, because it increases the angle of attack, will increase the rate of descent, unless the extra drag is compensated by more thrust.

The jet engine responds more slowly than the propeller engine does; the acceleration time for a typical high bypass-ratio turbofan from idle to full thrust is up to eight seconds. There is none of the slip-stream effect of the propeller-driven aeroplane, when an increase in power immediately produces an improvement in both control and lift. Opening jet throttles to correct a sink, or a low or slow approach, can involve considerable height loss before the required effect is achieved.

The importance of speed stability on the approach is paramount. Critical to the assessment of approach speed is the basic stalling speed, Vs. The normal gentle stall, generally termed the 1g stall, is the basis on which the approach speed is calculated. An approach speed of 1.3 times the 1g stalling speed, Vs, theoretically gives a speed margin 30 per cent over the stall. In practice this margin is eroded by different computations of Vs. Instead of the 1g stalling speed (that is to say the minimum speed at which the lift is equal to the weight in level flight) commercial pressures for better load-carrying performance have led to the acceptance of a Vs of 0.94 the 1g stalling speed. This is the minimum speed recorded during the stall and recovery, and it can be five or ten knots below the 1g stalling speed. Because of this "phoney" stalling speed many pilots add five or ten knots to the recommended threshold speed, even though this will result in increased landing distance. Some authorities maintain that this "phoney" stalling speed is at the root of many landing incidents.

APPROACH TECHNIQUE There is no international standard flight-deck approach procedure. The most widely used is the one in which the handling pilot — either the captain or the copilot — "flies the needles" while the other monitors the operation and looks out for the approach lights.

Decision Height (page 208) is pre-determined for the particular airport and conditions. If when Decision Height is called out no lights are in sight then the handling pilot will automatically overshoot. There is no transfer of control at a critical moment; the pilot who has been flying the aircraft, and who has the feel of it, keeps flying it during what may be vital seconds as the ground comes up.

British Airways European Division's monitored-approach procedure has been evolved by an operator which makes high-frequency flights over short sectors in the bad weather of Northern Europe. The division has had no fatal jet accidents during the approach and landing. The British Airways European Division philosphy is that command must always remain with the captain; he must make all the major decisions throughout the flight.

This operator's monitored approach is based on the belief that it is wrong for the captain to become totally involved in handling the aircraft while the copilot (P2) does nothing except operate levers and switches on command. In the monitored approach one pilot, P2, flies the instruments and handles the aircraft while the captain, P1, oversees everything that P2 does, ensures that procedures are correctly followed, and generally manages and monitors the operation.

At 100ft above Decision Height, an "alert call" gives the captain, the non-handling pilot, time to look out through the windscreen and "make the transition to visual" — in other words, to adjust his eyes from the instrument panel to the outside world. Depending on whether he can see the approach lights clearly, he makes a command decision, calling out LAND if the lights are in view or OVERSHOOT if they are not. Meanwhile the copilot P2 — the handling pilot — is flying the aircraft on instruments. He automatically overshoots at Decision Height unless he has heard the command LAND. At the very low Decision Heights, when the aircraft is only a few feet from touchdown, the co-pilot completes the landing in the absence of any call from the captain.

British Airways European Division claims that in the monitored approach command decisions remain always with the captain. Other professionals agree with the concept of a handling pilot and a decision-making pilot who monitors the whole operation, but feel that the procedure diminishes the captain's authority. For example, the copilot overshoots, or can overshoot, without being ordered to do so by the captain.

The airline's senior pilots believe in the importance of withdrawing the captain from the physical activity of flying the aircraft, and freeing him to do the critical management. Other airlines find the concept difficult to sell to captains who for many years have always made their own approaches and landings, and taken pride in them, and who were trained thus as copilots.

British Airways European Division believes that its monitored approach procedure ensures that a Cockpit Voice Recorder (CVR) readout will never contain the words, recorded in so many approach-accident reports: "You're too low, captain". The division claims that its weather minima are the lowest in the world with the exception of the French domestic airline, Air Inter, which has similar monitored-approach and command procedures.

Although British Airways European Division uses its procedures in

218

all visibilities, in good weather the captain may reverse roles to give the copilot command and landing practice.

The procedure provides for a third pilot, P3 or the second officer, as a further monitor. If the captain has not called OVERSHOOT, and if P2 has not initiated the overshoot procedure at Decision Height, P3 is required to call out the command. It is also his job at 500ft to call out altimeter information; at 300ft (Alert Height, or Equipment Decision Height) P3 is required to report on the status of the aircraft systems, especially automatic landing. On this report rests the decision whether to go to Category 2 or 3 minima — the latter being the worst visibility, with a Decision Height of 20ft for the TriStar and 12ft for the Trident.

ANGLE OF ATTACK Another approach technique is to "fly alpha", the Angle of Attack. This is the angle between the chord line of the wing and the airflow. It is not to be confused with pitch attitude, which is the angle between the chord line of the wing and the earth's horizon.

If at low speeds, that is to say during the approach or climb-out, angle of attack is flown precisely, airspeed is accurately controlled for a given weight. Flying angle of attack, or alpha, eliminates the need in theory for both airspeed indicator and artificial horizon, or attitude direction indicator (ADI). On the approach, for example, the descent path of the aircraft will be at an angle of alpha minus the pitch attitude angle. This is sometimes known as net flight path, or the Velocity Vector.

This velocity vector can be shown electro-optically "in the windscreen" by a head-up display (HUD) (see page 214). The horizon line on the HUD is aligned with the true horizon, and the velocity vector line below it with the aiming point on the runway. Electronics then provide a small reference triangle on the display which, if kept on the velocity vector, ensures that the correct alpha and hence airspeed are flown. The HUD provides another symbol to denote power. When thrust is the same as drag, this symbol is on the velocity vector line of the display. If it moves above, the pilot knows that he must reduce power, and vice versa.

Thus the pilot can in theory fly without looking down at either his airspeed indicator or ADI or power settings. He looks ahead through his windscreen and flies the angle-of-attack and power symbols electro-optically projected by the HUD. This system could be useful during an overshoot or an engine failure on climb-out, when the pilot has an instant read-out of his situation, and in particular his angle of attack.

The angle-of-attack or alpha HUD display is useful also for showing pilots the effects of wind-shear (see below). Any sudden change of wind velocity and direction changes the angle of attack and this is immediately apparent to the pilot as a change in his velocity vector. He applies power to move the power symbol up to the runway aiming point, at the same time pulling back the stick to raise the velocity vector to coincide with it.

The "fly-alpha" and HUD techniques will require development before becoming accepted. The "fly-airspeed-and-altitude" principle remains deeply ingrained.

WIND-SHEAR Cool air settles over an airport in a valley overnight. Day dawns, warms up, and a current of warm air passes over the cool, still air. A zone of turbulence may now form where the two air masses meet. The result can be wind-shear.

It forms in many other ways too, especially when there are thunderstoms about. It was around before the aeroplane. But for some reason as yet un-clear it is getting more and more into the accident reports.

Suppose that an aircraft climbs through a front just after take-off. If the direction of the upper warm wind is the same as that of the aircraft, the aircraft will, on passing out of the cool air, experience an abrupt loss of airspeed and rate of climb as it flies through the wind-shear. This can be dangerous near the ground, and even more so on the approach.

Most incidents associated with wind-shear have been during the approach. During this phase of flight power-settings are low: and if the aircraft has the usual headwind while descending towards the airport, and if this suddenly becomes a tailwind as the aircraft passes through the shear, there will be a loss of lift and airspeed which, unless power is applied immediately, may result in a critical loss of altitude. Another accident report will say: "The pilot did not recognise the need to correct an excessive rate of descent," or words to that effect. Wind-shears involving changes of 180° and velocity changes of 50kt or more within 200 ft of the ground have been experienced.

Most fronts contain gradual changes in wind direction and velocity. But some have sharp transition zones which can produce significant shear. If the meteorologist knows that there is a temperature difference of 5°C or more across a front, and that the front is moving at a speed of 30kt or more, then the tower can warn pilots that shear is probable.

Wind-shear is most often associated with thunderstorms. Although the squall line may be as much as ten miles ahead of a thunderstorm, a clue to the pilot that shear may be lying in wait is the presence of the thunderstorm itself.

During the approach, captains who suspect wind-shear will carefully monitor their INS/Doppler wind readings and compare them with surface winds. The crew will add a few knots to the normal approach speed, perhaps take over the auto-throttle manually, and keep an especially careful eye on thrust, pitch attitude, rate of descent and IAS.

A sudden increase in headwind during an approach will require reduced auto-throttle and an increased rate of descent. Thrust will reduce initially to reduce indicated speed, but will later have to be increased to maintain speed, once it has settled. If thrust is not applied quickly enough, the rate of sink will rapidly increase, causing the aircraft to strike the approach lights or perhaps to make a very hard landing.

A sudden increase in tailwind during the approach will cause increased thrust from the auto-throttle and a decreased rate of descent. A very fast, long and eventful landing may result.

Wind-shear near the ground requires very rapid changes of thrust and a good general rule is not to allow thrust to get too low when on finals — especially when wind-shear conditions, so often associated with thunderstorms, are about.

A good rule of thumb when approaching and landing a big jet in windy gusty conditions or when thunderstorms are about is to add half the forecast wind to the scheduled approach speed plus all the forecast gusts, and hold this speed to touchdown — though never adding more than 20kt. If too much is added to the approach speed an overrun may result. The object is to achieve the correct target threshold speed, allowing for the natural "bleed-off" as the runway is approached and for unexpected wind-shear and eddies, especially if big buildings are up-wind. Allowance also has to be made for the "boundary layer" near the ground, as the general free-stream wind slows down when in friction with the ground.

Rapid changes of barometric pressure often precede thunderstorms and their associated wind-shear conditions. A pressure change of up to 4 millibars in one minute can be detected by a special "pressure-jump" sensor. A triangular array of three such sensors mounted on telephone poles approximately 1km apart, and up to 10km from the runway threshold, have shown experimentally that they can forecast wind-shear conditions, detecting them even before the airport weather radar.

The US Federal Aviation Administration has experimented with pressure-jump sensors at Chicago O'Hare, Washington Dulles and at Tinker Air Force Base in Oklahoma, an area of heavy thunderstorm activity. The sensors are also used to detect wake vortices (Chapter 9). Experiements with acoustic Doppler and laser radars are more expensive, but are continuing to built up a mass of measured data which will enable airports to warn pilots of potentially dangerous wind-shear and wake vortices.

There is a need for wind sensors to give pilots better information about wind-shear during the last 1,000ft, especially when thunderstorms are about. The met man, as always, is the pilot's best friend.

HUMAN FACTORS Research is tending to concentrate on the last 100ft. What are the ear, eye and hand activities? What did the pilot see compared with what he expected to see on cloud-break? What was the difference between his "psychological set" — what he was expecting to see — and what he actually saw? Fixation, or psychological set, is a curious human phenomenon, from which airline pilots are not immune.

It occurs when the mind is convinced that it understands a situation, and chooses to ignore all evidence to the contrary, and to misinterpret evidence to the contrary to confirm the original incorrect conviction. This is of course common enough in politicians; among pilots it can be fatal.

After an accident or an incident, says the US Air Line Pilots Association: "we have to get the true story, the full story. We have to invent a way of getting it. We all know as car drivers that people don't want to put down for everyone to read that they were listening to the radio or going too fast. We have to make a method available so that the stuff comes out.

"At the moment we suspend a pilot so that he has 30 days at home getting bitter instead of 30 days doing landings."

SUMMARY Because half the world's air-transport accidents happen during the approach and landing, and because such accidents are so often attributed to crew error, there is no doubt where the major accident-prevention effort and budget should be concentrated. The most fruitful research would be into crew reports of incidents. Surviving crews provide more evidence than recordings of dead men's voices, and incidents provide a bigger sample and therefore a better basis for technical and operational reforms.

Such research must be well funded. Money spent on showpiece public inquiries, and on "crash" safety measures following a disaster, is seldom money well spent. Unfortunately, politicians and Governments sometimes seem to react only to catastrophes. The money spent on just one public inquiry could produce a lot of safety if diverted into incident research.

The reporting of incidents via a neutral third party, which ensures immunity from punishment, could be the answer. In the United States incident reports go to the Federal Aviation Administration by way of Nasa, the National Aeronautics and Space Administration (Chapter 4). In fact, the reporting of incidents to intermediate, neutral experts could prove to be the greatest air-safety measure of all.

INDEX

225

Equi-signal 126, 129
Equity capital 180, 182
Equivalent Perceived Noise Decibel (EPNdB) 159-65
Escape: *see* Emergency Exits or Slides
Eureka 129
Evacuation: *see* Emergency Exits
"Exceedences" (Flight Data Recorders) 154, 192
Exemplary damages 115
Exits: *see* Emergency Exits or Slides
Extradition (hijackers) 62, 64

F.27/ F.28: *see* Fokker-VFW
Fail-safe design 203, 215
Fatigue, structure 41-3, 98
  crew 186, 188-9, 193-4
Feathering (propellers) 29, 48
Federal Aviation Administration (USA)
  Accident liability 114-117
  Airworthiness Directives (ADs) 55-6, 97, 114-7
  Bird Strikes 89
  Collisions 91
  Flight Data Recorders 104
  General 54, 59, 69, 98, 167, 221
  Ground Proximity Warning Systems (GPWSs) 209-10
  Hazardous cargo 119-20
  Incident-reporting 8-10, 20, 26-33, 222
  Licensing 59
  Pilot incapacitation 202
  Security 61, 65-6
  Service Difficulty Reports (SDRs) 28-32, 36-39
Ferrying 178-9
Fibre-optics (borescope) 149
Fines 8, 30
Finland 21
Fire 28-9, 59, 69-75, 80-1, 100, 103, 143-4, 190, 216
First Officer: *see* Co-pilot
Fixation: *see* Psychological set
Flammability 80
Flame-out (engines) 29
Flaps 10, 39, 42, 44-5, 48, 55, 67, 85-6, 164-6, 190, 210
Flashpoint (fuel) 70
Flight Foreword, 18, 20-2
Flight Data Recorders 10, 43-4, 96, 103-8, 149, 151, 153-4, 186, 191-3
  Despatch 36
  Engineers 38, 195-6
  envelope 44
  Information Regions (FIRs) 133
  inspector 7
  Level 133, 135

Manual 7, 12
  operations 39, 169, 174-6, 185, 191, 205
  planning 135-6, 163
  Progress Slip 135
  Safety Committee (UK) 9, 30, 35
  Safety Foundation (US) 9, 25-8
  Time Limitations 193-4
Floor strength (airliners) 12, 75-76
Flutter 45
Flying controls 43-7, 158, 189, 215
Flying Tiger 202
Flyover noise 159-60
Foam compound 143-4
Fog 141-2, 204, 208-9, 211-2
Fokker-VFW F.27/ F.28 63, 67, 83, 140
Food (crew) 201
Forgings (engine discs) 157
France 19-23, 64, 96-7, 109, 149, 153, 180, 218
Frangible airport lights 144
Freedom of Information Act (USA) 30, 36
Frequencies, radio and radar 125
Friction courses (runways) 142
Fuel 13, 29, 38, 43, 53-4, 69-71, 92-3, 121, 133, 148, 155-6, 161, 165, 176, 185, 189
Furnishing (flammability) 80

Gee 127, 129
General aviation 61, 89
General Dynamics 114-5
General Electric 149
General Flying Test (GFT) 14
Germany, West 19-23, 97, 99
Glideslope (or glidepath) 85, 139, 160-1, 164-5, 208-10, 212-4
Gordon-Burge, Hugh 28
Grooving (of runways) 142
Ground Controlled Approach (GCA) 126, 139
Ground Proximity Warning Systems (GPWs) 191-2, 205, 209-11
Guadalajara Convention 113-4, 117
Guatemala Protocol 113, 117
Gusts 43, 48, 221

Hague, The (Convention) (hijacking) 62-6
Hague, The (Protocol) 112-3, 117
Hamble 187
Hard-time component-lives 148-9, 153, 177
Hawaii 131-2
Hawker Siddeley (*see also* Comet and Trident) 4, 41, 67
Hawks (airport bird control) 88
Hazardous cargo 13, 119-23
Head-up Displays (HUD) 214, 219-20
Heart disease (pilots) 99, 196-204, 201-4

226